written and designed by STEVEN T. SEAGLE

sols

colored by BRAD SIMPSON

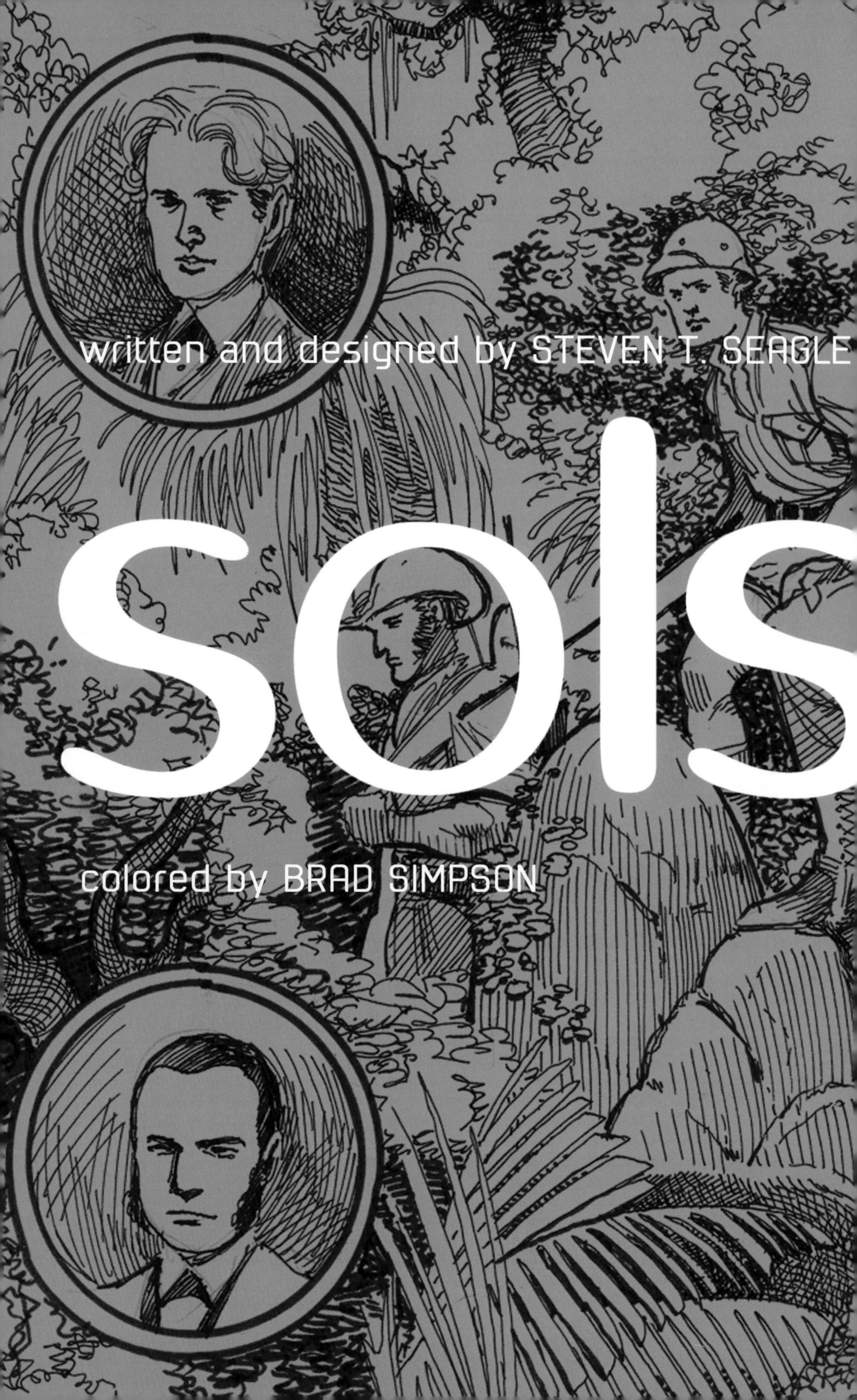

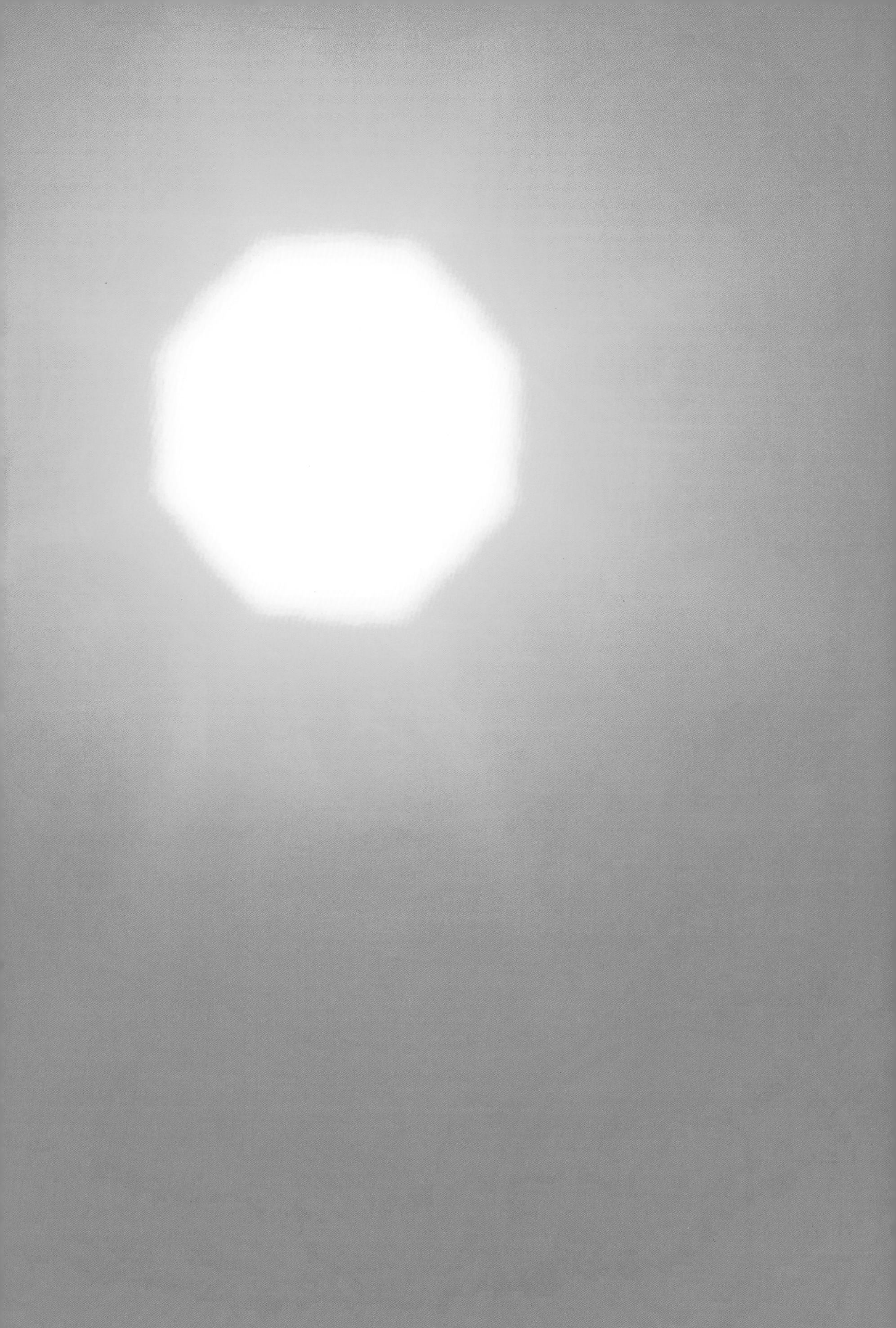

produced by MAN OF ACTION ENTERTAINMENT - LA, CA / NY, NY
published by IMAGE COMICS - Berkeley, CA,

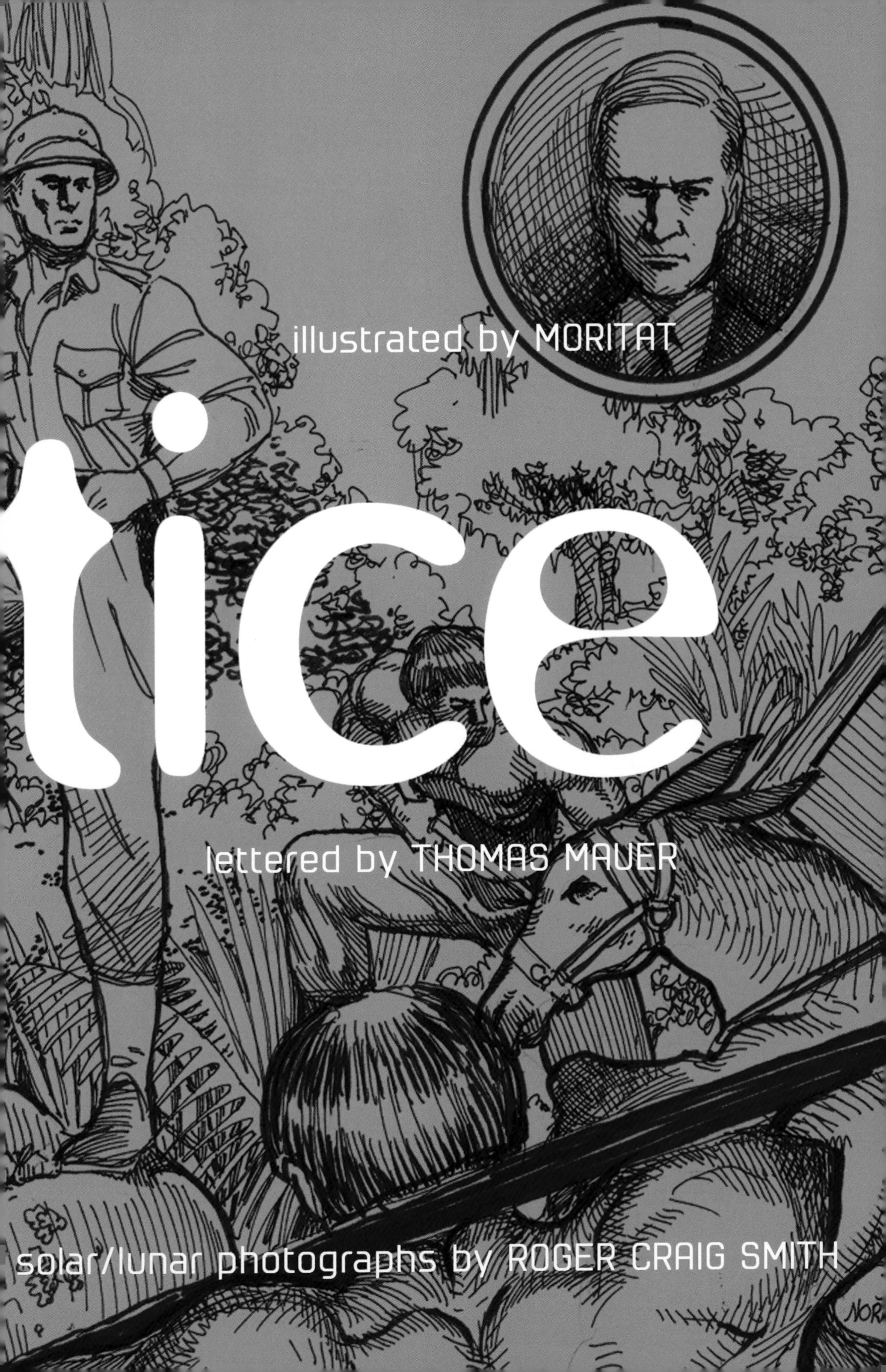
illustrated by MORITAT
tice
lettered by THOMAS MAUER
solar/lunar photographs by ROGER CRAIG SMITH

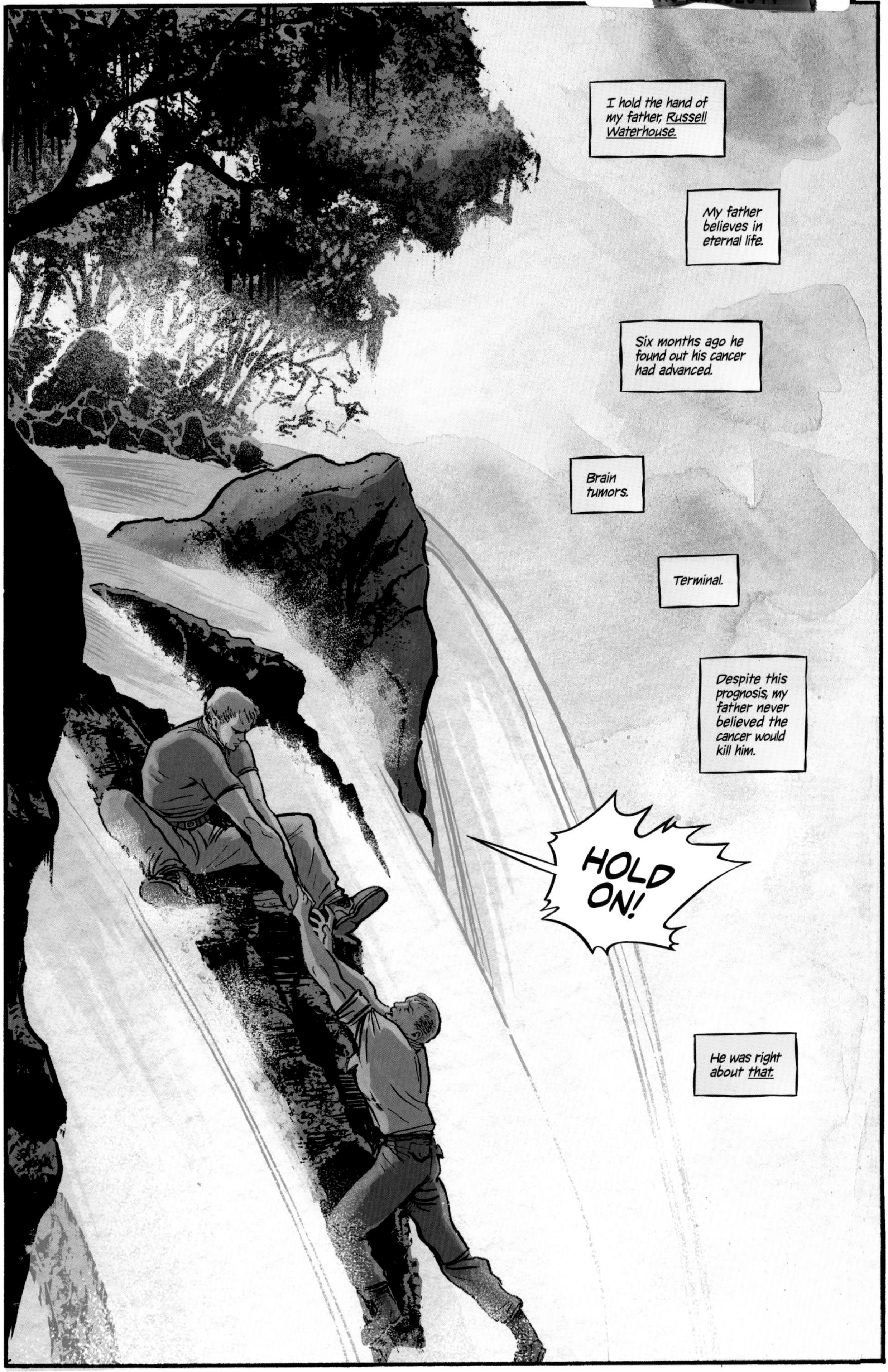
I hold the hand of my father, Russell Waterhouse.
My father believes in eternal life.
Six months ago he found out his cancer had advanced.
Brain tumors.
Terminal.
Despite this prognosis, my father never believed the cancer would kill him.
HOLD ON!
He was right about that.

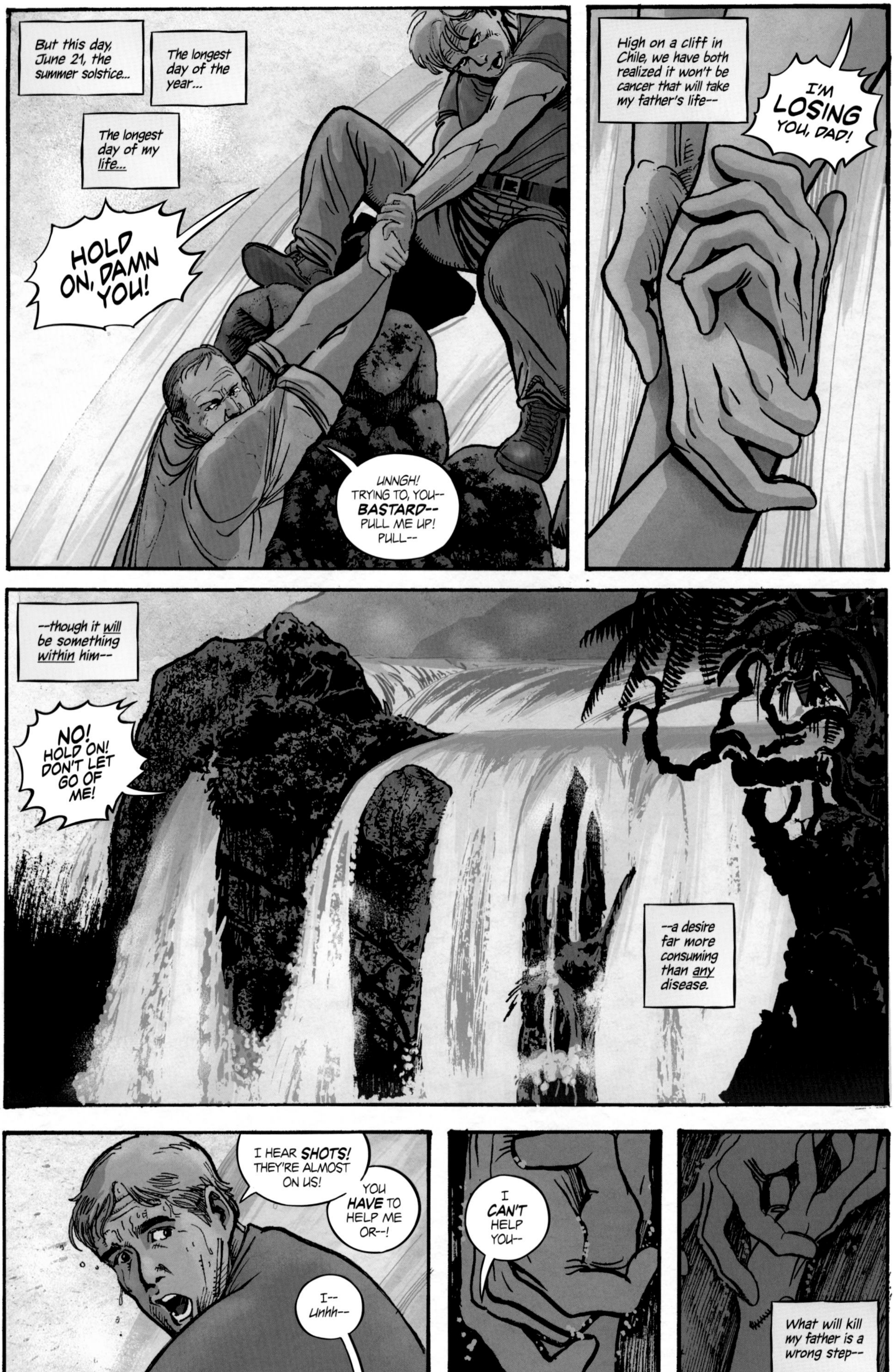

But this day, June 21, the summer solstice...
The longest day of the year...
The longest day of my life...
HOLD ON, DAMN YOU!
UNNGH! TRYING TO, YOU-- BASTARD-- PULL ME UP! PULL--
High on a cliff in Chile, we have both realized it won't be cancer that will take my father's life--
I'M LOSING YOU, DAD!
--though it will be something within him--
NO! HOLD ON! DON'T LET GO OF ME!
--a desire far more consuming than any disease.
I HEAR SHOTS! THEY'RE ALMOST ON US!
YOU HAVE TO HELP ME OR--!
I-- Unhh--
I CAN'T HELP YOU--
What will kill my father is a wrong step--

A wrong step on the path toward resolving his unnatural curiosity about living forever--

Eternal life.

NO!

NOOOOO!

And as my father falls to the very _certain_ end of his life--

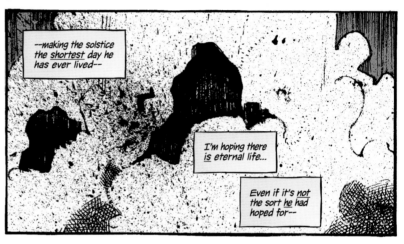

--making the solstice the _shortest_ day he has ever lived--

I'm hoping there _is_ eternal life...

Even if it's not the sort _he_ had hoped for--

The kind he had been so certain he'd find--

The eternal life which is probably _my_ only hope of surviving now...

The Fountain of Youth.

The mad dream I've heard about all my life...

All my life...

OH, IT'S **OUT** THERE. YOU CAN BET YOUR FUCKING **LIFE** IT'S OUT THERE. AND I'M **GOING** TO FIND IT!

RUSSELL! I'VE **TOLD** YOU NOT TO USE THAT LANGUAGE IN FRONT OF **HUGH!**

HE'LL HEAR IT SOONER OR LATER. BETTER **SOONER,** AS FAR AS I'M CONCERNED.

MAYBE IT'LL KEEP HIM FROM TURNING INTO A **FAG** LIKE THAT COUSIN OF YOURS--

THAT'S **ENOUGH!** I'VE ALWAYS STOOD BY YOU, RUSSELL--

YOU'RE A **BRILLIANT** MAN. BUT THE FOUNTAIN OF YOUTH IS **NOT** REAL. IT'S A **MYTH...** A **STORY.**

I'M ONE OF THE RICHEST GODDAMN MEN IN AMERICA. **THAT'S** WHY YOU'VE STOOD BY ME.

NOW YOU BETTER SHUT YOUR YAP, OR THE PURSE STRINGS YOU'RE SO ATTRACTED TO ARE GONNA CINCH UP, AND I MEAN **FAST.**

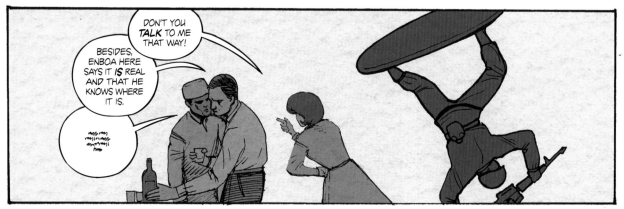

DON'T YOU **TALK** TO ME THAT WAY!

BESIDES, ENBOA HERE SAYS IT **IS** REAL AND THAT HE KNOWS WHERE IT IS.

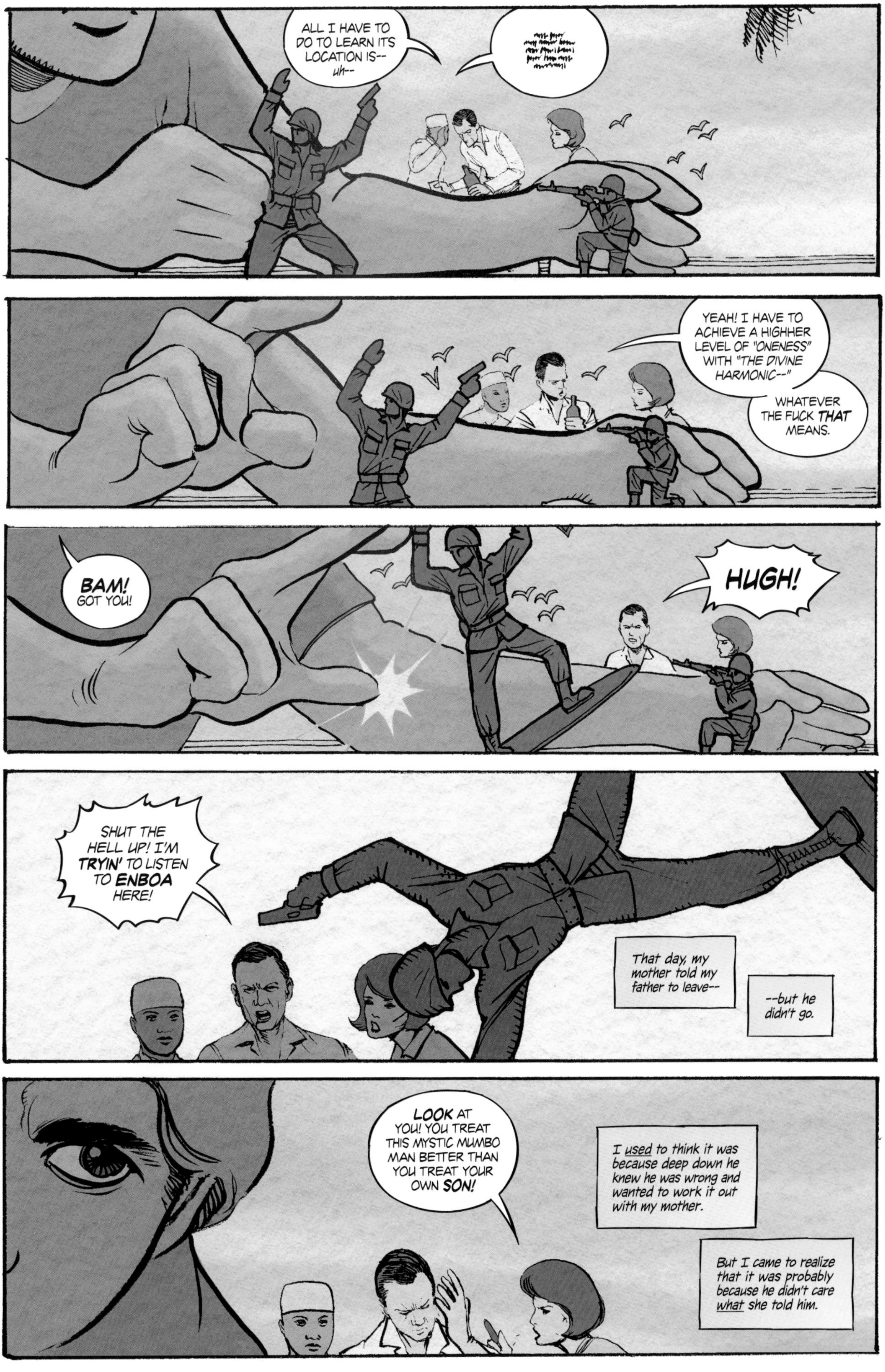
ALL I HAVE TO DO TO LEARN ITS LOCATION IS-- uh--
YEAH! I HAVE TO ACHIEVE A HIGHHER LEVEL OF "ONENESS" WITH "THE DIVINE HARMONIC--"
WHATEVER THE FUCK THAT MEANS.
BAM! GOT YOU!
HUGH!
SHUT THE HELL UP! I'M TRYIN' TO LISTEN TO ENBOA HERE!
That day, my mother told my father to leave--
--but he didn't go.
LOOK AT YOU! YOU TREAT THIS MYSTIC MUMBO MAN BETTER THAN YOU TREAT YOUR OWN SON!
I used to think it was because deep down he knew he was wrong and wanted to work it out with my mother.
But I came to realize that it was probably because he didn't care what she told him.

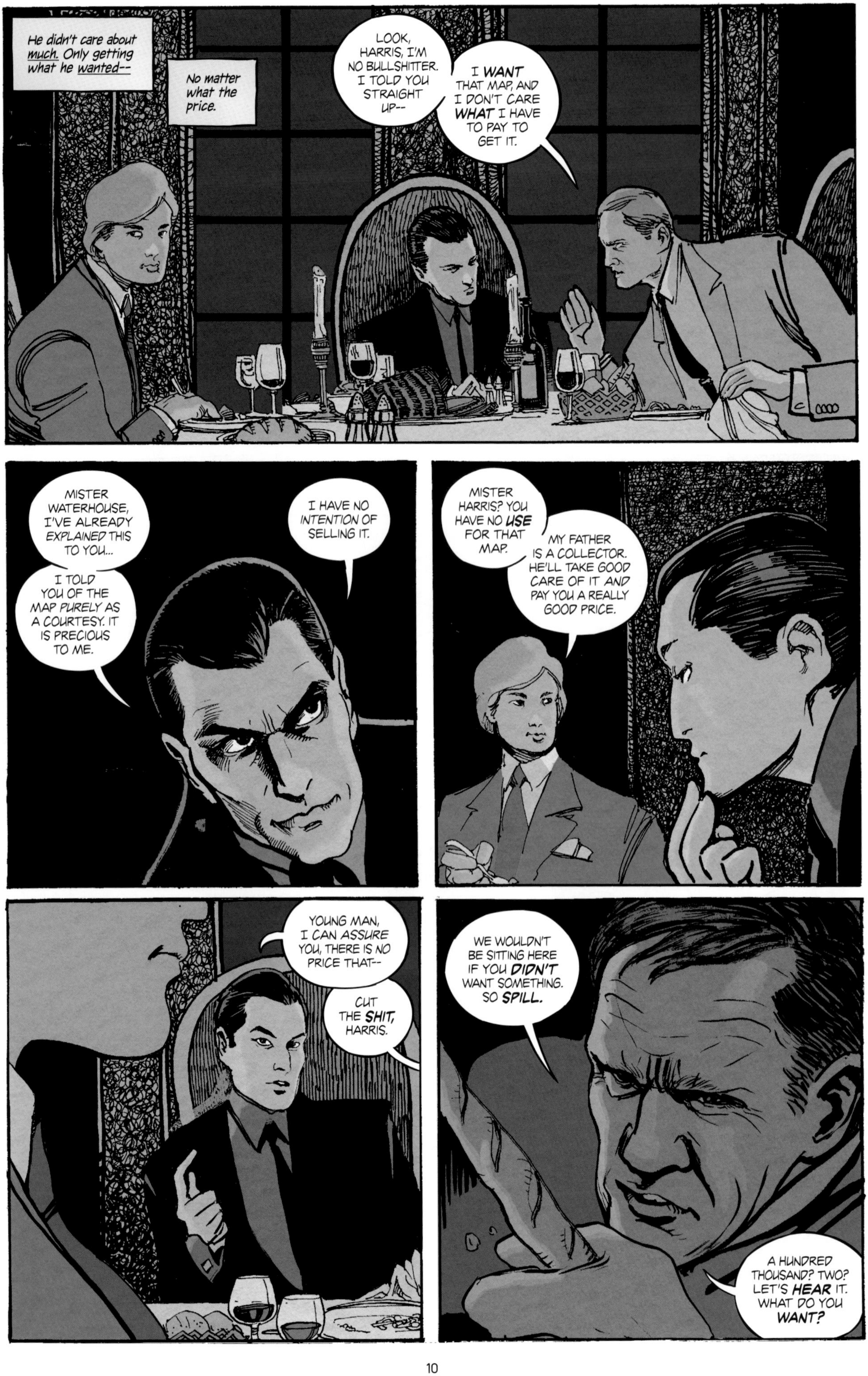
He didn't care about much. Only getting what he wanted--
No matter what the price.
LOOK, HARRIS, I'M NO BULLSHITTER. I TOLD YOU STRAIGHT UP--
I WANT THAT MAP, AND I DON'T CARE WHAT I HAVE TO PAY TO GET IT.
MISTER WATERHOUSE, I'VE ALREADY EXPLAINED THIS TO YOU...
I TOLD YOU OF THE MAP PURELY AS A COURTESY. IT IS PRECIOUS TO ME.
I HAVE NO INTENTION OF SELLING IT.
MISTER HARRIS? YOU HAVE NO USE FOR THAT MAP.
MY FATHER IS A COLLECTOR. HE'LL TAKE GOOD CARE OF IT AND PAY YOU A REALLY GOOD PRICE.
YOUNG MAN, I CAN ASSURE YOU, THERE IS NO PRICE THAT--
CUT THE SHIT, HARRIS.
WE WOULDN'T BE SITTING HERE IF YOU DIDN'T WANT SOMETHING. SO SPILL.
A HUNDRED THOUSAND? TWO? LET'S HEAR IT. WHAT DO YOU WANT?

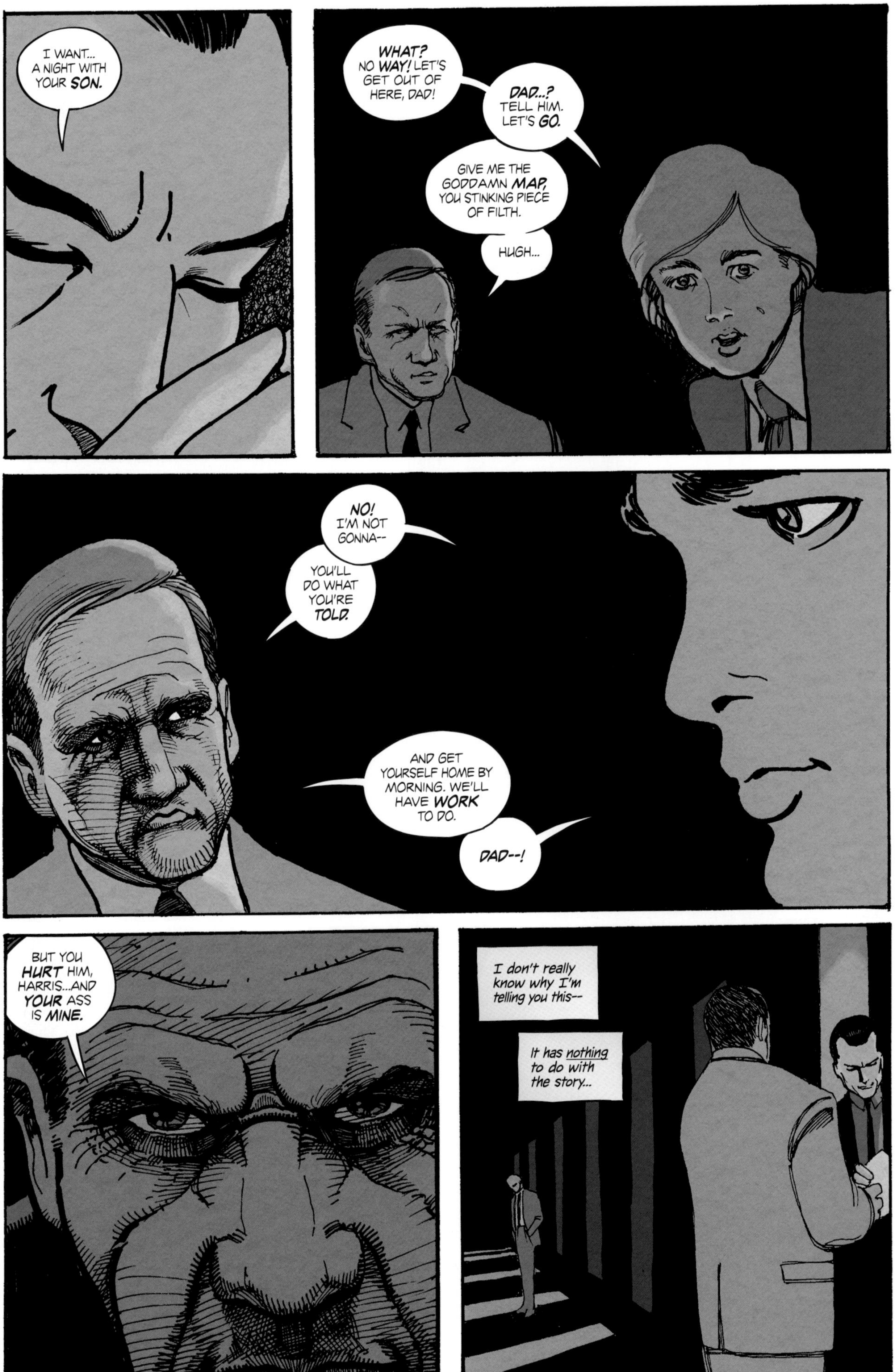
I WANT... A NIGHT WITH YOUR SON.
WHAT? NO WAY! LET'S GET OUT OF HERE, DAD!
DAD...? TELL HIM. LET'S GO.
GIVE ME THE GODDAMN MAP, YOU STINKING PIECE OF FILTH.
HUGH...
NO! I'M NOT GONNA--
YOU'LL DO WHAT YOU'RE TOLD.
AND GET YOURSELF HOME BY MORNING. WE'LL HAVE WORK TO DO.
DAD--!
BUT YOU HURT HIM, HARRIS...AND YOUR ASS IS MINE.
I don't really know why I'm telling you this--
It has nothing to do with the story...

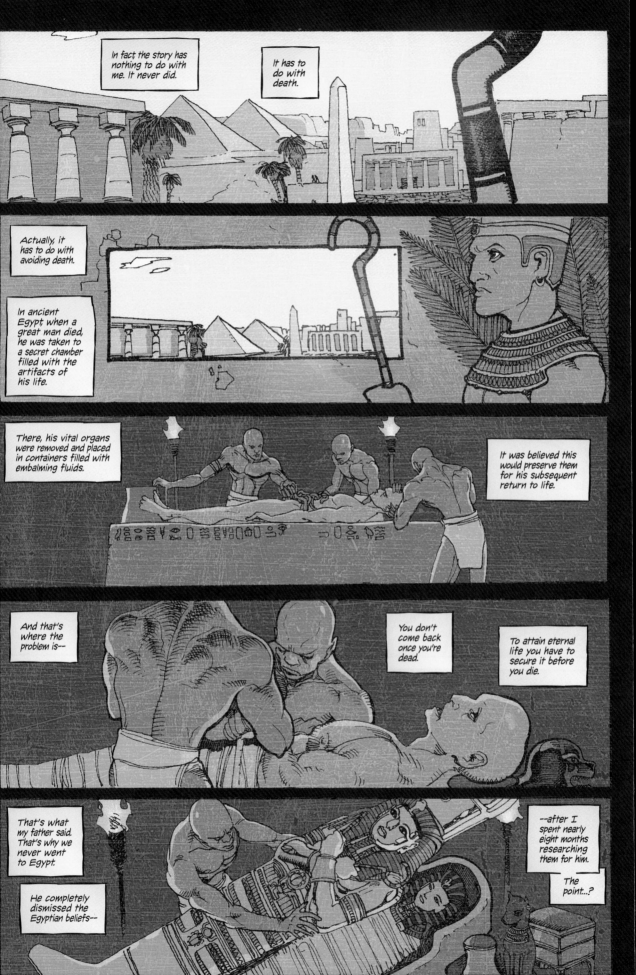

In fact the story has nothing to do with me. It never did.

It has to do with death.

Actually, it has to do with avoiding death.

In ancient Egypt, when a great man died, he was taken to a secret chamber filled with the artifacts of his life.

There, his vital organs were removed and placed in containers filled with embalming fluids.

It was believed this would preserve them for his subsequent return to life.

And that's where the problem is--

You don't come back once you're dead.

To attain eternal life you have to secure it before you die.

That's what my father said. That's why we never went to Egypt.

He completely dismissed the Egyptian beliefs--

--after I spent nearly eight months researching them for him.

The point...?

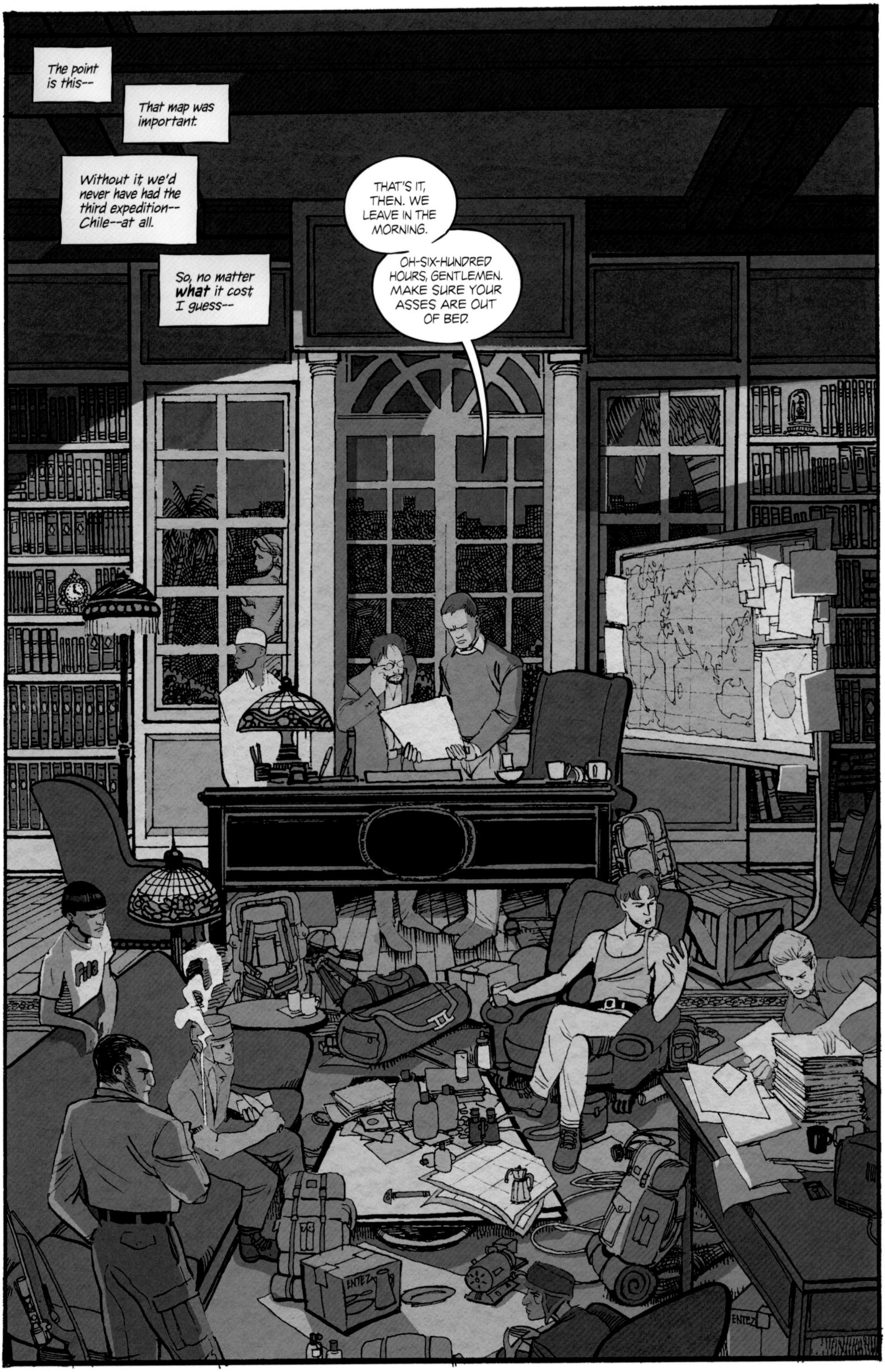
The point is this--
That map was important.
Without it we'd never have had the third expedition--Chile--at all.
So, no matter **what** it cost, I guess--
THAT'S IT, THEN. WE LEAVE IN THE MORNING.
OH-SIX-HUNDRED HOURS, GENTLEMEN. MAKE SURE YOUR ASSES ARE OUT OF BED.

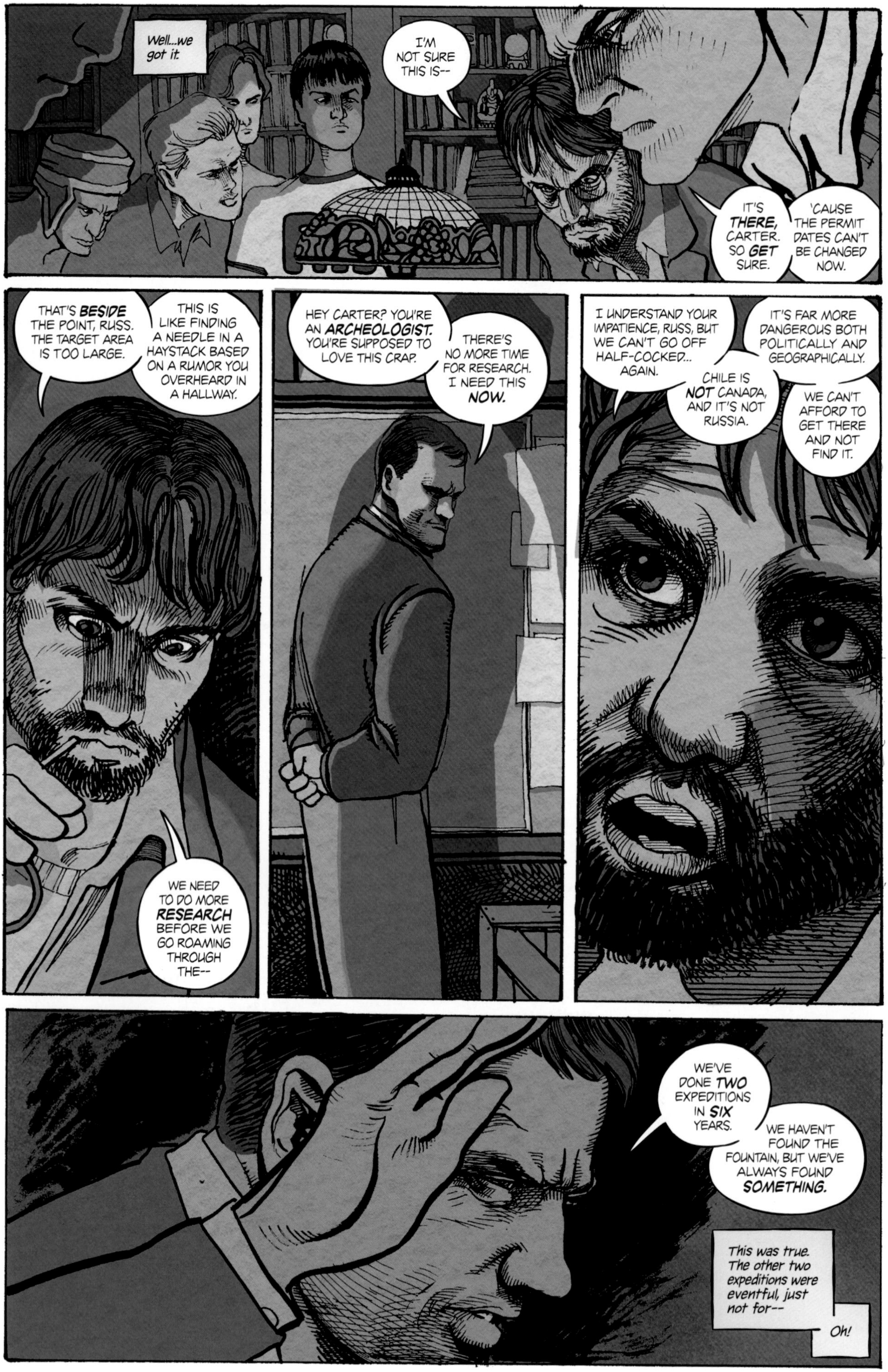
Well...we got it.
I'M NOT SURE THIS IS--
IT'S THERE, CARTER. SO GET SURE.
'CAUSE THE PERMIT DATES CAN'T BE CHANGED NOW.
THAT'S BESIDE THE POINT, RUSS. THE TARGET AREA IS TOO LARGE.
THIS IS LIKE FINDING A NEEDLE IN A HAYSTACK BASED ON A RUMOR YOU OVERHEARD IN A HALLWAY.
WE NEED TO DO MORE RESEARCH BEFORE WE GO ROAMING THROUGH THE--
HEY CARTER? YOU'RE AN ARCHEOLOGIST. YOU'RE SUPPOSED TO LOVE THIS CRAP.
THERE'S NO MORE TIME FOR RESEARCH. I NEED THIS NOW.
I UNDERSTAND YOUR IMPATIENCE, RUSS, BUT WE CAN'T GO OFF HALF-COCKED... AGAIN.
IT'S FAR MORE DANGEROUS BOTH POLITICALLY AND GEOGRAPHICALLY.
CHILE IS NOT CANADA, AND IT'S NOT RUSSIA.
WE CAN'T AFFORD TO GET THERE AND NOT FIND IT.
WE'VE DONE TWO EXPEDITIONS IN SIX YEARS.
WE HAVEN'T FOUND THE FOUNTAIN, BUT WE'VE ALWAYS FOUND SOMETHING.
This was true. The other two expeditions were eventful, just not for--
Oh!

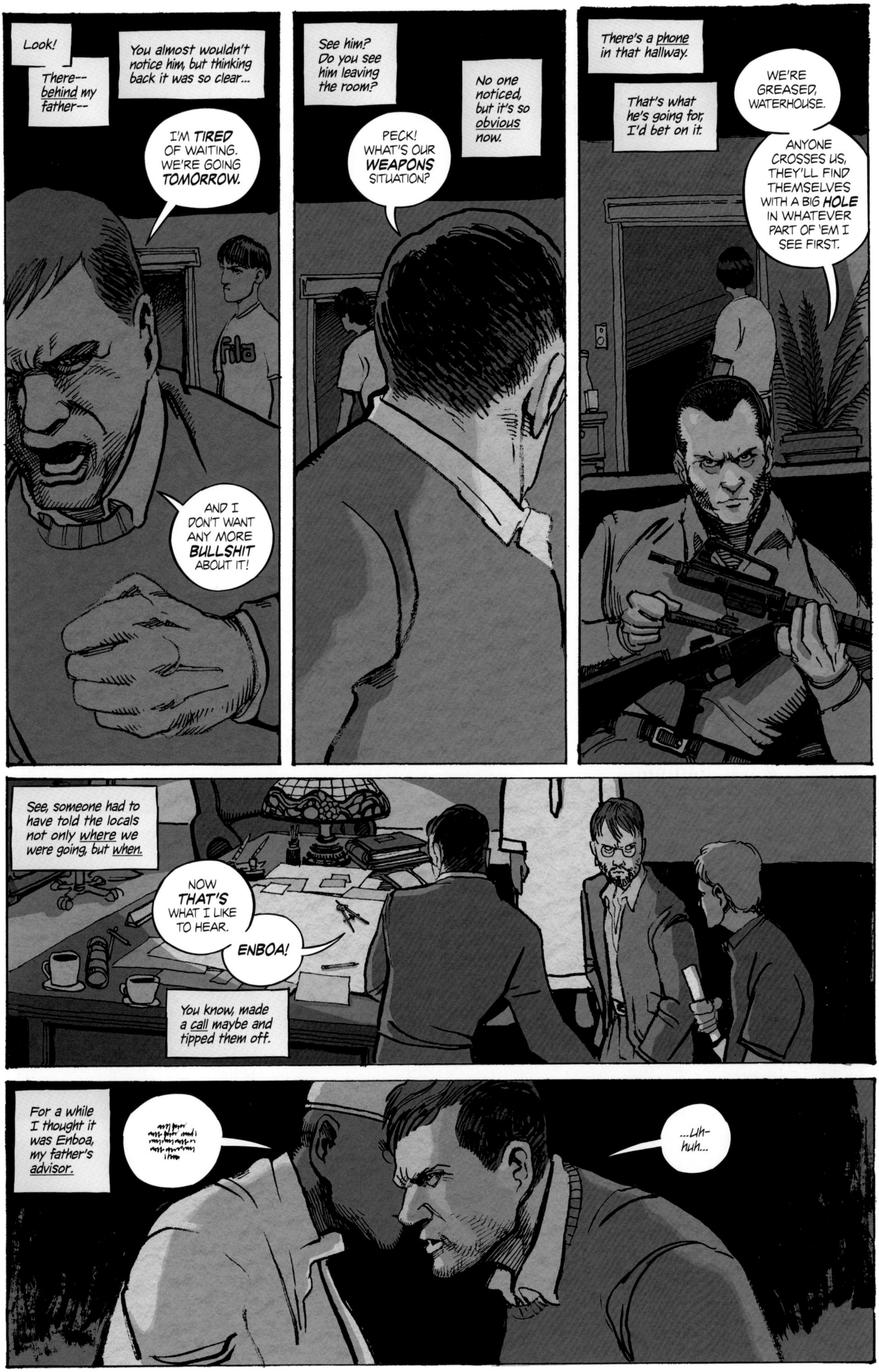

Look!
There-- behind my father--
You almost wouldn't notice him, but thinking back it was so clear...
I'M TIRED OF WAITING. WE'RE GOING TOMORROW.
AND I DON'T WANT ANY MORE BULLSHIT ABOUT IT!
See him? Do you see him leaving the room?
No one noticed, but it's so obvious now.
PECK! WHAT'S OUR WEAPONS SITUATION?
There's a phone in that hallway.
That's what he's going for, I'd bet on it.
WE'RE GREASED, WATERHOUSE.
ANYONE CROSSES US, THEY'LL FIND THEMSELVES WITH A BIG HOLE IN WHATEVER PART OF 'EM I SEE FIRST.
See, someone had to have told the locals not only where we were going, but when.
NOW THAT'S WHAT I LIKE TO HEAR.
ENBOA!
You know, made a call maybe and tipped them off.
For a while I thought it was Enboa, my father's advisor.
...Uh-huh...

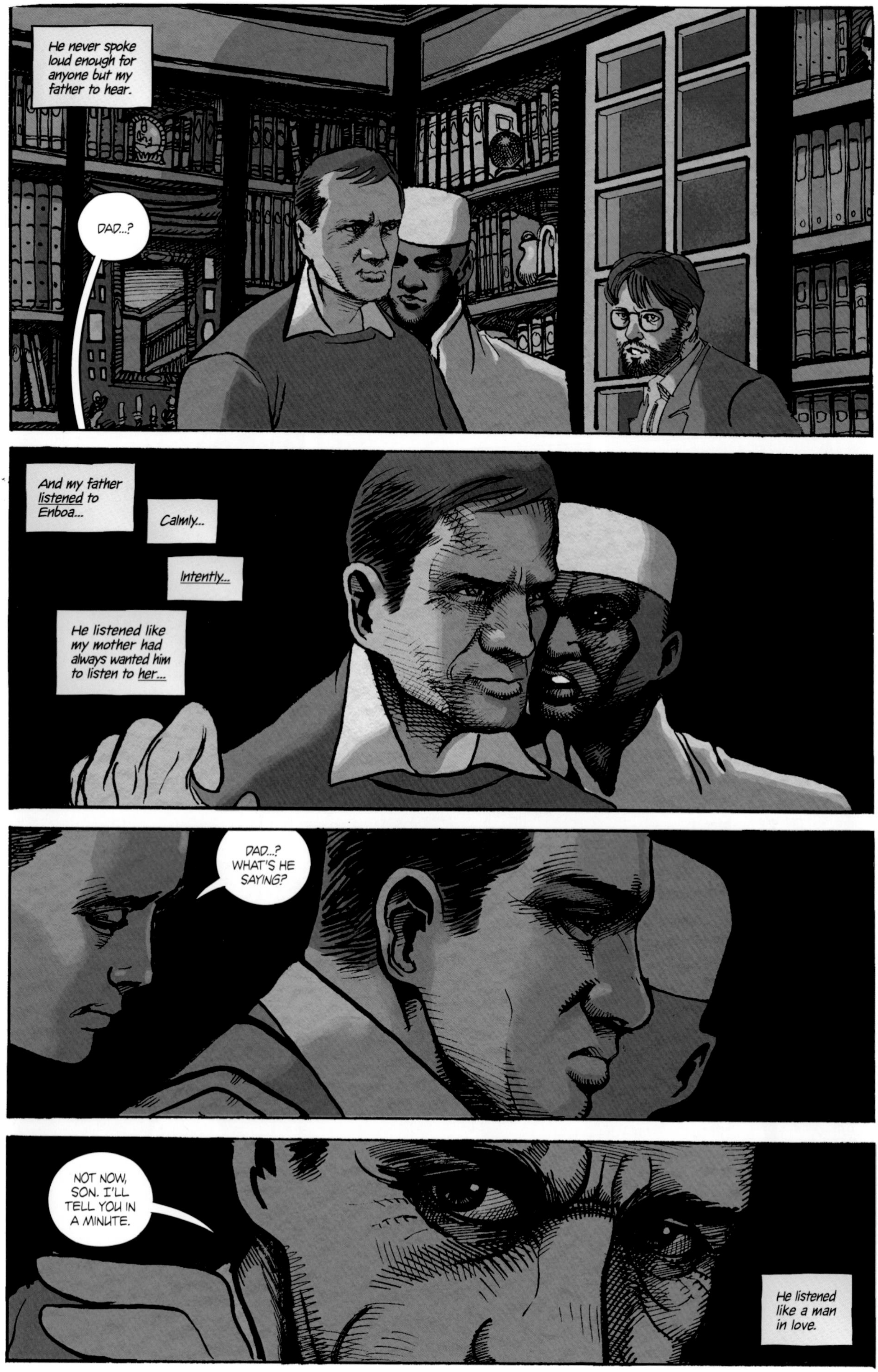
He never spoke loud enough for anyone but my father to hear.
DAD...?
And my father listened to Enboa...
Calmly...
Intently...
He listened like my mother had always wanted him to listen to her...
DAD...? WHAT'S HE SAYING?
NOT NOW, SON. I'LL TELL YOU IN A MINUTE.
He listened like a man in love.

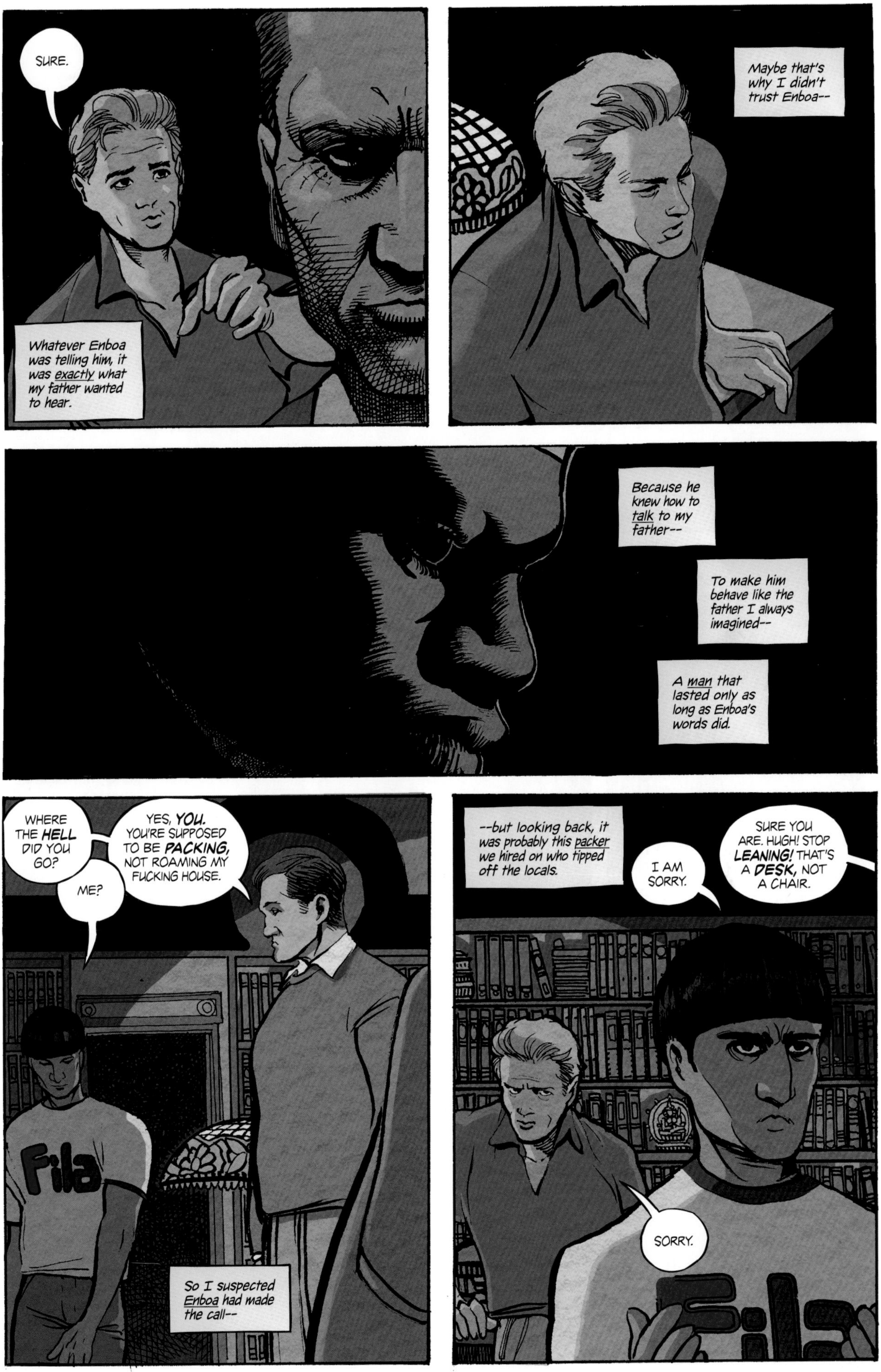
SURE.
Whatever Enboa was telling him, it was exactly what my father wanted to hear.
Maybe that's why I didn't trust Enboa--
Because he knew how to talk to my father--
To make him behave like the father I always imagined--
A man that lasted only as long as Enboa's words did.
WHERE THE HELL DID YOU GO?
ME?
YES, YOU. YOU'RE SUPPOSED TO BE PACKING, NOT ROAMING MY FUCKING HOUSE.
So I suspected Enboa had made the call--
--but looking back, it was probably this packer we hired on who tipped off the locals.
I AM SORRY.
SURE YOU ARE. HUGH! STOP LEANING! THAT'S A DESK, NOT A CHAIR.
SORRY.

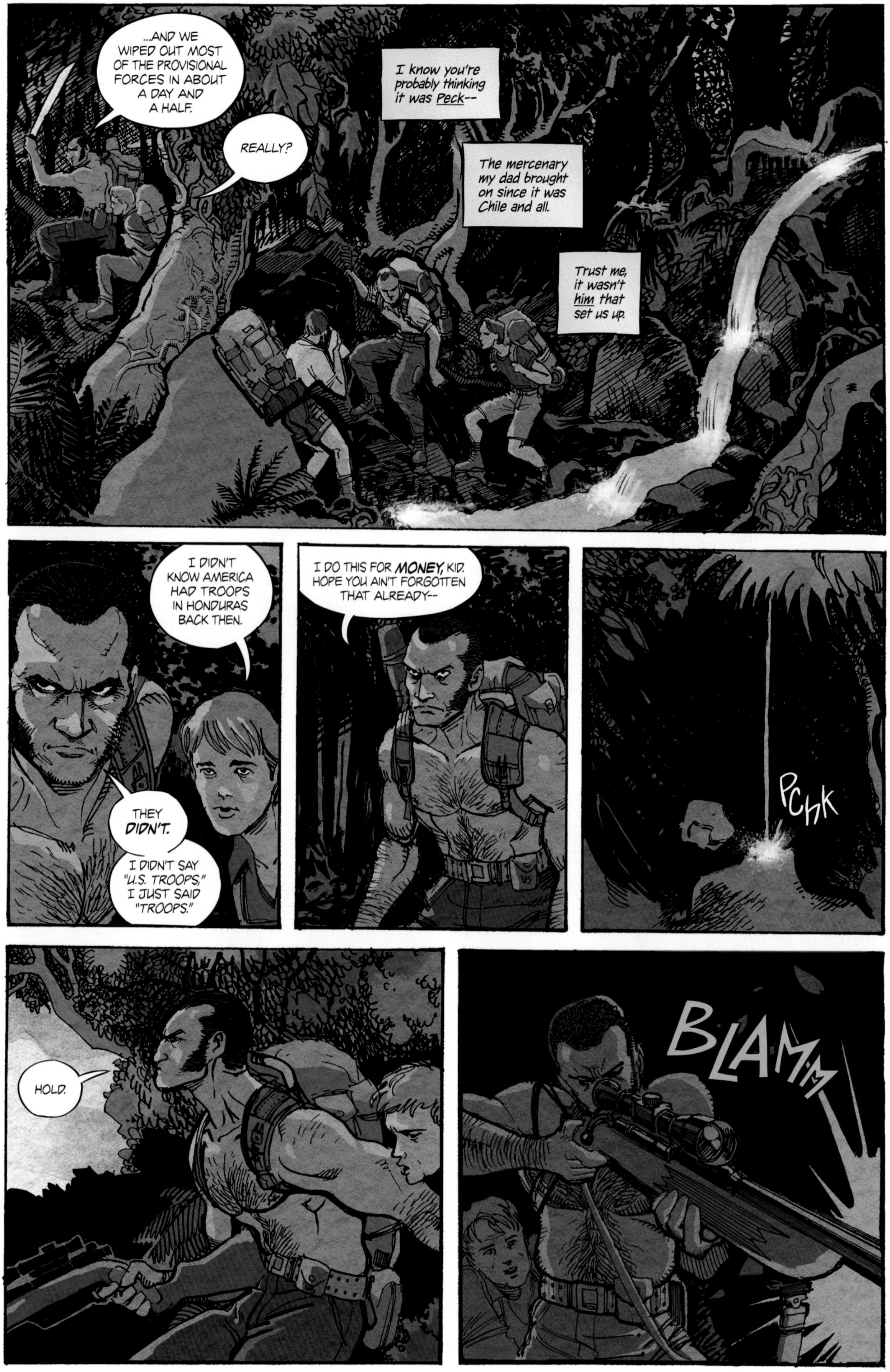
...AND WE WIPED OUT MOST OF THE PROVISIONAL FORCES IN ABOUT A DAY AND A HALF.
REALLY?
I know you're probably thinking it was Peck--
The mercenary my dad brought on since it was Chile and all.
Trust me, it wasn't him that set us up.
I DIDN'T KNOW AMERICA HAD TROOPS IN HONDURAS BACK THEN.
THEY DIDN'T.
I DIDN'T SAY "U.S. TROOPS," I JUST SAID "TROOPS."
I DO THIS FOR MONEY, KID. HOPE YOU AIN'T FORGOTTEN THAT ALREADY--
PCHK
HOLD.
BLAMM

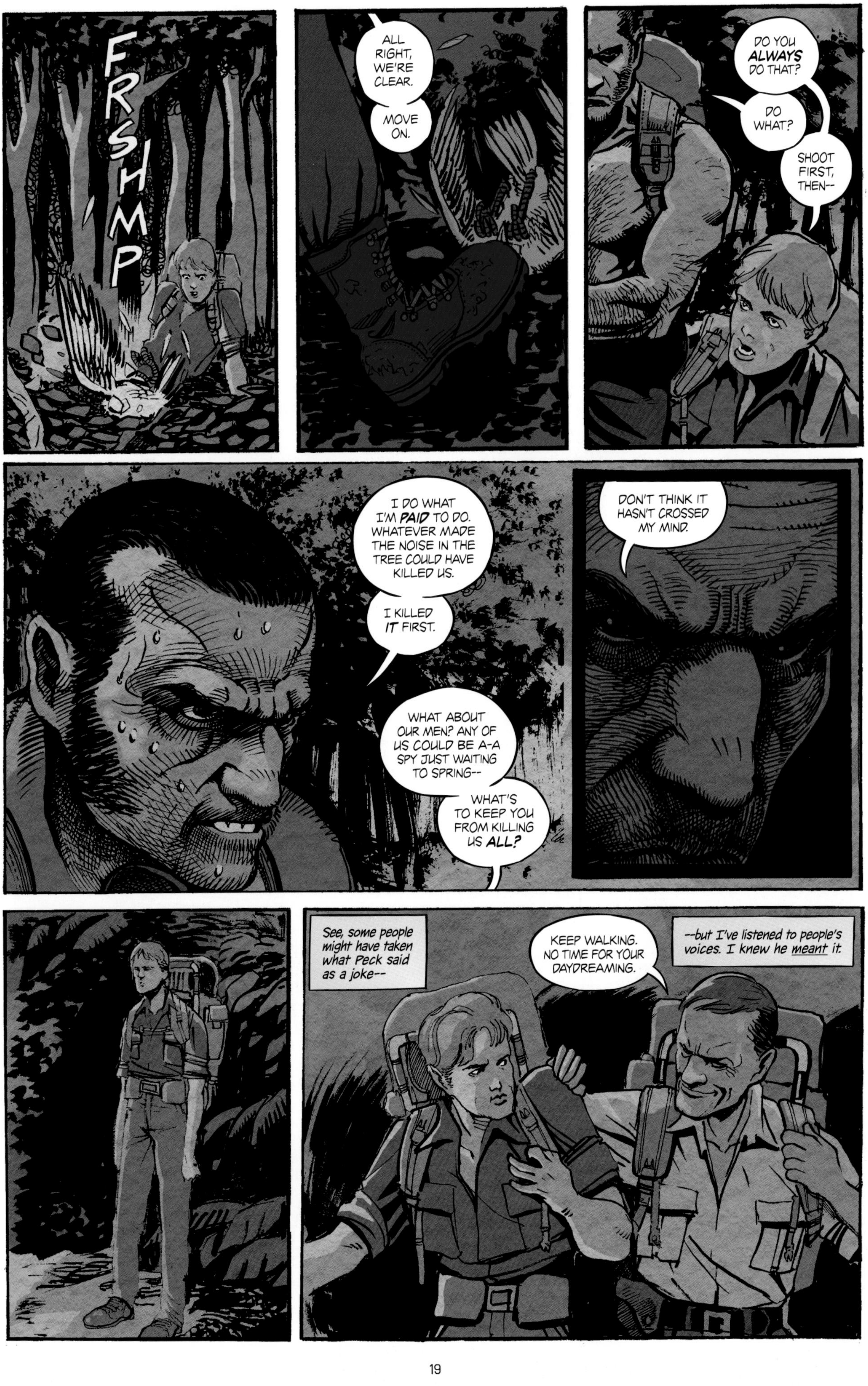
FRSHMP
ALL RIGHT, WE'RE CLEAR.
MOVE ON.
DO YOU ALWAYS DO THAT?
DO WHAT?
SHOOT FIRST, THEN--
I DO WHAT I'M PAID TO DO. WHATEVER MADE THE NOISE IN THE TREE COULD HAVE KILLED US.
I KILLED IT FIRST.
WHAT ABOUT OUR MEN? ANY OF US COULD BE A-A SPY JUST WAITING TO SPRING--
WHAT'S TO KEEP YOU FROM KILLING US ALL?
DON'T THINK IT HASN'T CROSSED MY MIND.
See, some people might have taken what Peck said as a joke--
KEEP WALKING. NO TIME FOR YOUR DAYDREAMING.
--but I've listened to people's voices. I knew he meant it.

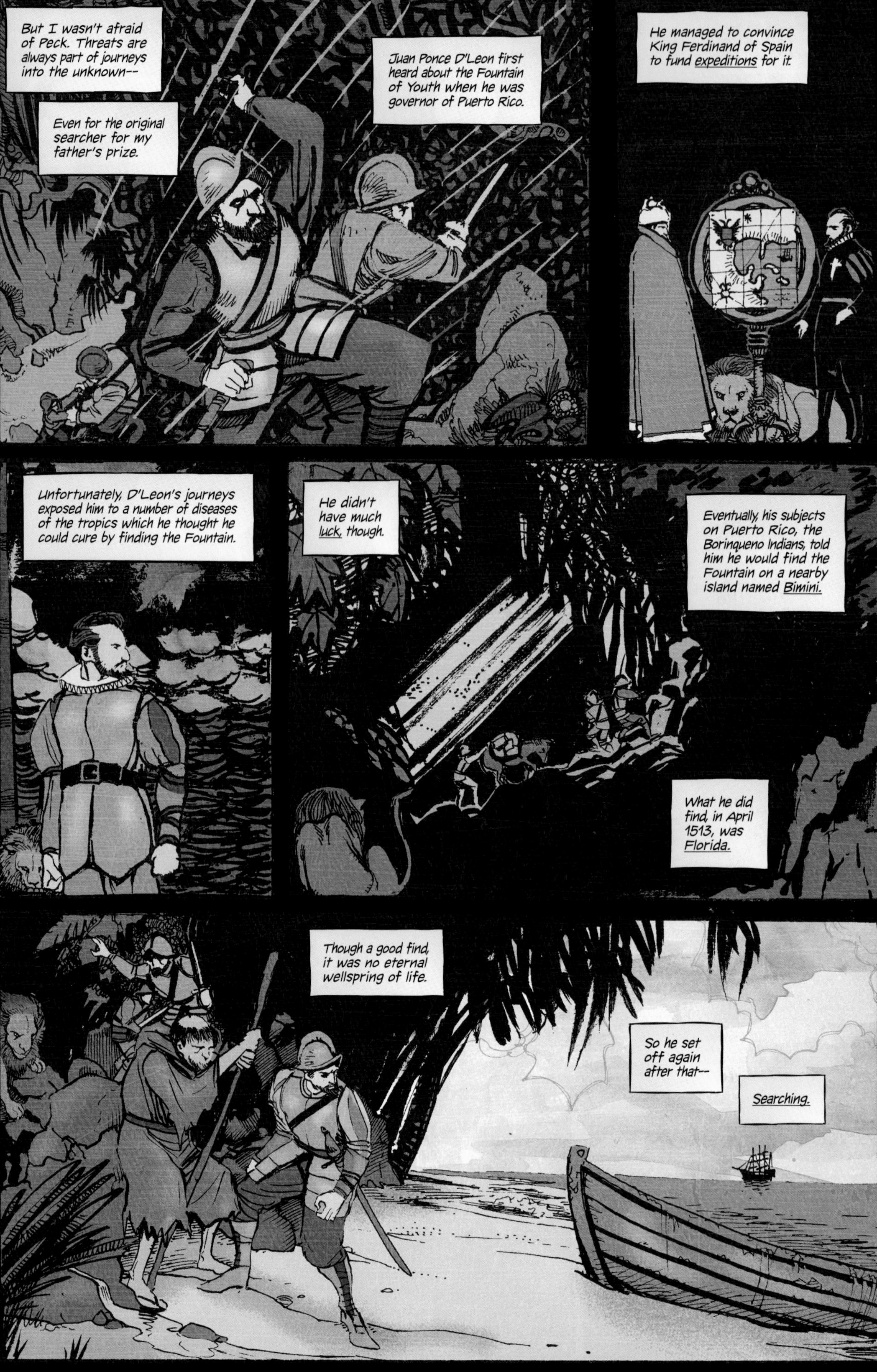
But I wasn't afraid of Peck. Threats are always part of journeys into the unknown--
Even for the original searcher for my father's prize.
Juan Ponce D'Leon first heard about the Fountain of Youth when he was governor of Puerto Rico.
He managed to convince King Ferdinand of Spain to fund expeditions for it.
Unfortunately, D'Leon's journeys exposed him to a number of diseases of the tropics which he thought he could cure by finding the Fountain.
He didn't have much luck, though.
Eventually, his subjects on Puerto Rico, the Borinqueno Indians, told him he would find the Fountain on a nearby island named Bimini.
What he did find, in April 1513, was Florida.
Though a good find, it was no eternal wellspring of life.
So he set off again after that--
Searching.

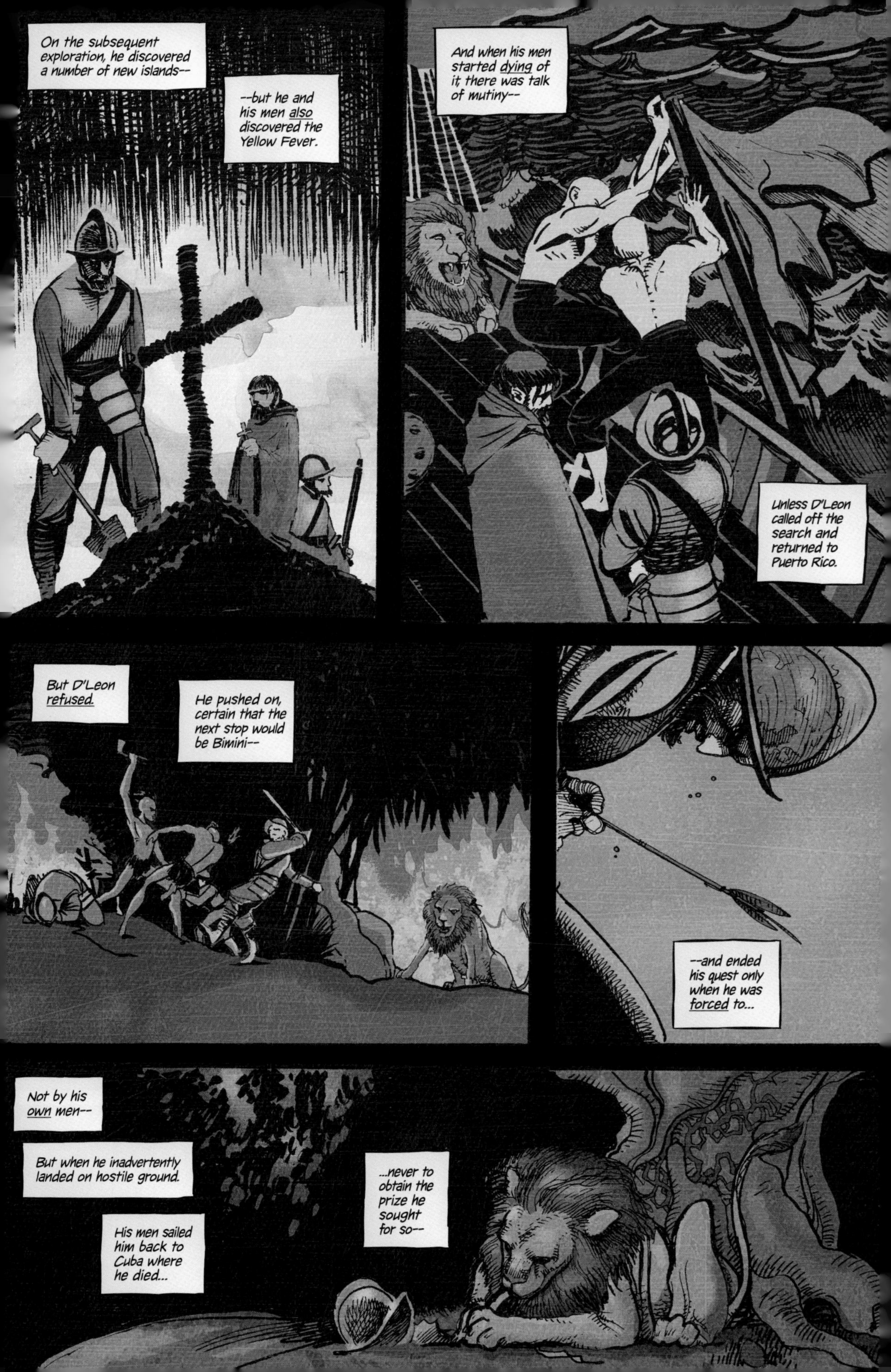
On the subsequent exploration, he discovered a number of new islands--
--but he and his men also discovered the Yellow Fever.
And when his men started dying of it, there was talk of mutiny--
Unless D'Leon called off the search and returned to Puerto Rico.
But D'Leon refused.
He pushed on, certain that the next stop would be Bimini--
--and ended his quest only when he was forced to...
Not by his own men--
But when he inadvertently landed on hostile ground.
His men sailed him back to Cuba where he died...
...never to obtain the prize he sought for so--

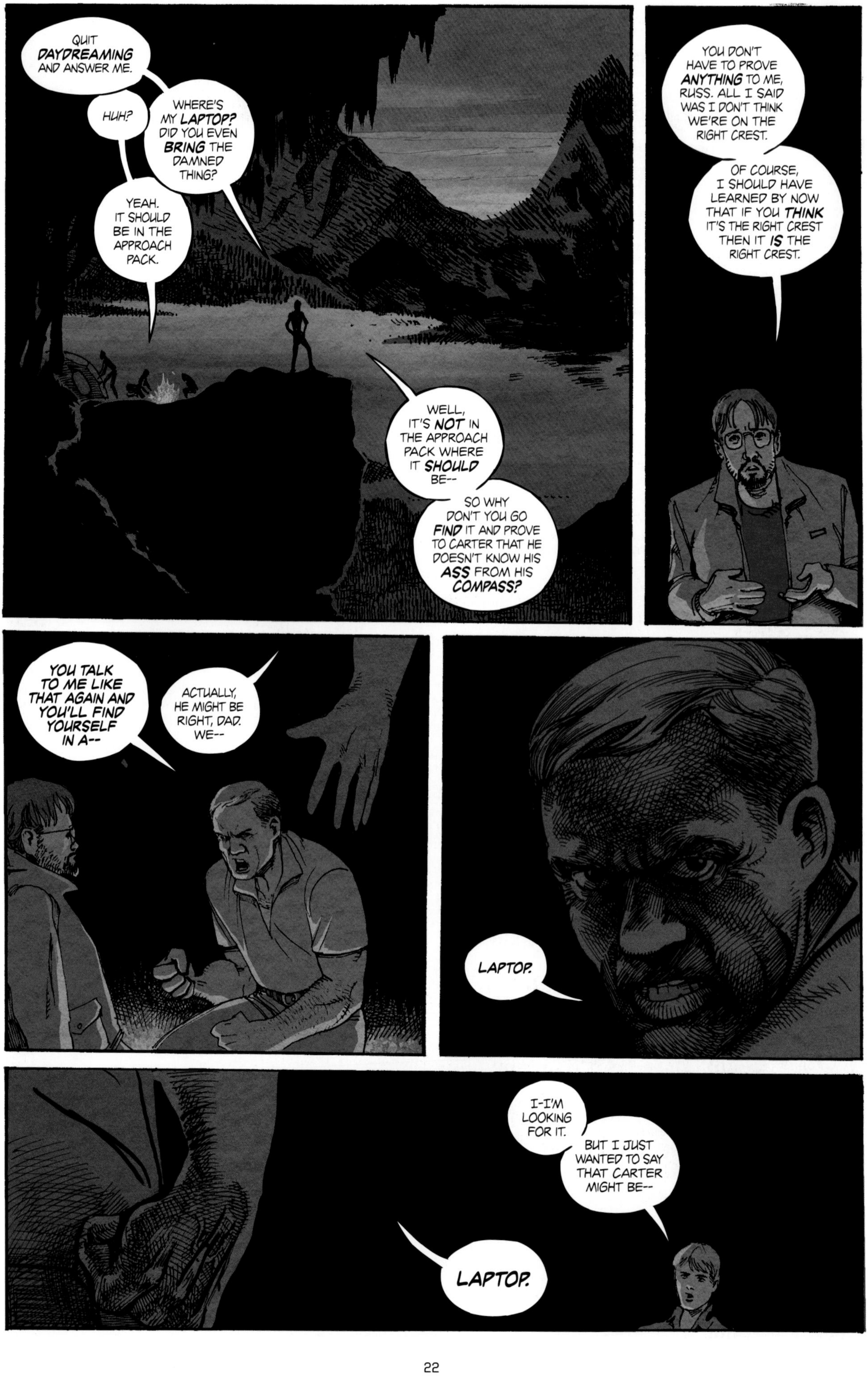
QUIT DAYDREAMING AND ANSWER ME.
HUH?
WHERE'S MY LAPTOP? DID YOU EVEN BRING THE DAMNED THING?
YEAH. IT SHOULD BE IN THE APPROACH PACK.
WELL, IT'S NOT IN THE APPROACH PACK WHERE IT SHOULD BE--
SO WHY DON'T YOU GO FIND IT AND PROVE TO CARTER THAT HE DOESN'T KNOW HIS ASS FROM HIS COMPASS?
YOU DON'T HAVE TO PROVE ANYTHING TO ME, RUSS. ALL I SAID WAS I DON'T THINK WE'RE ON THE RIGHT CREST.
OF COURSE, I SHOULD HAVE LEARNED BY NOW THAT IF YOU THINK IT'S THE RIGHT CREST THEN IT IS THE RIGHT CREST.
YOU TALK TO ME LIKE THAT AGAIN AND YOU'LL FIND YOURSELF IN A--
ACTUALLY, HE MIGHT BE RIGHT, DAD. WE--
LAPTOP.
I-I'M LOOKING FOR IT.
BUT I JUST WANTED TO SAY THAT CARTER MIGHT BE--
LAPTOP.

LAPTOP.

LAP--

UNNH!

HNNH...

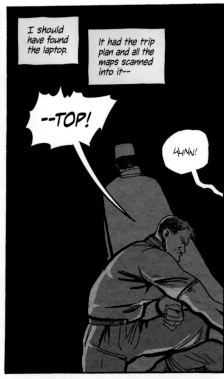

I should have found the laptop.

It had the trip plan and all the maps scanned into it--

--TOP!

UHNN!

Which was a really good idea--

THAT'S ENOUGH.

Computerized maps make it...

THIS IS NONE OF YOUR DAMNED BUSINESS, PECK!

IS NOW.

MOVE! OR I'LL MAKE YOU WISH YOU HAD.

BACK OFF FROM THE BOY UNTIL YOU'VE COOLED DOWN.

UHH...

...NHH...

AND DON'T EVER THREATEN ME. UNDERSTOOD?

See, I'll do this if you let me.

Tell stuff to get you on my side when all you really need to know is what happened--

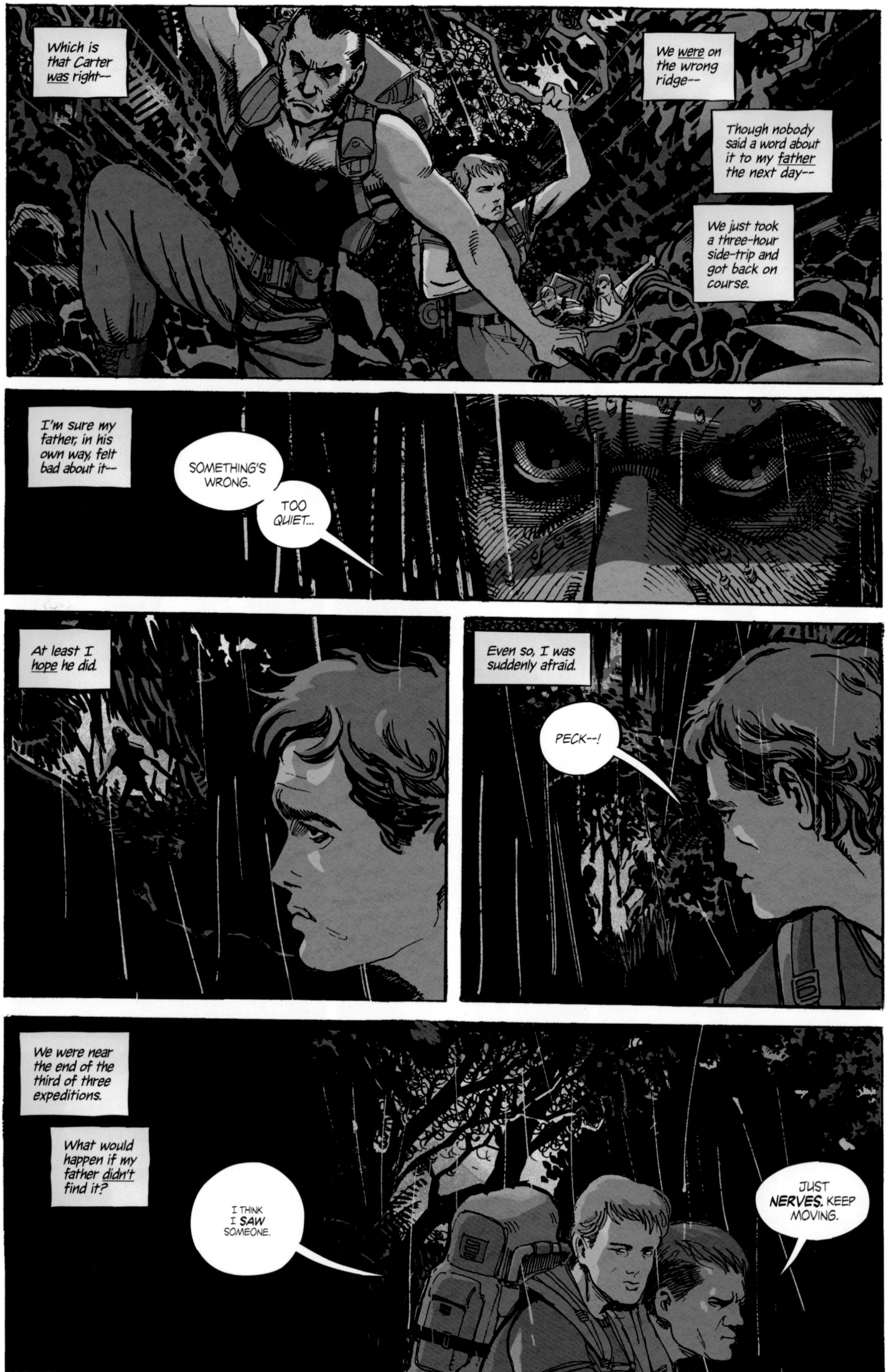
Which is that Carter was right--
We were on the wrong ridge--
Though nobody said a word about it to my father the next day--
We just took a three-hour side-trip and got back on course.
I'm sure my father, in his own way, felt bad about it--
SOMETHING'S WRONG.
TOO QUIET...
At least I hope he did.
Even so, I was suddenly afraid.
PECK--!
We were near the end of the third of three expeditions.
What would happen if my father didn't find it?
I THINK I SAW SOMEONE.
JUST NERVES. KEEP MOVING.

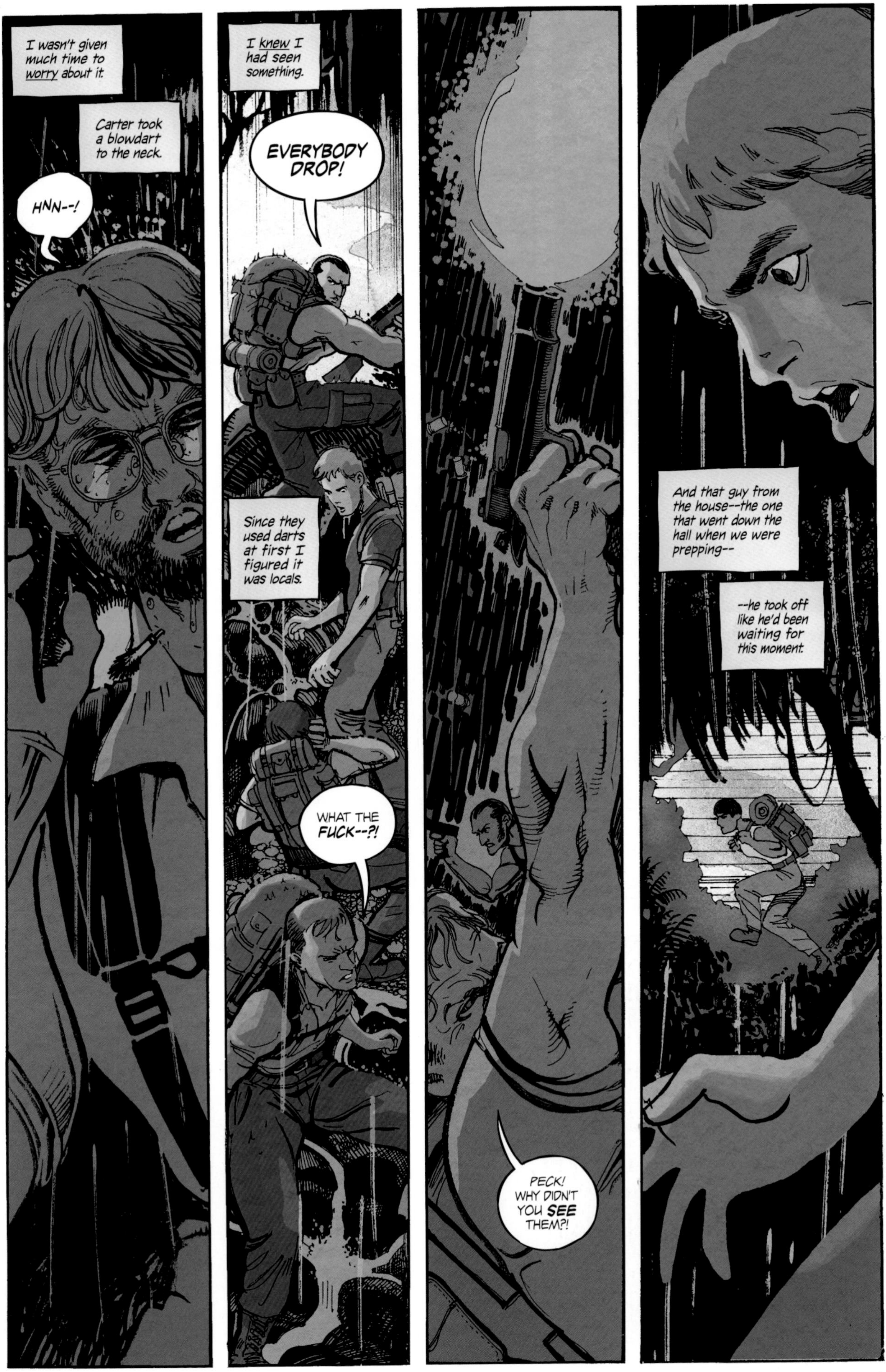
I wasn't given much time to worry about it.
Carter took a blowdart to the neck.
HNN--!
I knew I had seen something.
EVERYBODY DROP!
Since they used darts at first I figured it was locals.
WHAT THE FUCK--?!
PECK! WHY DIDN'T YOU SEE THEM?!
And that guy from the house--the one that went down the hall when we were prepping--
--he took off like he'd been waiting for this moment.

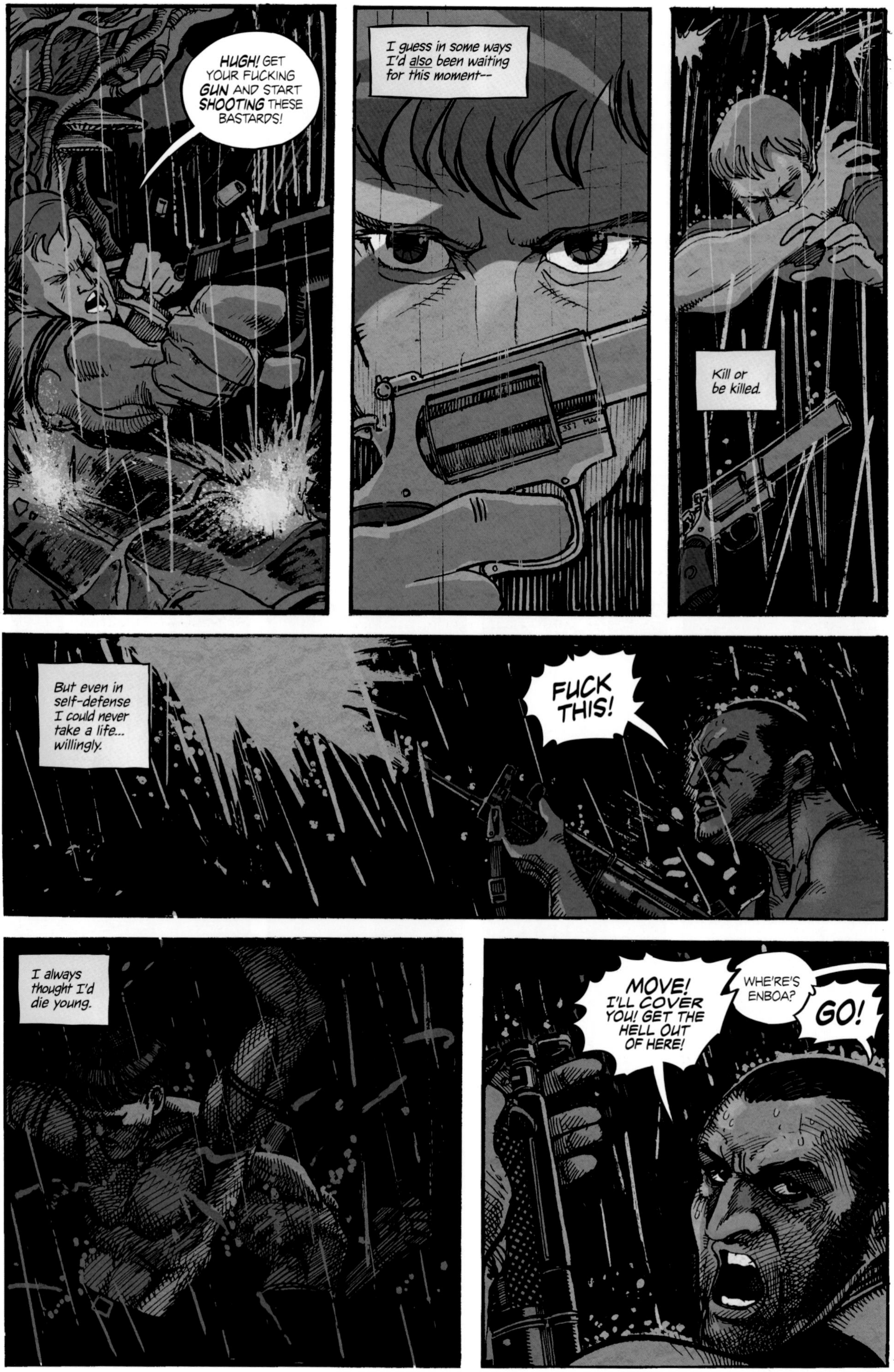
HUGH! GET YOUR FUCKING GUN AND START SHOOTING THESE BASTARDS!
I guess in some ways I'd also been waiting for this moment--
Kill or be killed.
But even in self-defense I could never take a life... willingly.
FUCK THIS!
I always thought I'd die young.
MOVE! I'LL COVER YOU! GET THE HELL OUT OF HERE!
WHE'RE'S ENBOA?
GO!

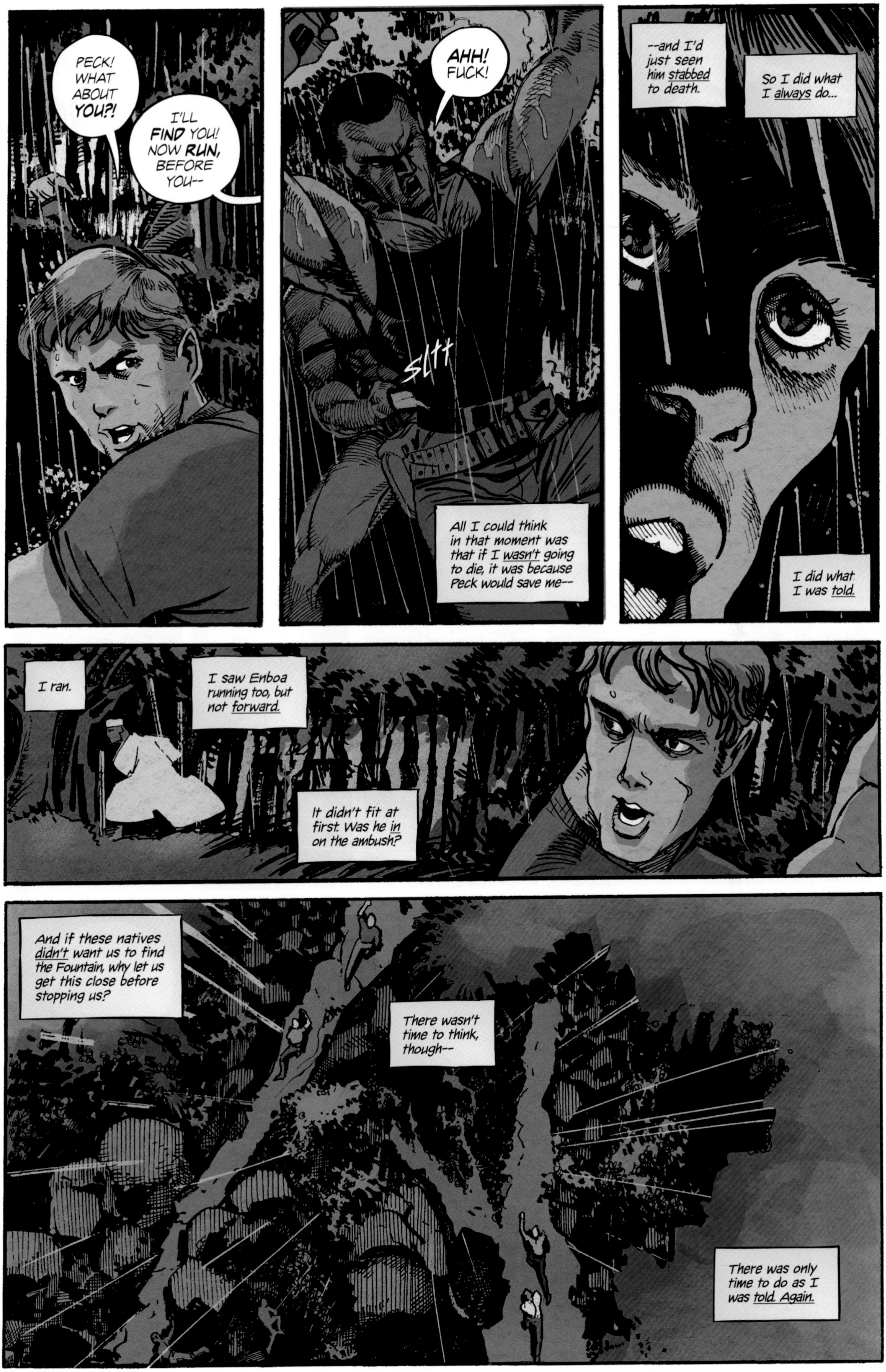
PECK! WHAT ABOUT YOU?!
I'LL FIND YOU! NOW RUN, BEFORE YOU--
AHH! FUCK!
SLTT
All I could think in that moment was that if I wasn't going to die, it was because Peck would save me--
--and I'd just seen him stabbed to death.
So I did what I always do...
I did what I was told.
I ran.
I saw Enboa running too, but not forward.
It didn't fit at first. Was he in on the ambush?
And if these natives didn't want us to find the Fountain, why let us get this close before stopping us?
There wasn't time to think, though--
There was only time to do as I was told. Again.

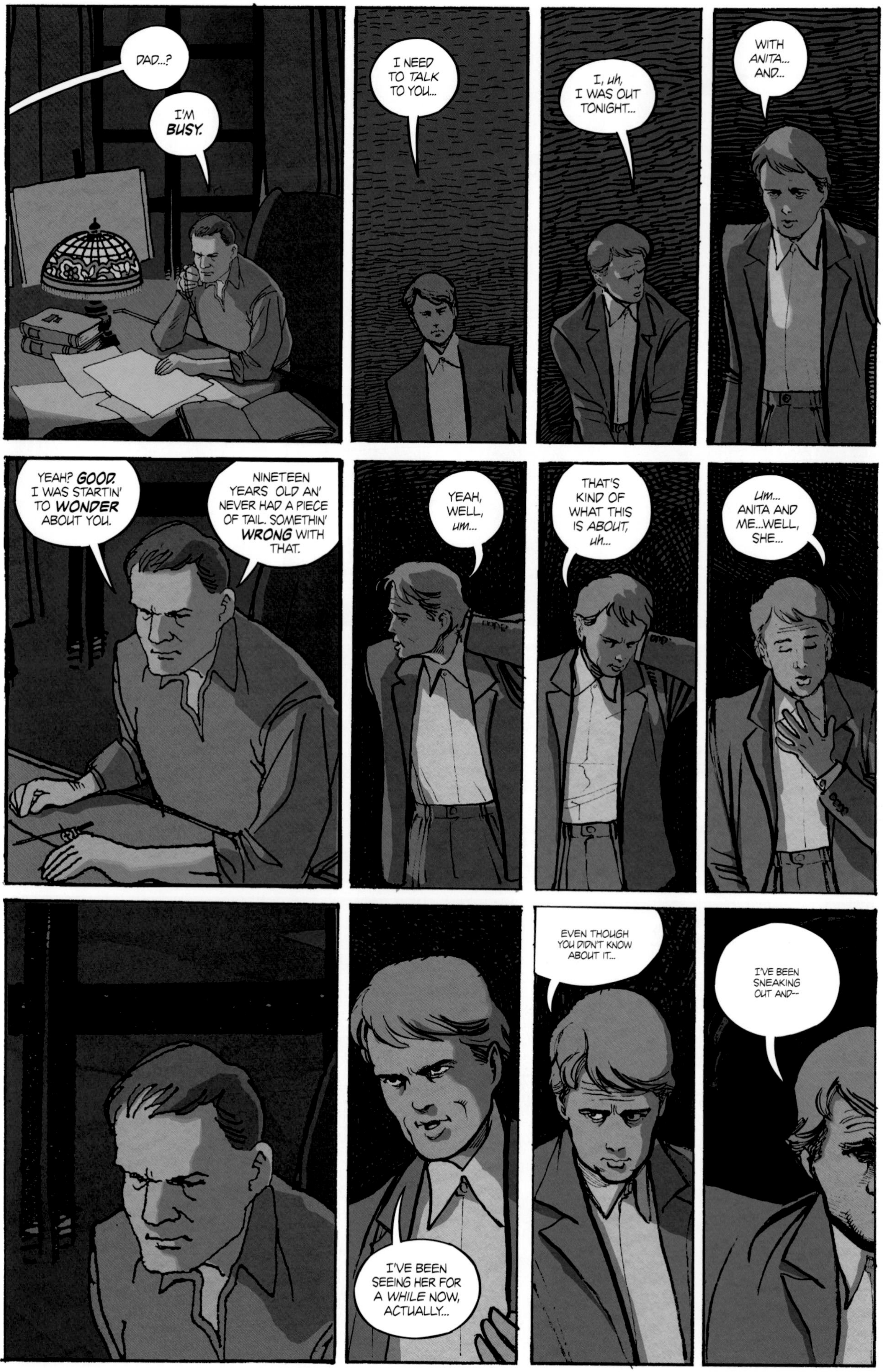
DAD...?
I'M BUSY.
I NEED TO TALK TO YOU...
I, uh, I WAS OUT TONIGHT...
WITH ANITA... AND...
YEAH? GOOD. I WAS STARTIN' TO WONDER ABOUT YOU.
NINETEEN YEARS OLD AN' NEVER HAD A PIECE OF TAIL. SOMETHIN' WRONG WITH THAT.
YEAH, WELL, um...
THAT'S KIND OF WHAT THIS IS ABOUT, uh...
um... ANITA AND ME...WELL, SHE...
I'VE BEEN SEEING HER FOR A WHILE NOW, ACTUALLY...
EVEN THOUGH YOU DIDN'T KNOW ABOUT IT...
I'VE BEEN SNEAKING OUT AND--

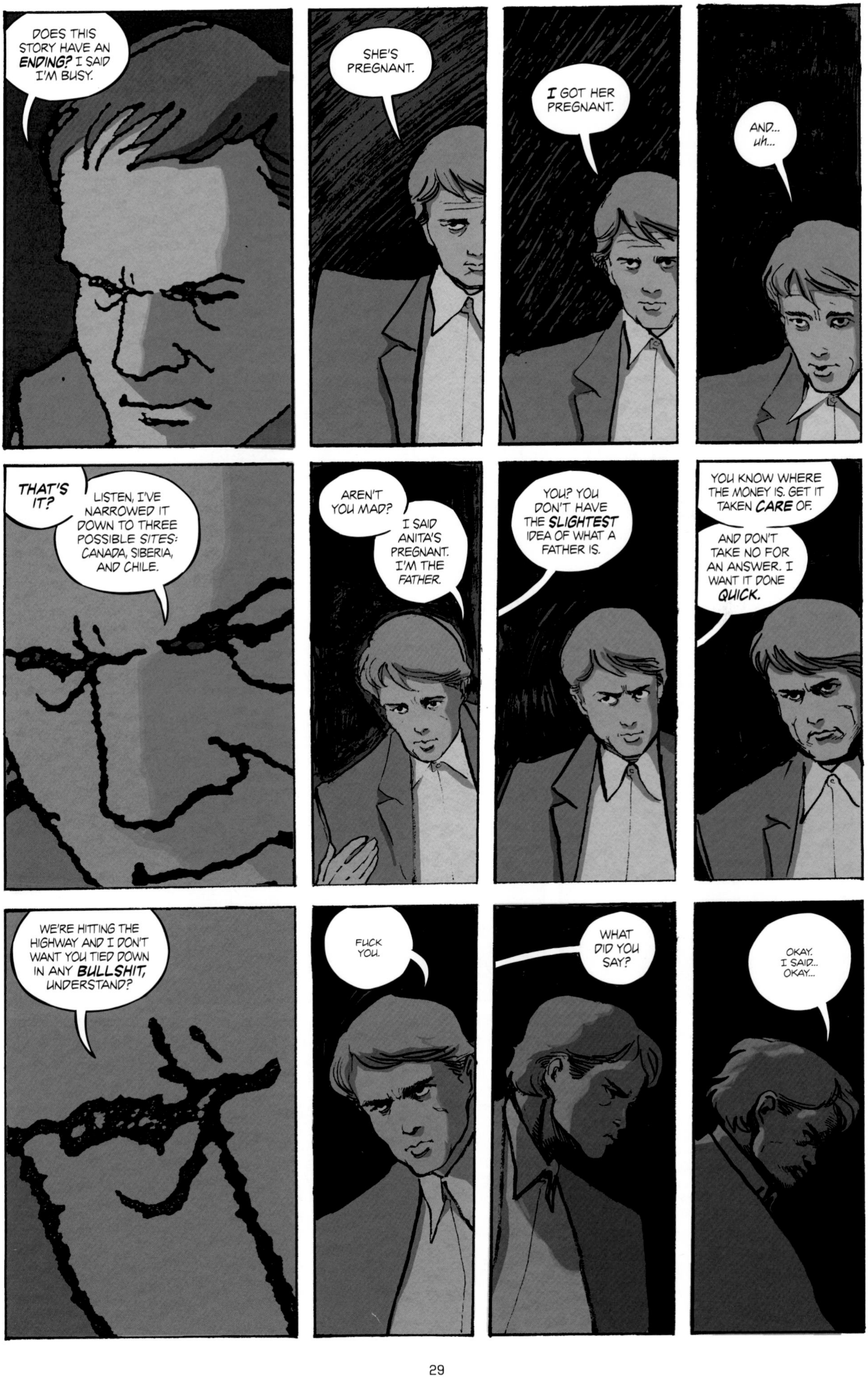
DOES THIS STORY HAVE AN ENDING? I SAID I'M BUSY.
SHE'S PREGNANT.
I GOT HER PREGNANT.
AND... uh...
THAT'S IT?
LISTEN, I'VE NARROWED IT DOWN TO THREE POSSIBLE SITES: CANADA, SIBERIA, AND CHILE.
AREN'T YOU MAD?
I SAID ANITA'S PREGNANT. I'M THE FATHER.
YOU? YOU DON'T HAVE THE SLIGHTEST IDEA OF WHAT A FATHER IS.
YOU KNOW WHERE THE MONEY IS. GET IT TAKEN CARE OF.
AND DON'T TAKE NO FOR AN ANSWER. I WANT IT DONE QUICK.
WE'RE HITTING THE HIGHWAY AND I DON'T WANT YOU TIED DOWN IN ANY BULLSHIT, UNDERSTAND?
FUCK YOU.
WHAT DID YOU SAY?
OKAY. I SAID... OKAY...

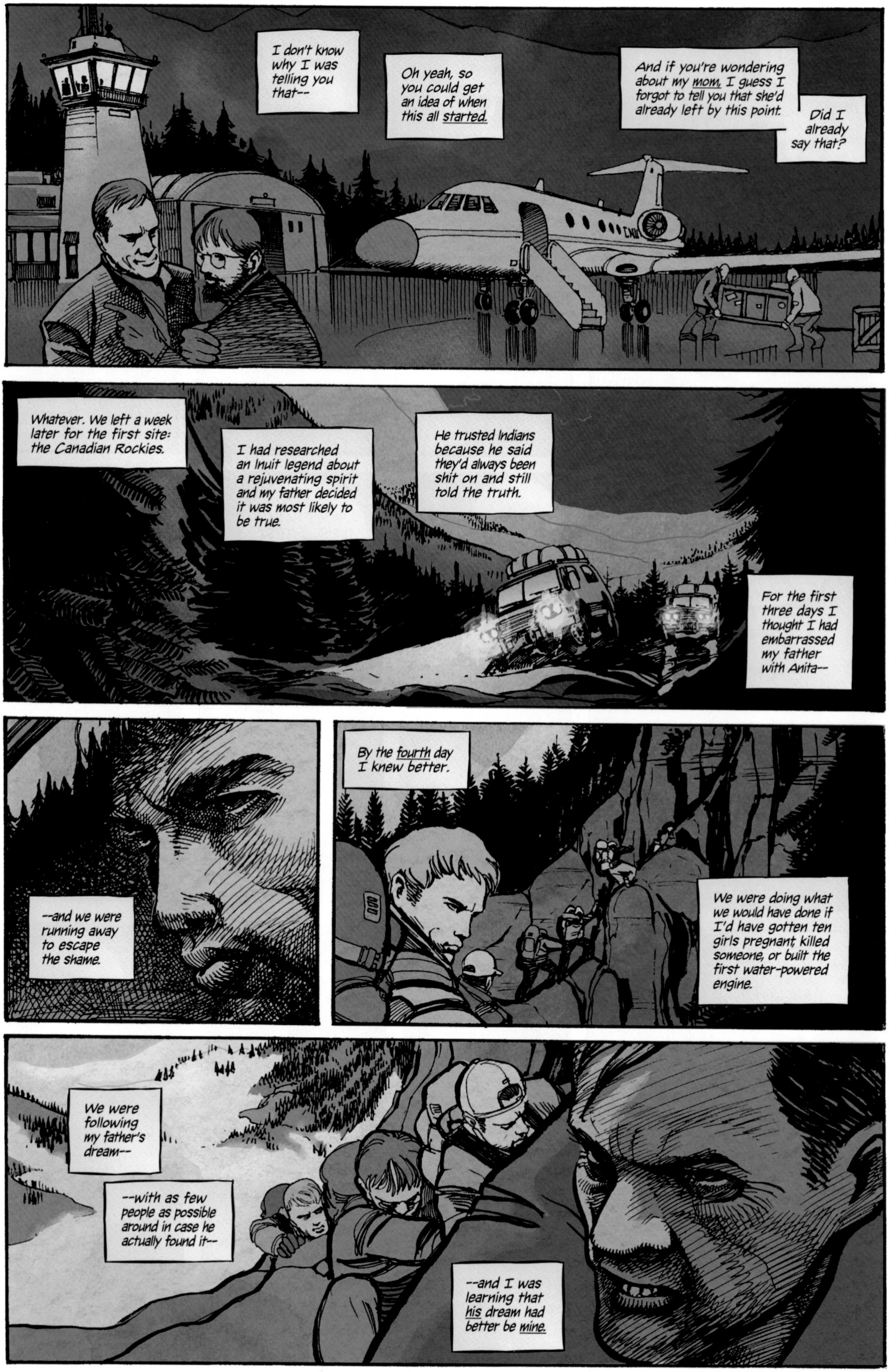
I don't know why I was telling you that--
Oh yeah, so you could get an idea of when this all started.
And if you're wondering about my mom, I guess I forgot to tell you that she'd already left by this point.
Did I already say that?
Whatever. We left a week later for the first site: the Canadian Rockies.
I had researched an Inuit legend about a rejuvenating spirit and my father decided it was most likely to be true.
He trusted Indians because he said they'd always been shit on and still told the truth.
For the first three days I thought I had embarrassed my father with Anita--
--and we were running away to escape the shame.
By the fourth day I knew better.
We were doing what we would have done if I'd have gotten ten girls pregnant, killed someone, or built the first water-powered engine.
We were following my father's dream--
--with as few people as possible around in case he actually found it--
--and I was learning that his dream had better be mine.

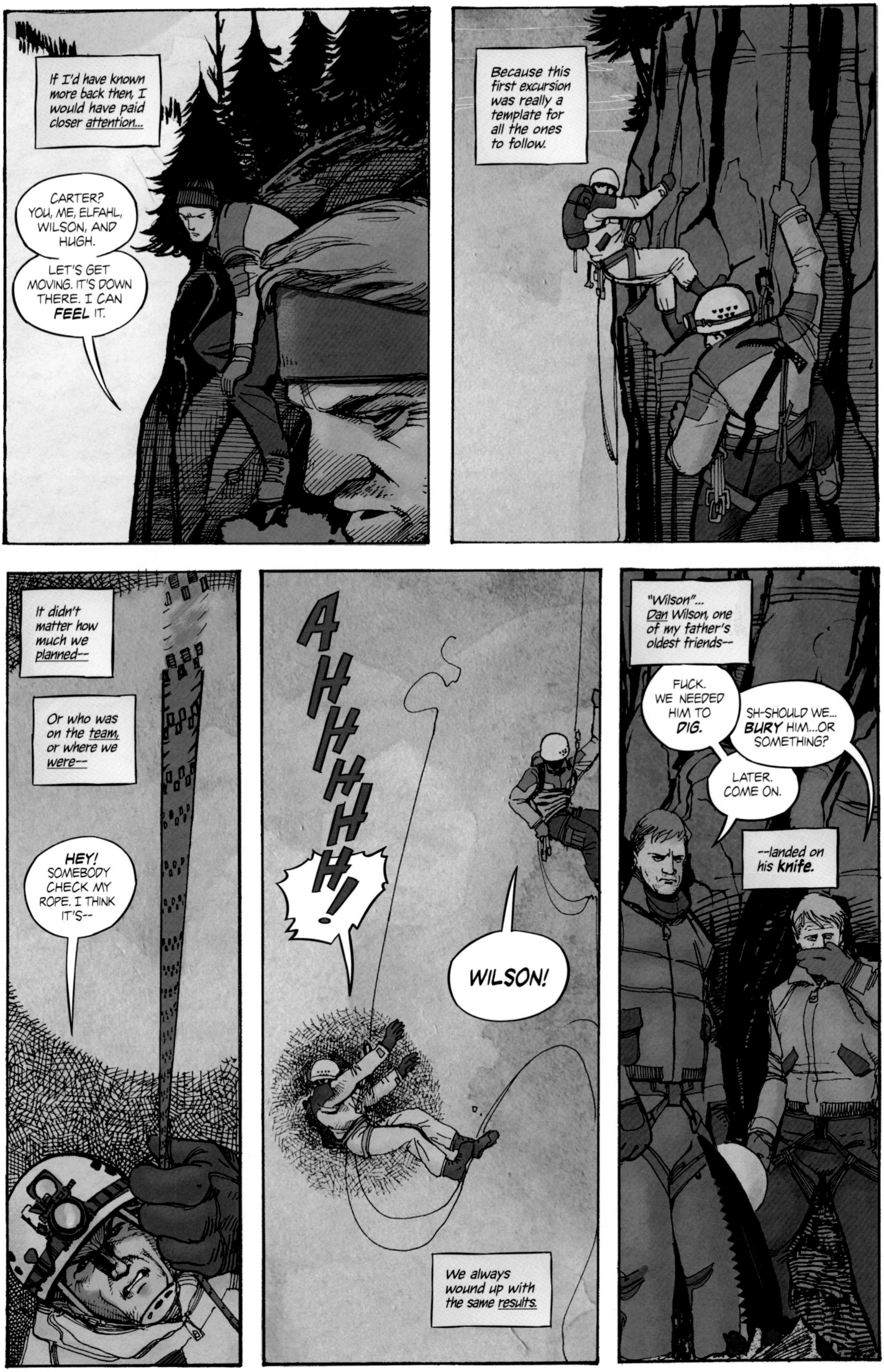
If I'd have known more back then, I would have paid closer attention...
CARTER? YOU, ME, ELFAHL, WILSON, AND HUGH.
LET'S GET MOVING. IT'S DOWN THERE. I CAN FEEL IT.
Because this first excursion was really a template for all the ones to follow.
It didn't matter how much we planned--
Or who was on the team, or where we were--
HEY! SOMEBODY CHECK MY ROPE. I THINK IT'S--
AHHHHH!
WILSON!
We always wound up with the same results.
"Wilson"... Dan Wilson, one of my father's oldest friends--
FUCK. WE NEEDED HIM TO DIG.
SH-SHOULD WE... BURY HIM...OR SOMETHING?
LATER. COME ON.
--landed on his knife.

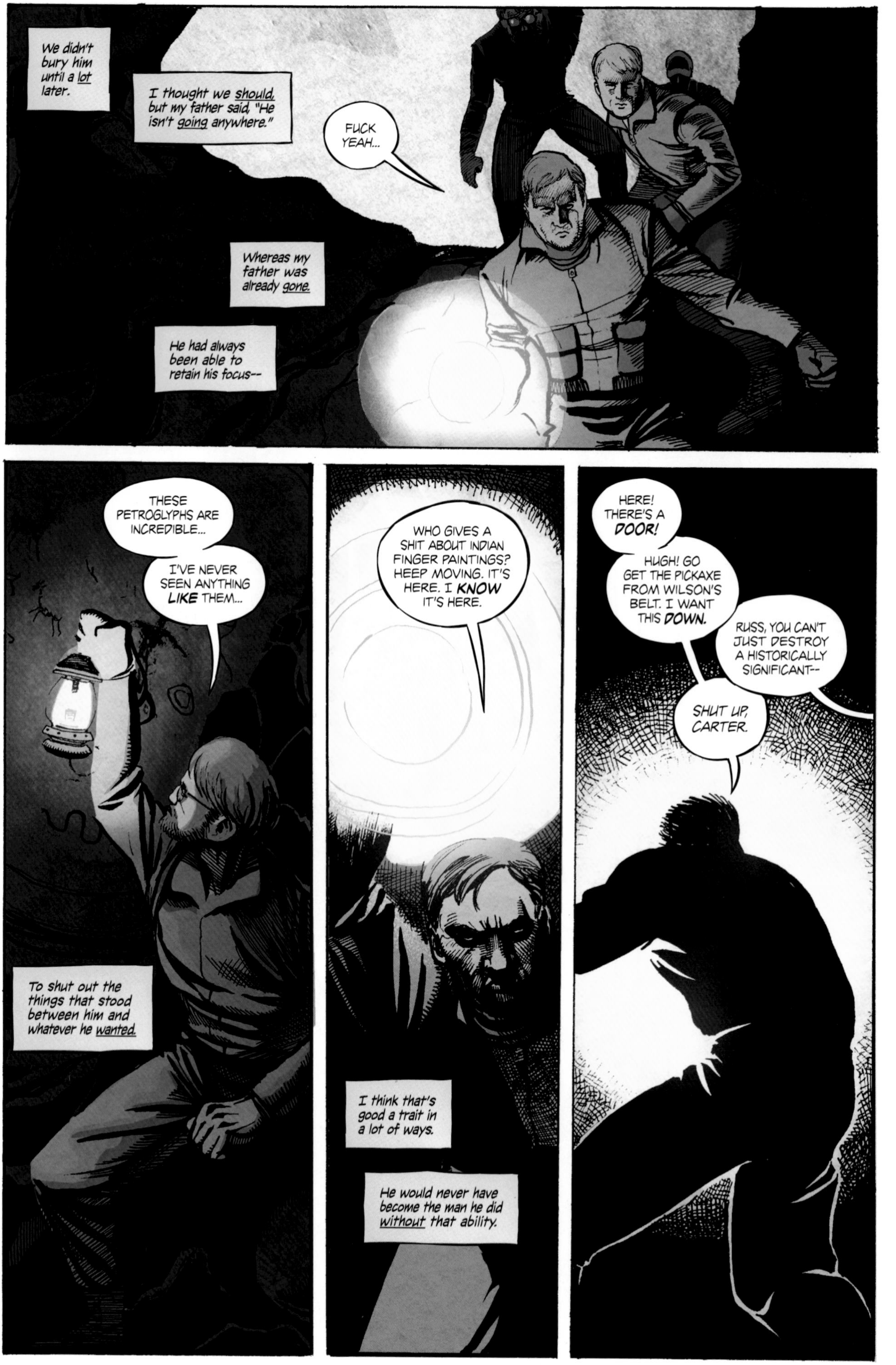
We didn't bury him until a lot later.
I thought we should, but my father said, "He isn't going anywhere."
FUCK YEAH...
Whereas my father was already gone.
He had always been able to retain his focus--
THESE PETROGLYPHS ARE INCREDIBLE...
I'VE NEVER SEEN ANYTHING LIKE THEM...
To shut out the things that stood between him and whatever he wanted.
WHO GIVES A SHIT ABOUT INDIAN FINGER PAINTINGS? KEEP MOVING. IT'S HERE. I KNOW IT'S HERE.
I think that's good a trait in a lot of ways.
He would never have become the man he did without that ability.
HERE! THERE'S A DOOR!
HUGH! GO GET THE PICKAXE FROM WILSON'S BELT. I WANT THIS DOWN.
RUSS, YOU CAN'T JUST DESTROY A HISTORICALLY SIGNIFICANT--
SHUT UP, CARTER.

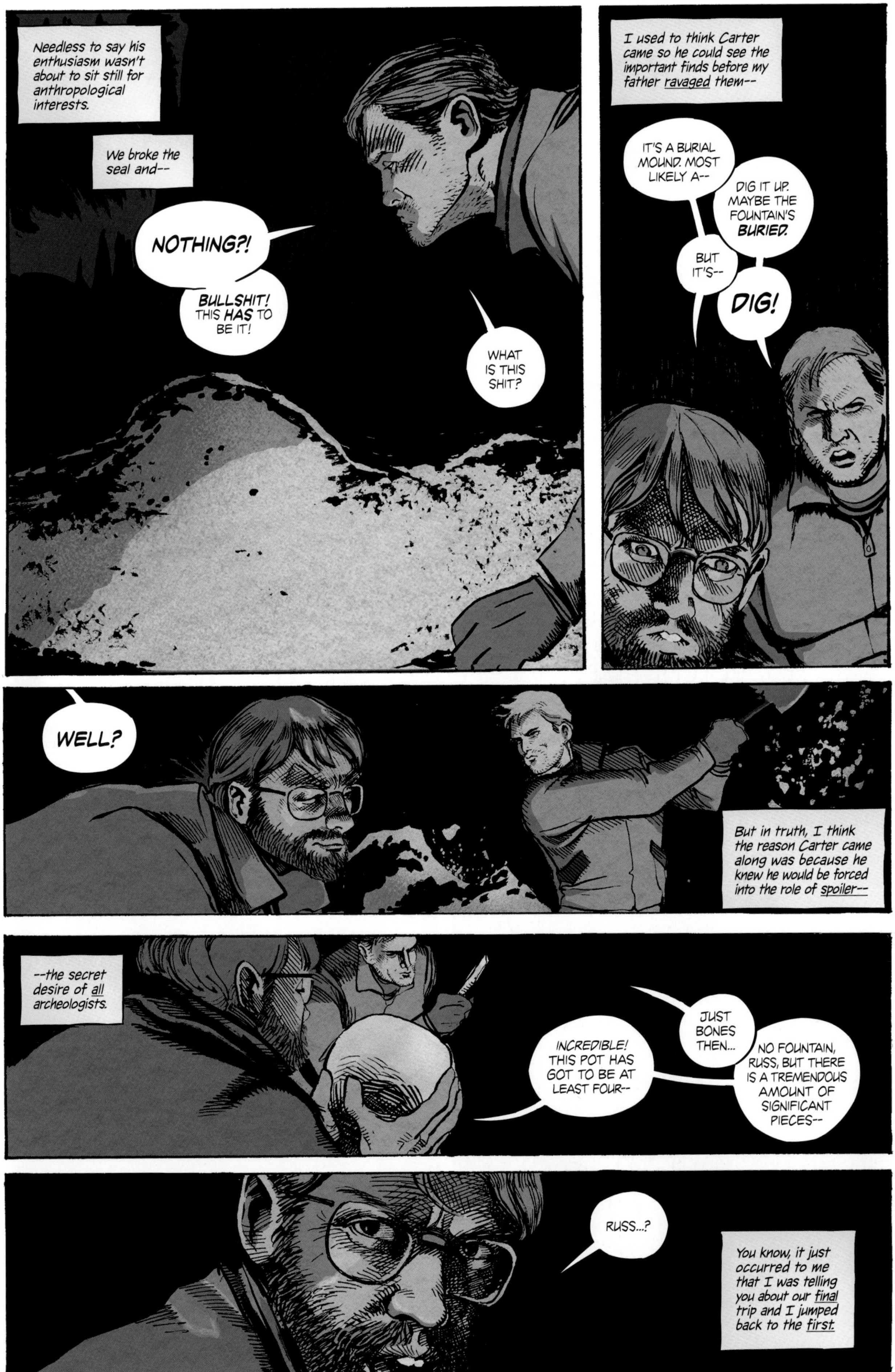
Needless to say his enthusiasm wasn't about to sit still for anthropological interests.
We broke the seal and--
NOTHING?!
BULLSHIT! THIS HAS TO BE IT!
WHAT IS THIS SHIT?
I used to think Carter came so he could see the important finds before my father ravaged them--
IT'S A BURIAL MOUND. MOST LIKELY A--
DIG IT UP. MAYBE THE FOUNTAIN'S BURIED.
BUT IT'S--
DIG!
WELL?
But in truth, I think the reason Carter came along was because he knew he would be forced into the role of spoiler--
--the secret desire of all archeologists.
INCREDIBLE! THIS POT HAS GOT TO BE AT LEAST FOUR--
JUST BONES THEN...
NO FOUNTAIN, RUSS, BUT THERE IS A TREMENDOUS AMOUNT OF SIGNIFICANT PIECES--
RUSS...?
You know, it just occurred to me that I was telling you about our final trip and I jumped back to the first.

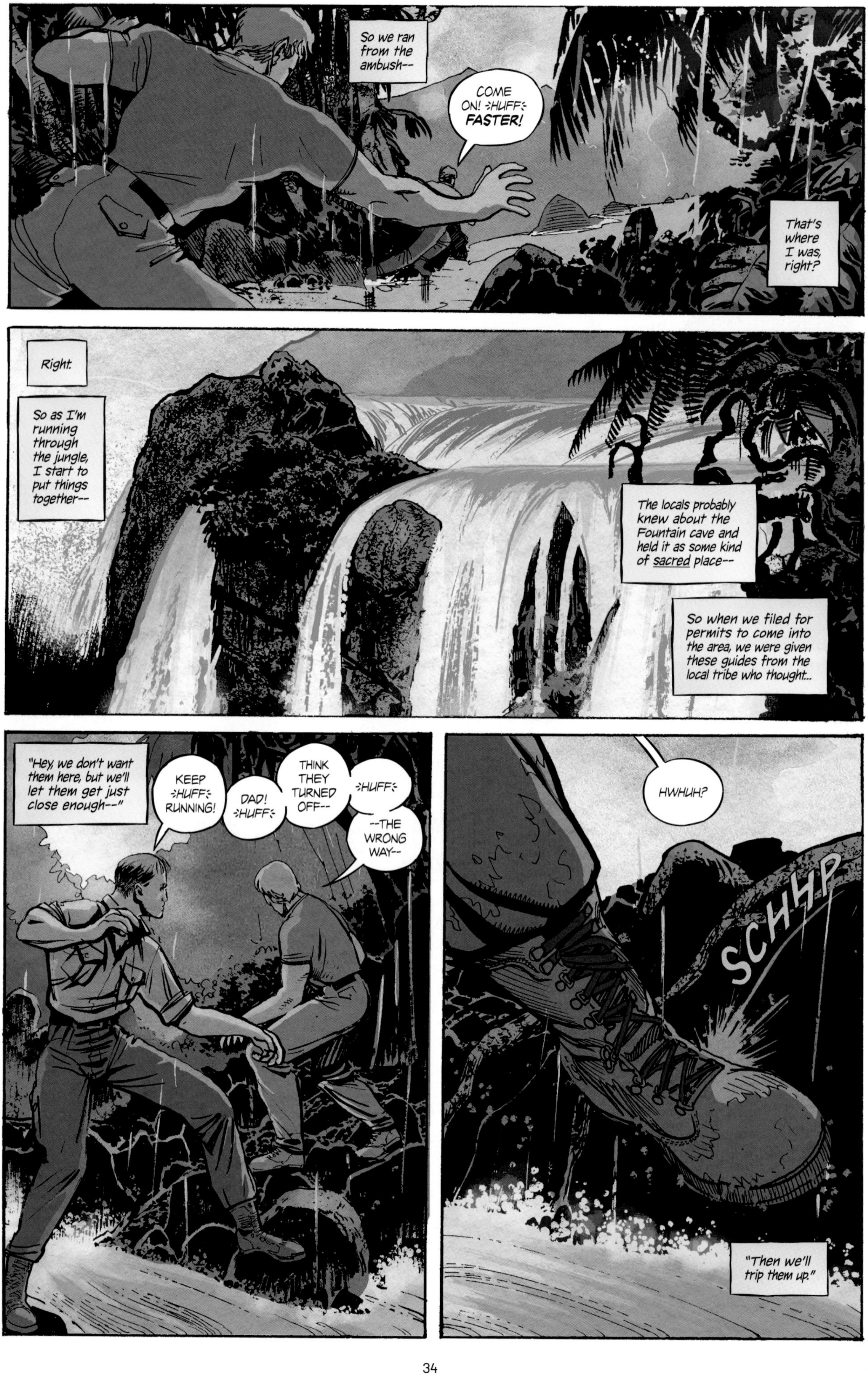
So we ran from the ambush--
COME ON! ⁝HUFF⁝ FASTER!
That's where I was, right?
Right.
So as I'm running through the jungle, I start to put things together--
The locals probably knew about the Fountain cave and held it as some kind of sacred place--
So when we filed for permits to come into the area, we were given these guides from the local tribe who thought...
"Hey, we don't want them here, but we'll let them get just close enough--"
KEEP ⁝HUFF⁝ RUNNING!
DAD! ⁝HUFF⁝
THINK THEY TURNED OFF--
⁝HUFF⁝
--THE WRONG WAY--
HWHUH?
SCHYP
"Then we'll trip them up."

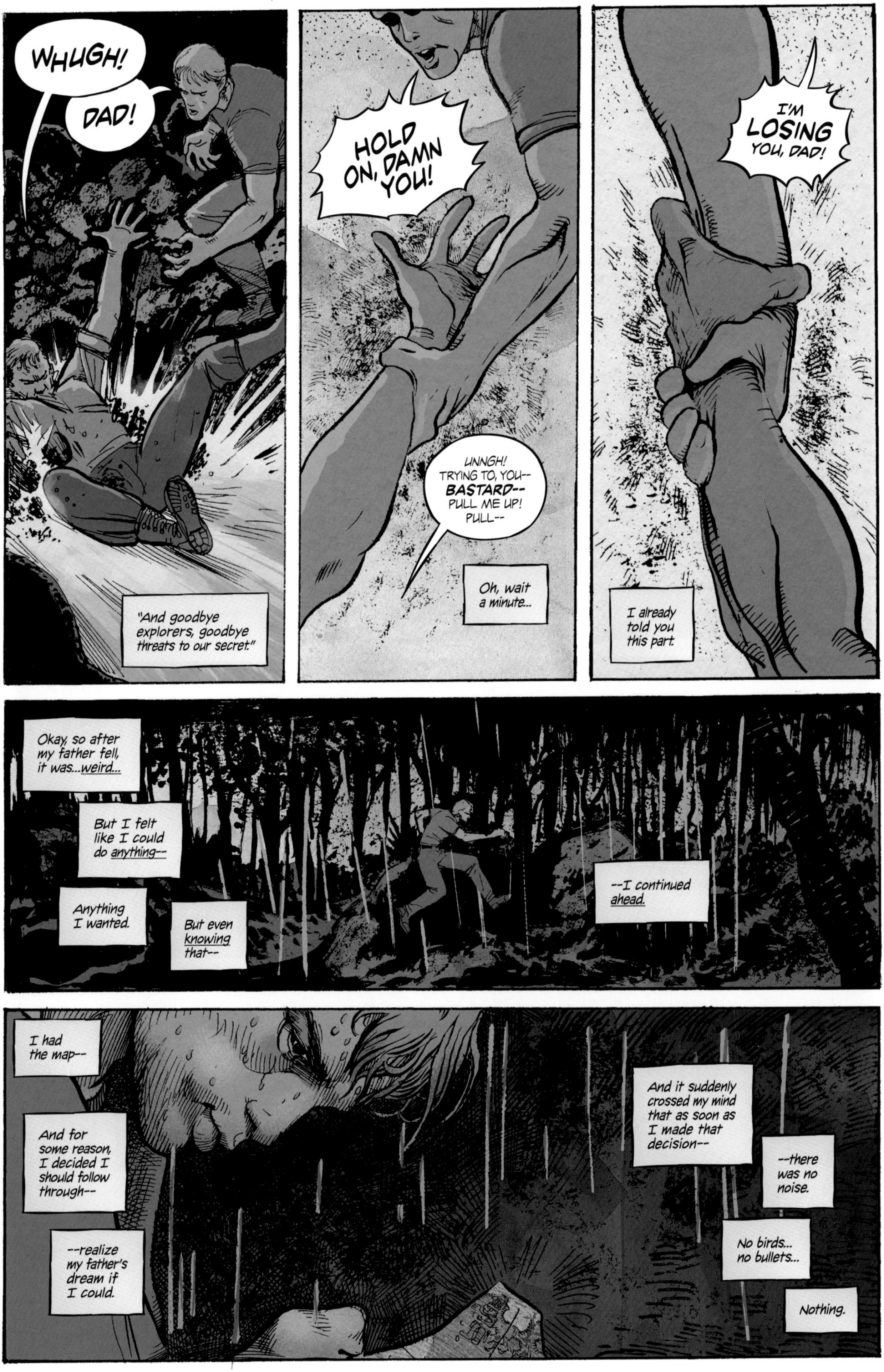
WHUGH!
DAD!
"And goodbye explorers, goodbye threats to our secret."
HOLD ON, DAMN YOU!
UNNGH! TRYING TO, YOU-- BASTARD-- PULL ME UP! PULL--
Oh, wait a minute...
I'M LOSING YOU, DAD!
I already told you this part.
Okay, so after my father fell, it was...weird...
But I felt like I could do anything--
Anything I wanted.
But even knowing that--
--I continued ahead.
I had the map--
And for some reason, I decided I should follow through--
--realize my father's dream if I could.
And it suddenly crossed my mind that as soon as I made that decision--
--there was no noise.
No birds... no bullets...
Nothing.

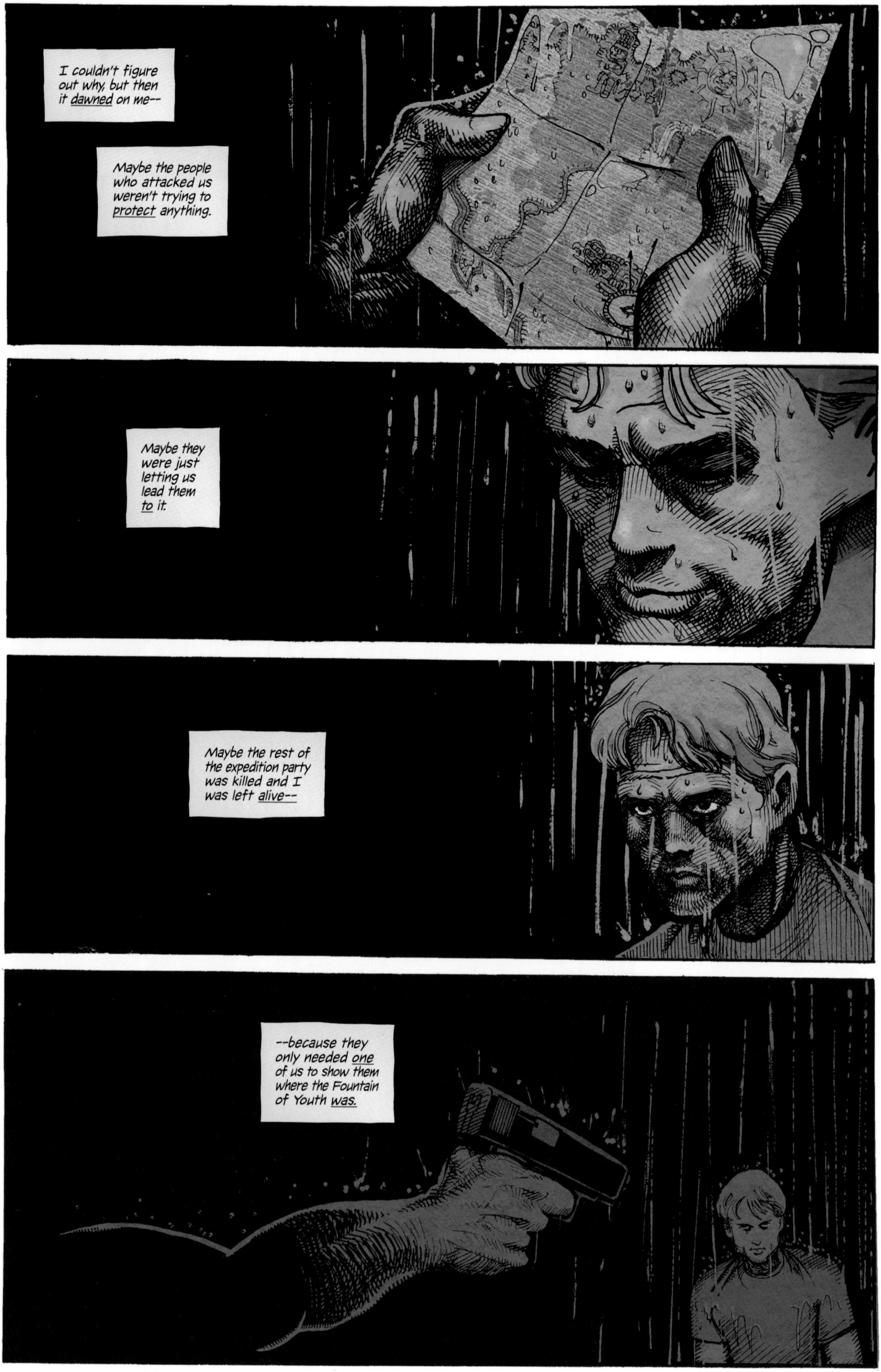
I couldn't figure out why, but then it dawned on me--
Maybe the people who attacked us weren't trying to protect anything.
Maybe they were just letting us lead them to it.
Maybe the rest of the expedition party was killed and I was left alive--
--because they only needed one of us to show them where the Fountain of Youth was.

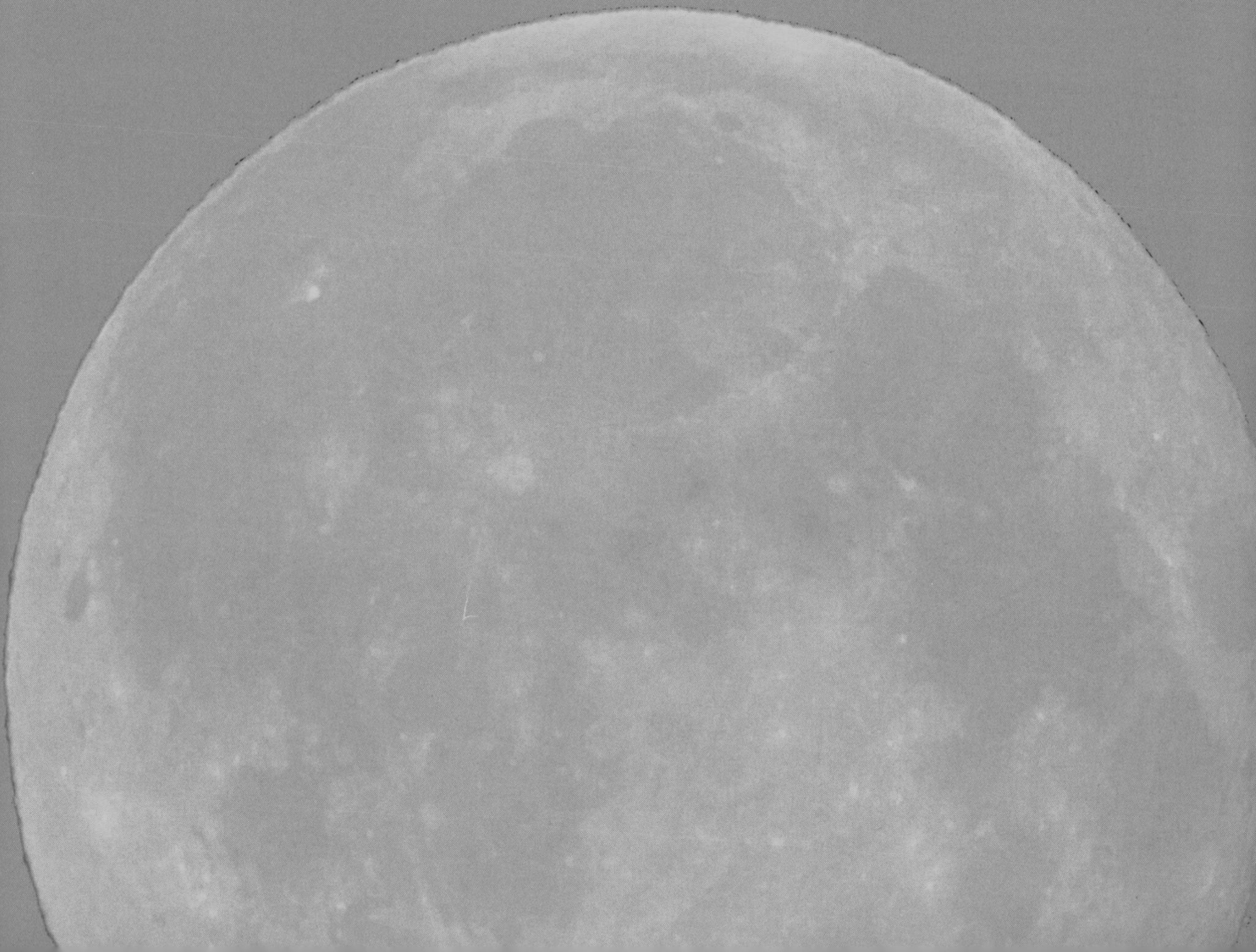

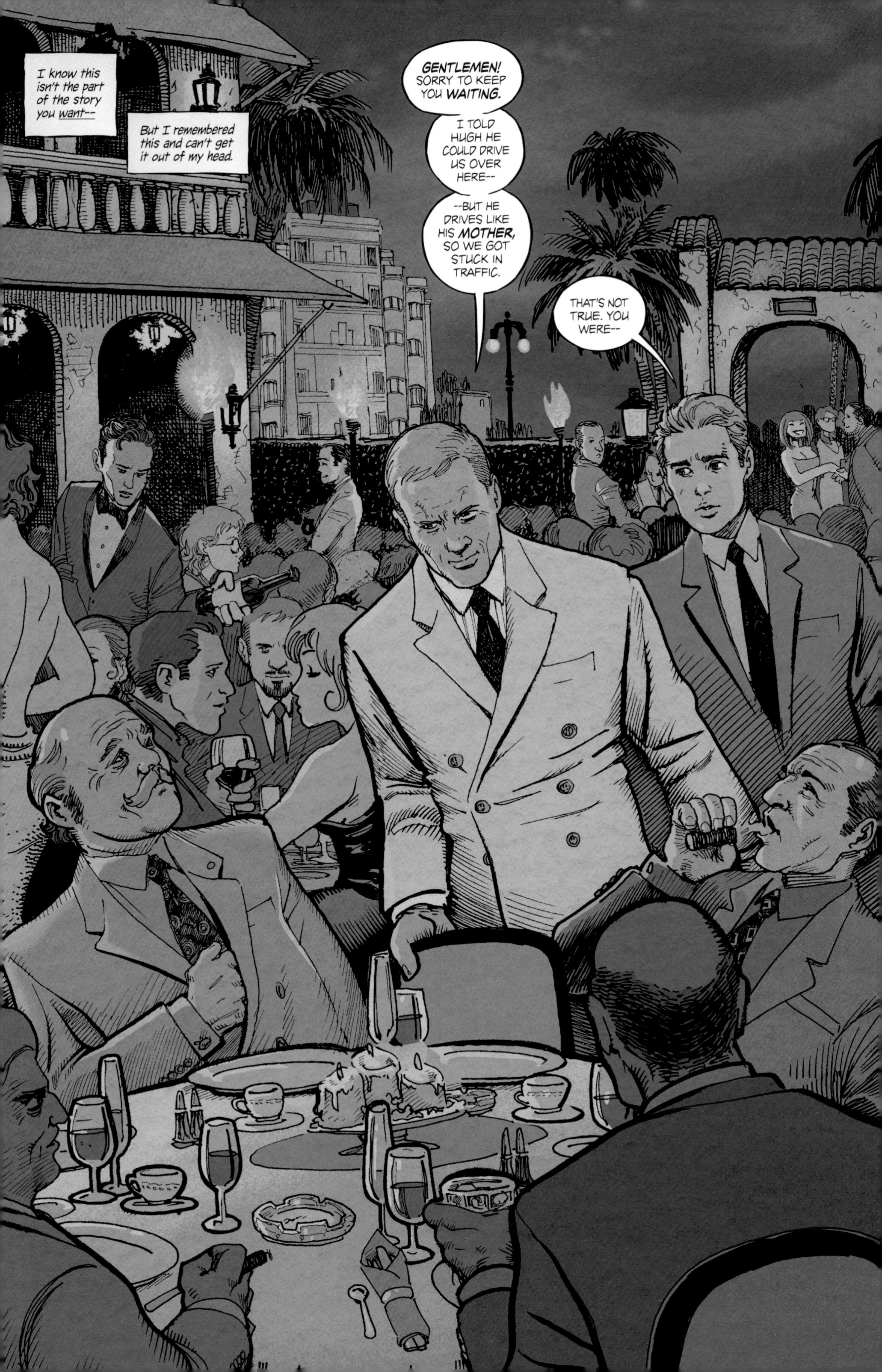
I know this isn't the part of the story you want--
But I remembered this and can't get it out of my head.
GENTLEMEN! SORRY TO KEEP YOU WAITING.
I TOLD HUGH HE COULD DRIVE US OVER HERE--
--BUT HE DRIVES LIKE HIS MOTHER, SO WE GOT STUCK IN TRAFFIC.
THAT'S NOT TRUE. YOU WERE--

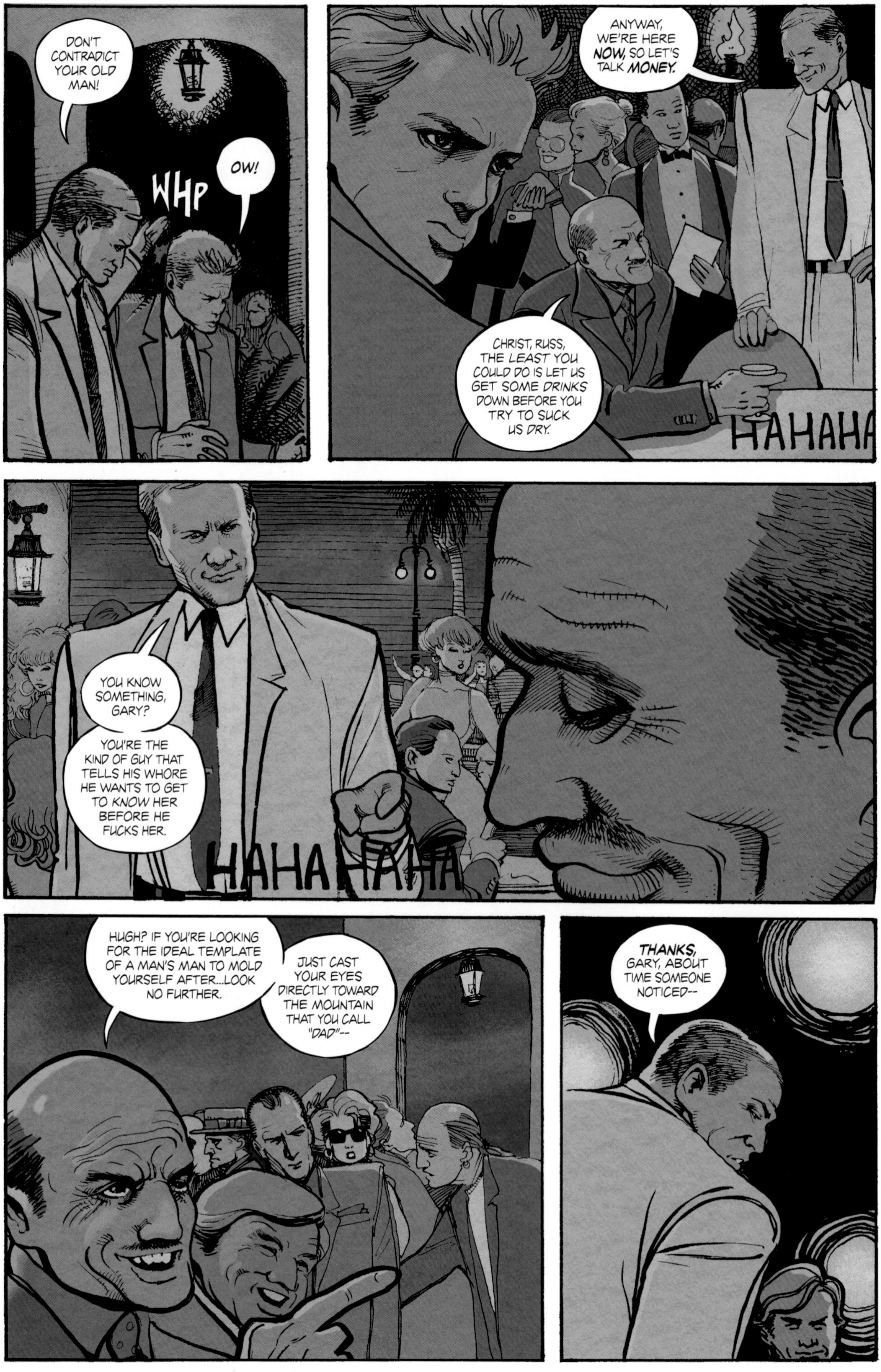
DON'T CONTRADICT YOUR OLD MAN!
WHP
OW!
ANYWAY, WE'RE HERE NOW, SO LET'S TALK MONEY.
CHRIST, RUSS, THE LEAST YOU COULD DO IS LET US GET SOME DRINKS DOWN BEFORE YOU TRY TO SUCK US DRY.
HAHAHA
YOU KNOW SOMETHING, GARY?
YOU'RE THE KIND OF GUY THAT TELLS HIS WHORE HE WANTS TO GET TO KNOW HER BEFORE HE FUCKS HER.
HAHAHAHAHA
HUGH? IF YOU'RE LOOKING FOR THE IDEAL TEMPLATE OF A MAN'S MAN TO MOLD YOURSELF AFTER...LOOK NO FURTHER.
JUST CAST YOUR EYES DIRECTLY TOWARD THE MOUNTAIN THAT YOU CALL "DAD"--
THANKS, GARY, ABOUT TIME SOMEONE NOTICED--

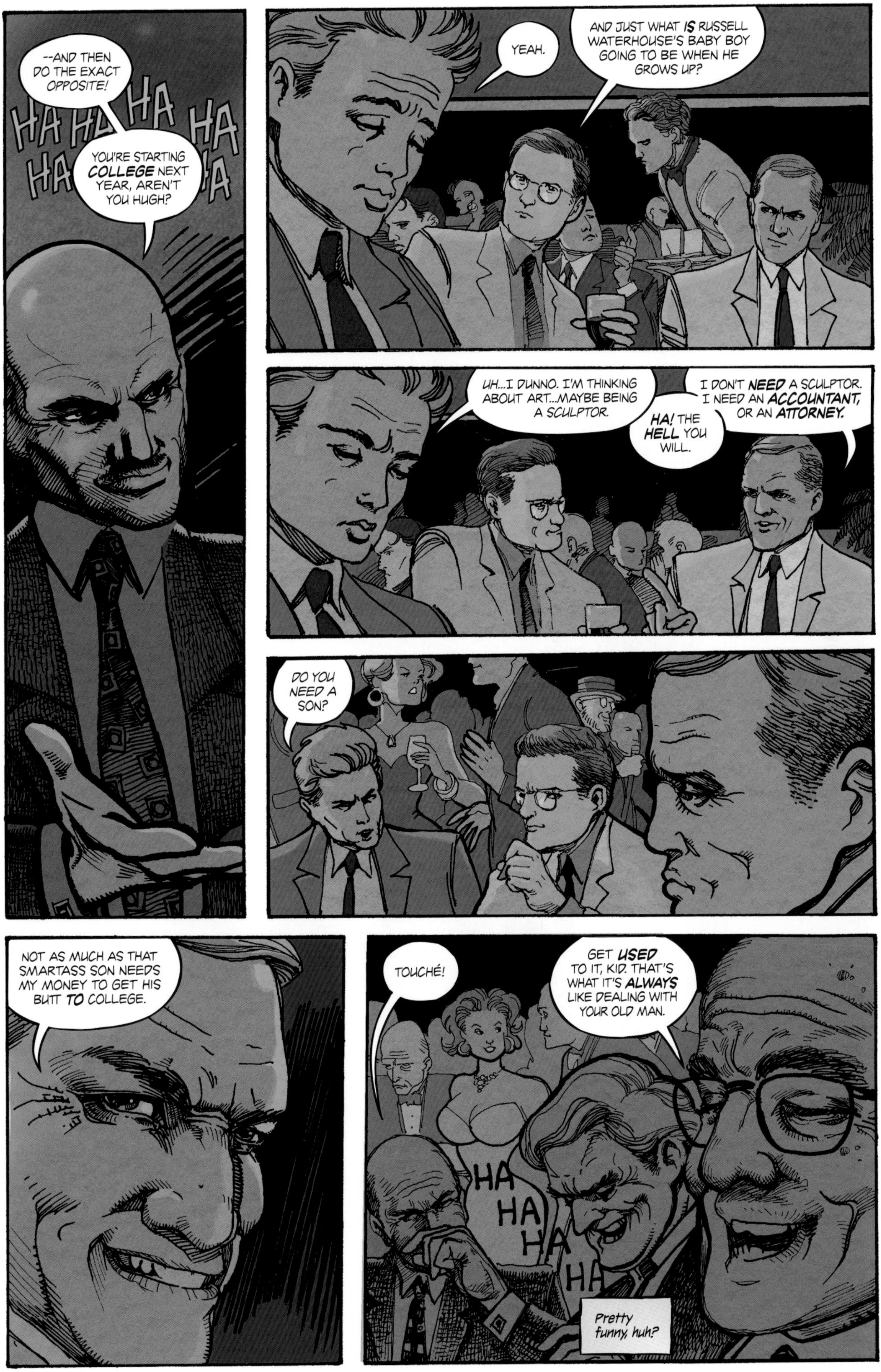
--AND THEN DO THE EXACT OPPOSITE!
HA HA HA HA HA HA HA
YOU'RE STARTING COLLEGE NEXT YEAR, AREN'T YOU HUGH?
YEAH.
AND JUST WHAT IS RUSSELL WATERHOUSE'S BABY BOY GOING TO BE WHEN HE GROWS UP?
UH...I DUNNO. I'M THINKING ABOUT ART...MAYBE BEING A SCULPTOR.
HA! THE HELL YOU WILL.
I DON'T NEED A SCULPTOR. I NEED AN ACCOUNTANT, OR AN ATTORNEY.
DO YOU NEED A SON?
NOT AS MUCH AS THAT SMARTASS SON NEEDS MY MONEY TO GET HIS BUTT TO COLLEGE.
TOUCHÉ!
GET USED TO IT, KID. THAT'S WHAT IT'S ALWAYS LIKE DEALING WITH YOUR OLD MAN.
HA HA HA HA
Pretty funny, huh?

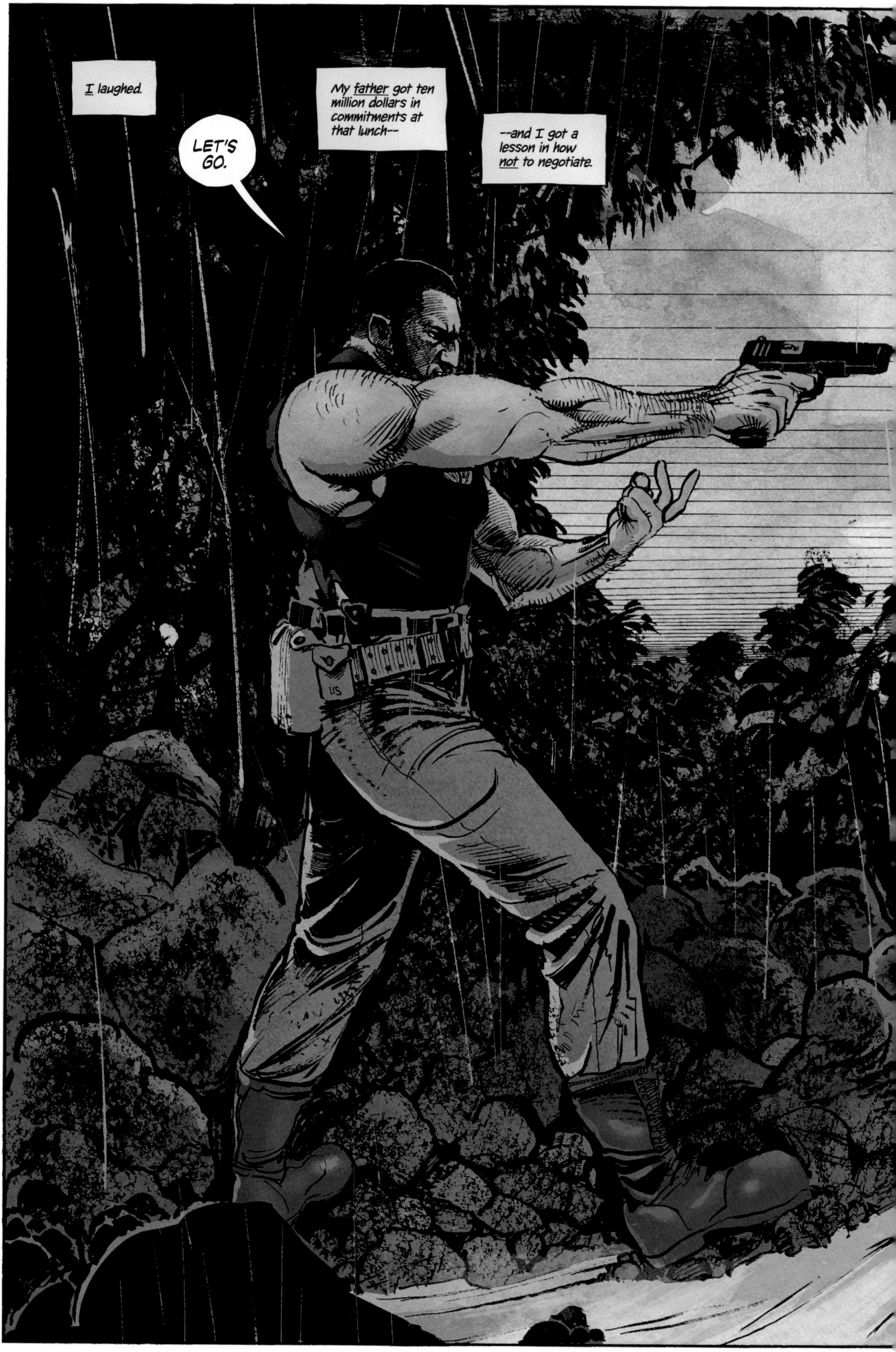
I laughed.
LET'S GO.
My father got ten million dollars in commitments at that lunch--
--and I got a lesson in how not to negotiate.
US

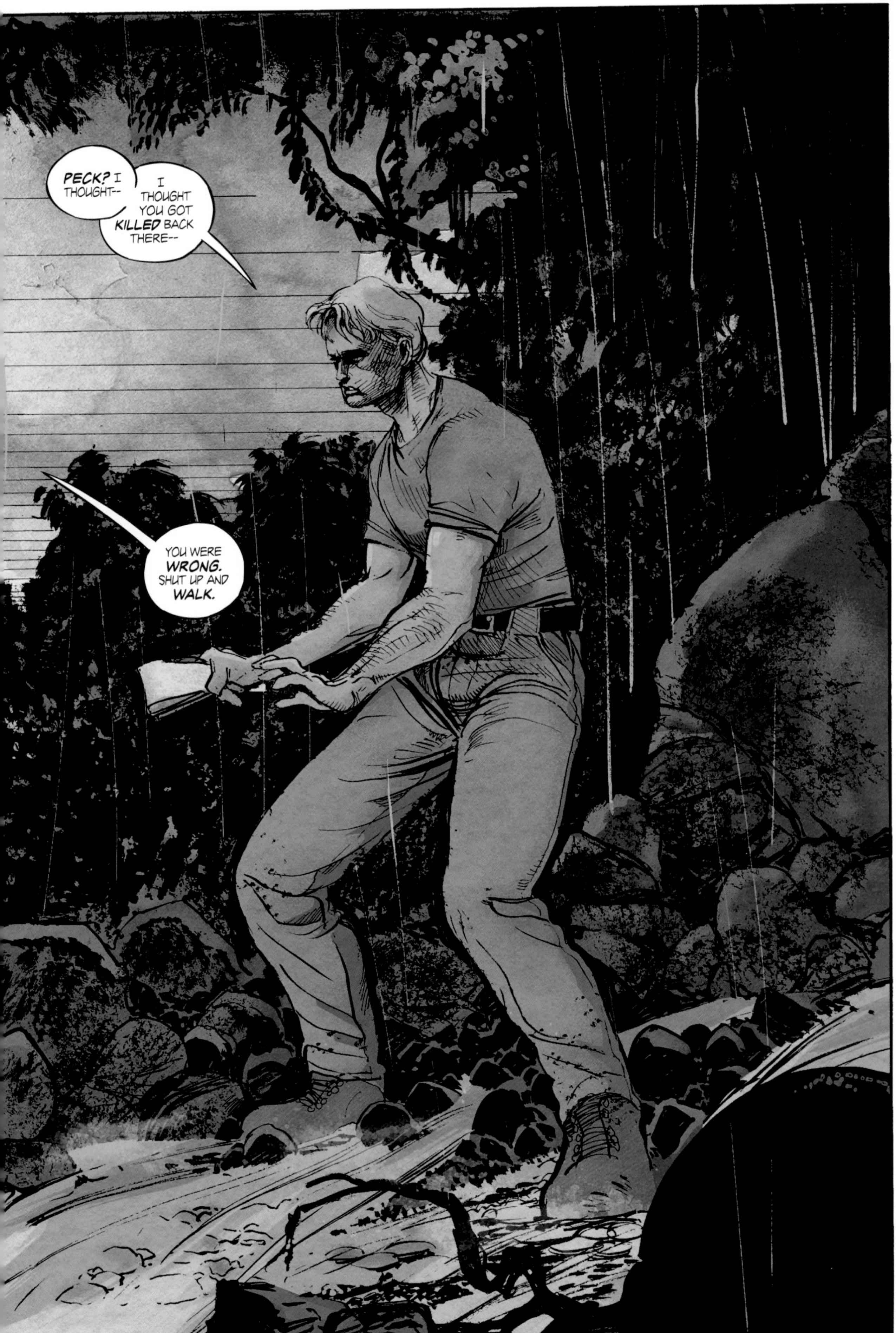
PECK? I THOUGHT--
I THOUGHT YOU GOT KILLED BACK THERE--
YOU WERE WRONG. SHUT UP AND WALK.

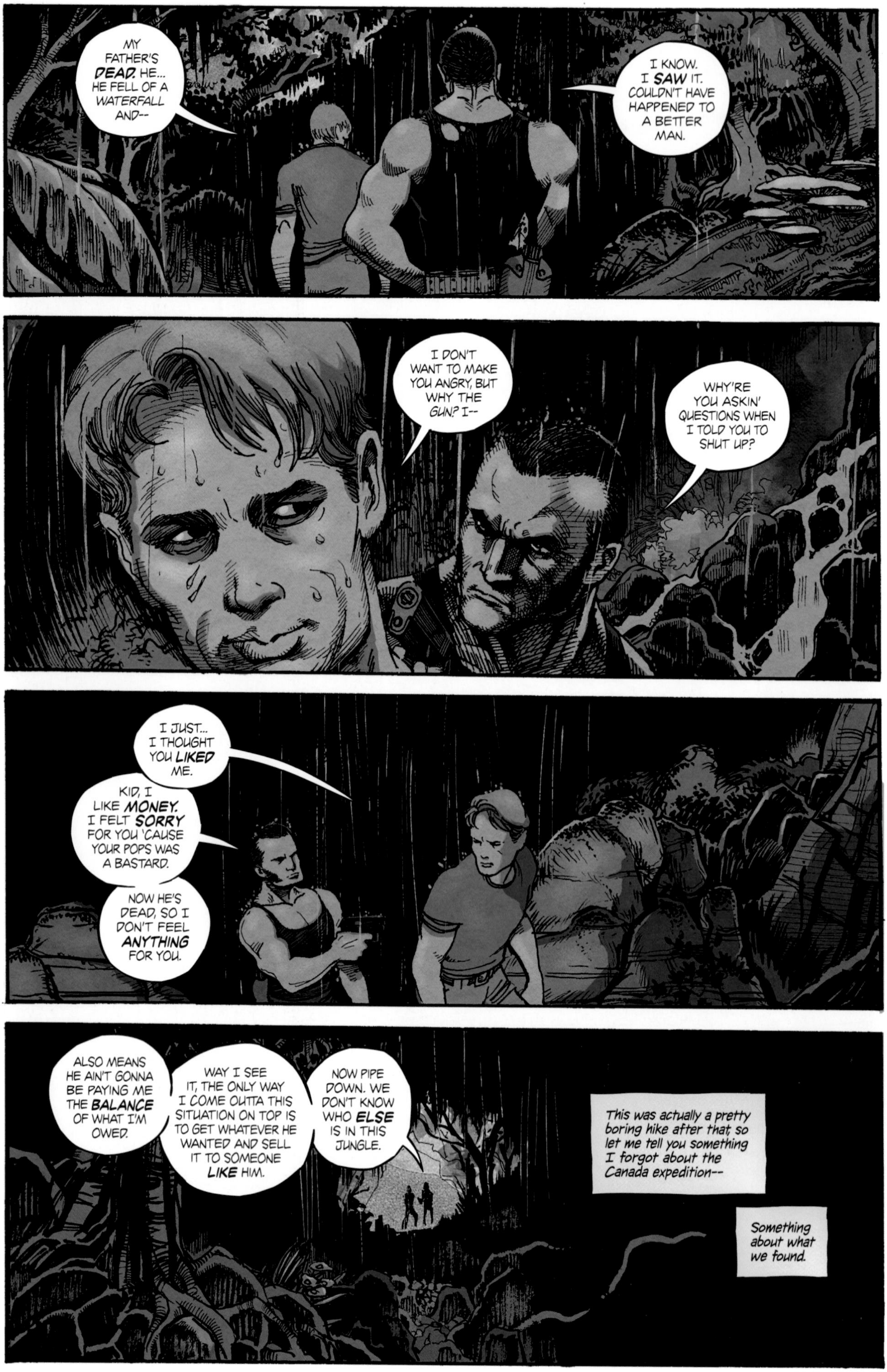
MY FATHER'S DEAD. HE... HE FELL OF A WATERFALL AND--
I KNOW. I SAW IT. COULDN'T HAVE HAPPENED TO A BETTER MAN.
I DON'T WANT TO MAKE YOU ANGRY, BUT WHY THE GUN? I--
WHY'RE YOU ASKIN' QUESTIONS WHEN I TOLD YOU TO SHUT UP?
I JUST... I THOUGHT YOU LIKED ME.
KID, I LIKE MONEY. I FELT SORRY FOR YOU 'CAUSE YOUR POPS WAS A BASTARD.
NOW HE'S DEAD, SO I DON'T FEEL ANYTHING FOR YOU.
ALSO MEANS HE AIN'T GONNA BE PAYING ME THE BALANCE OF WHAT I'M OWED.
WAY I SEE IT, THE ONLY WAY I COME OUTTA THIS SITUATION ON TOP IS TO GET WHATEVER HE WANTED AND SELL IT TO SOMEONE LIKE HIM.
NOW PIPE DOWN. WE DON'T KNOW WHO ELSE IS IN THIS JUNGLE.
This was actually a pretty boring hike after that, so let me tell you something I forgot about the Canada expedition--
Something about what we found.

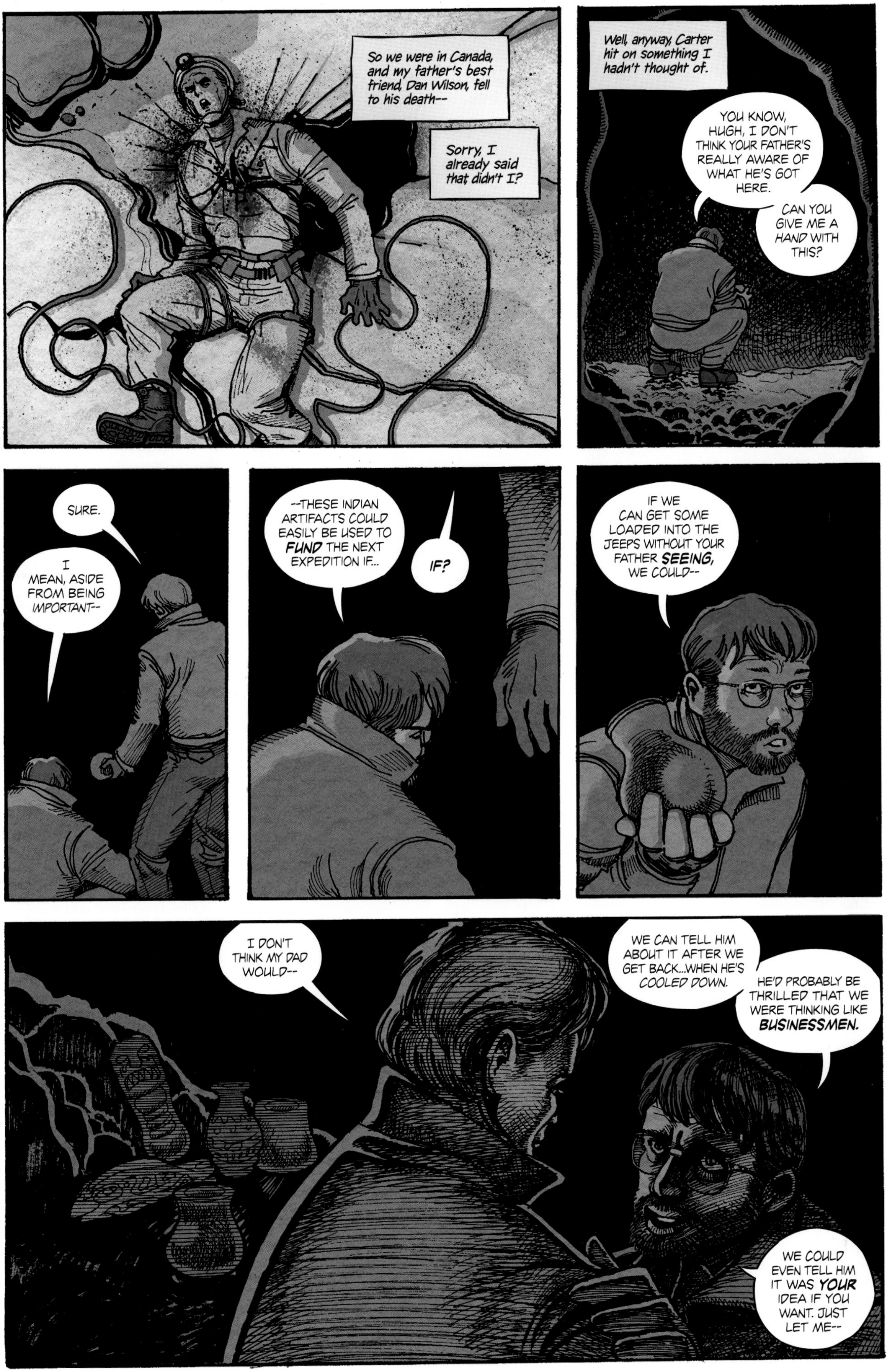
So we were in Canada, and my father's best friend, Dan Wilson, fell to his death--
Sorry, I already said that didn't I?
Well, anyway, Carter hit on something I hadn't thought of.
YOU KNOW, HUGH, I DON'T THINK YOUR FATHER'S REALLY AWARE OF WHAT HE'S GOT HERE.
CAN YOU GIVE ME A HAND WITH THIS?
SURE.
I MEAN, ASIDE FROM BEING IMPORTANT--
--THESE INDIAN ARTIFACTS COULD EASILY BE USED TO FUND THE NEXT EXPEDITION IF...
IF?
IF WE CAN GET SOME LOADED INTO THE JEEPS WITHOUT YOUR FATHER SEEING, WE COULD--
I DON'T THINK MY DAD WOULD--
WE CAN TELL HIM ABOUT IT AFTER WE GET BACK...WHEN HE'S COOLED DOWN.
HE'D PROBABLY BE THRILLED THAT WE WERE THINKING LIKE BUSINESSMEN.
WE COULD EVEN TELL HIM IT WAS YOUR IDEA IF YOU WANT. JUST LET ME--

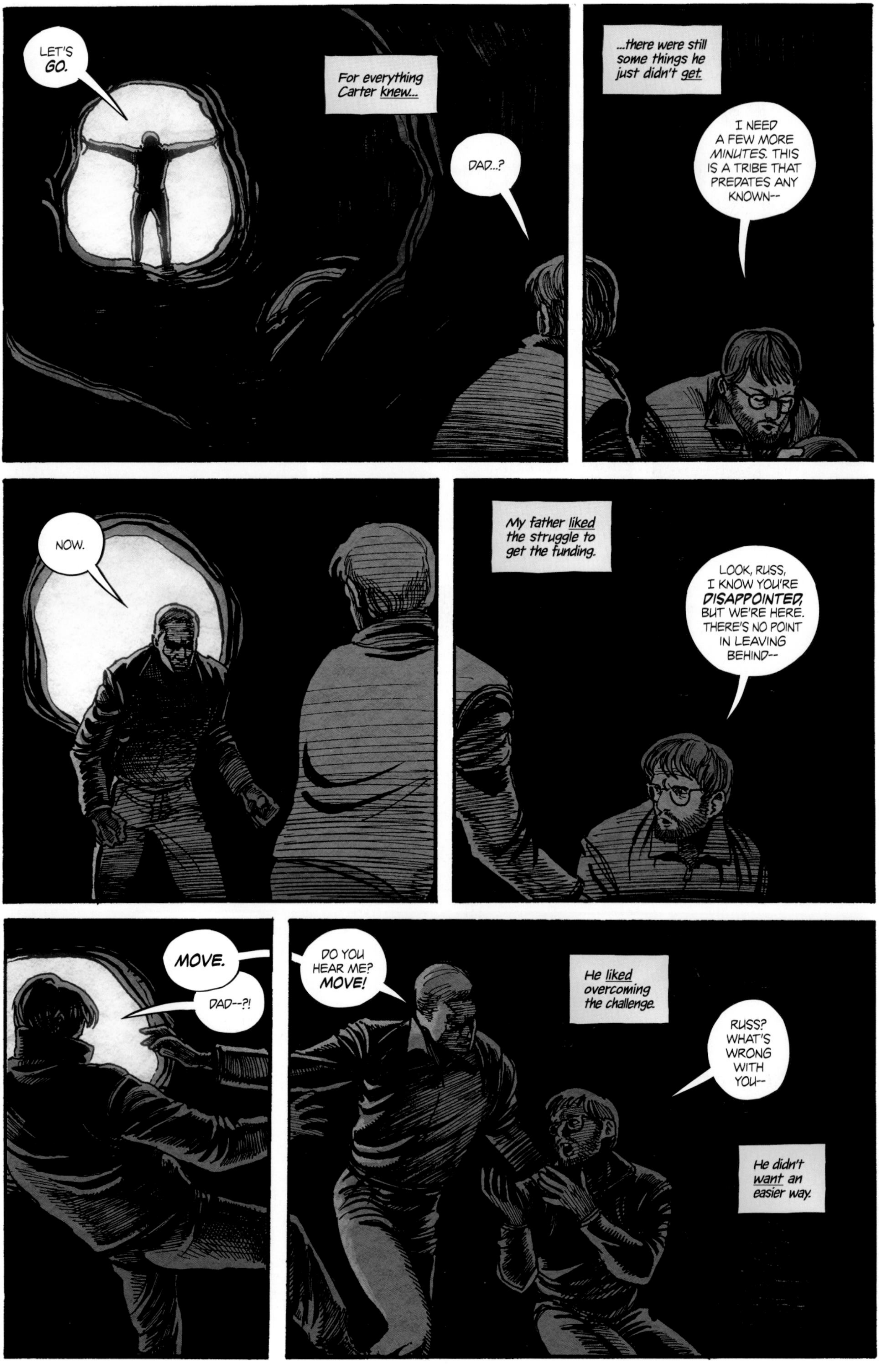
LET'S GO.
For everything Carter knew...
DAD...?
...there were still some things he just didn't get.
I NEED A FEW MORE MINUTES. THIS IS A TRIBE THAT PREDATES ANY KNOWN--
NOW.
My father liked the struggle to get the funding.
LOOK, RUSS, I KNOW YOU'RE DISAPPOINTED, BUT WE'RE HERE. THERE'S NO POINT IN LEAVING BEHIND--
MOVE.
DAD--?!
DO YOU HEAR ME? MOVE!
He liked overcoming the challenge.
RUSS? WHAT'S WRONG WITH YOU--
He didn't want an easier way.

I'M PAYING FOR THIS, CARTER. ME.

NOT SOME FUCKED UP, HEAD-IN-THEIR-ASS ADVISORY COMMITTEE AT A LOUSY EXCUSE FOR AN IVY LEAGUE SCHOOL THAT YOU'RE *LUCKY* TO BE WORKING AT.

He wanted it *his* way.

WE ARE HERE TO FIND ONE THING AND IT'S *NOT* POTTERY!

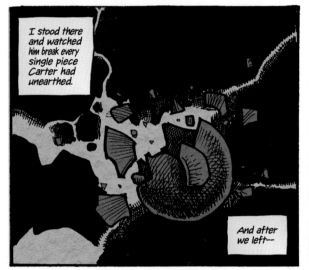

I stood there and watched him break every single piece Carter had unearthed.

And after we left--

That's when it hit me...

Canada is a beautiful country.

Beautiful.

47

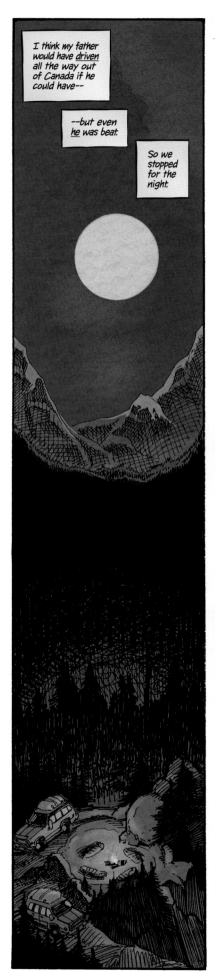

I think my father would have _driven_ all the way out of Canada if he could have--

--but even _he_ was beat.

So we stopped for the night.

And I _watched._

I watched my father struggle with the fact that his illness had won this first round.

I think he was crying.

I thought about _going_ to him...

Telling him I _understood_ how he felt...

But I didn't think he would take it the right way, so...

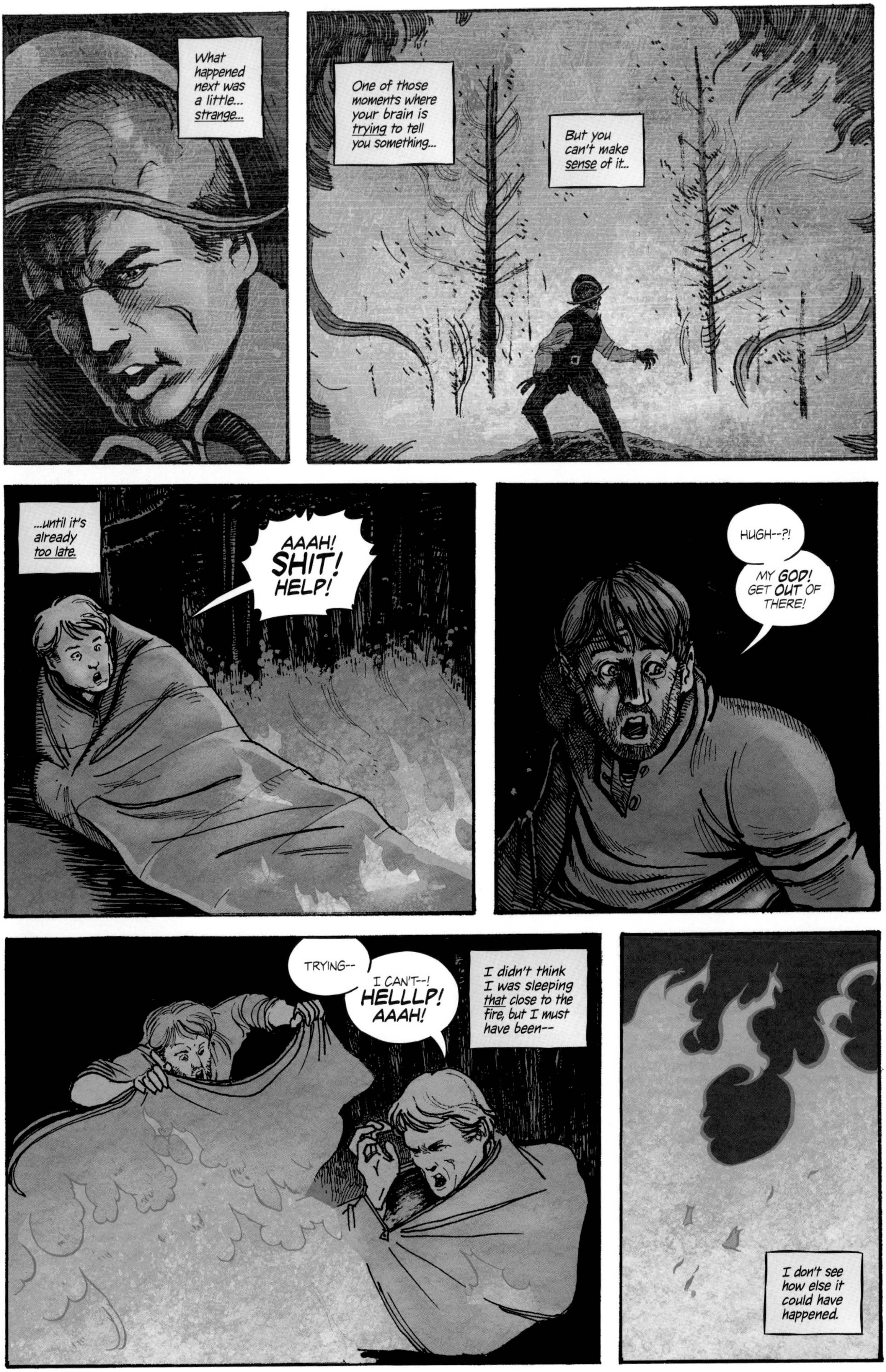
What happened next was a little... strange...
One of those moments where your brain is trying to tell you something...
But you can't make sense of it...
...until it's already too late.
AAAH! SHIT! HELP!
HUGH--?!
MY GOD! GET OUT OF THERE!
TRYING--
I CAN'T--! HELLLP! AAAH!
I didn't think I was sleeping that close to the fire, but I must have been--
I don't see how else it could have happened.

My father was nowhere to be found that night.

He'd just... wandered off.

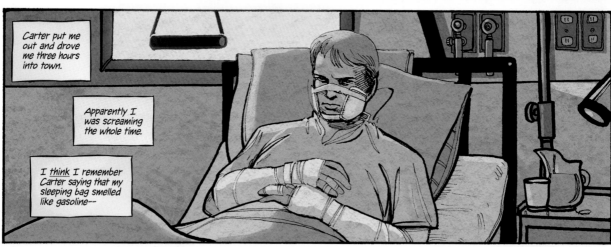

Carter put me out and drove me three hours into town.

Apparently I was screaming the whole time.

I think I remember Carter saying that my sleeping bag smelled like gasoline--

But he probably just said that to get me as mad at my father as he was.

Besides, my father made it to the hospital about thirty minutes after I went into the emergency room.

He had obviously left right after he found out what happened from the others.

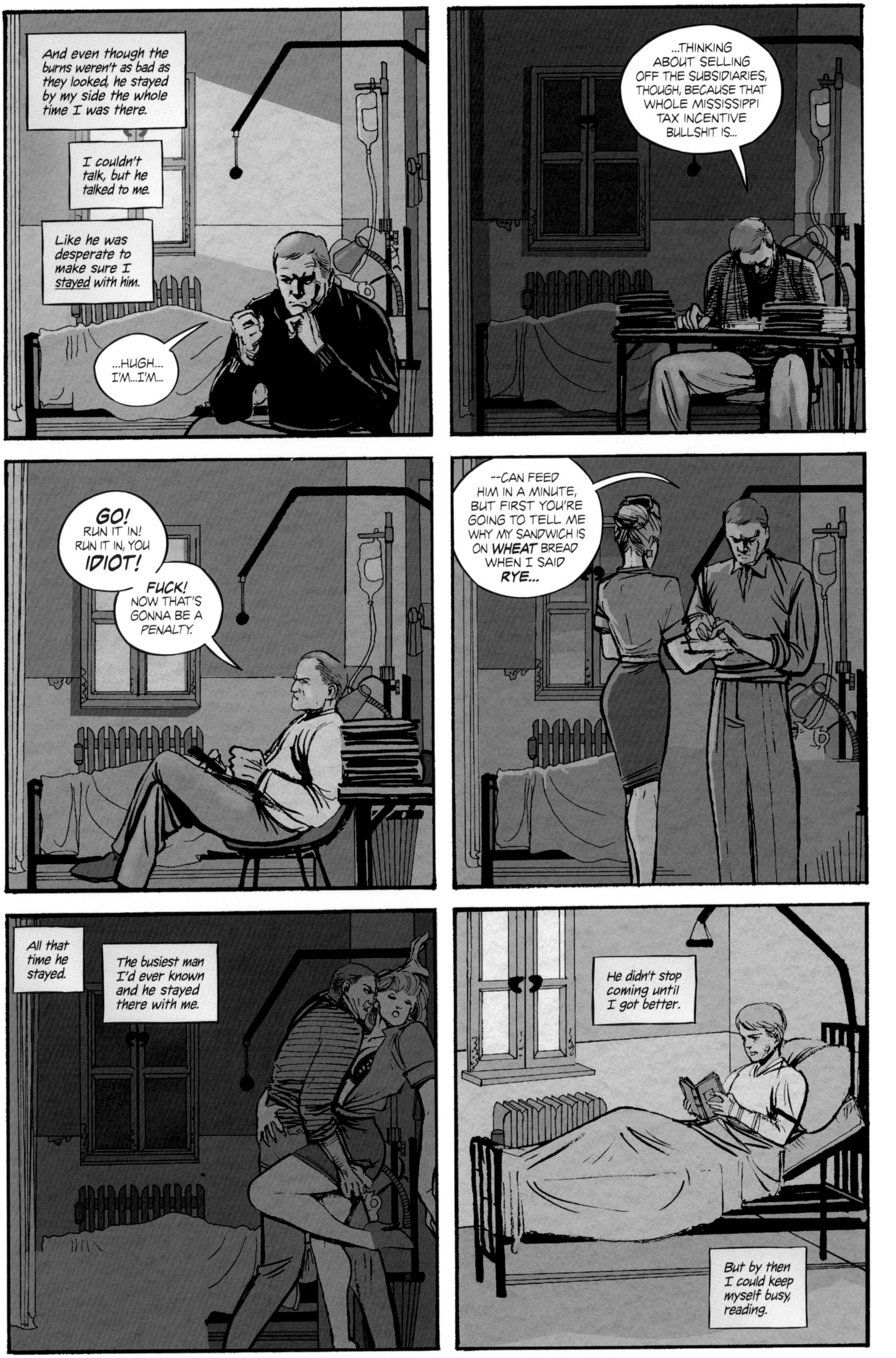
And even though the burns weren't as bad as they looked, he stayed by my side the whole time I was there.
I couldn't talk, but he talked to me.
Like he was desperate to make sure I stayed with him.
...HUGH... I'M...I'M...
...THINKING ABOUT SELLING OFF THE SUBSIDIARIES, THOUGH, BECAUSE THAT WHOLE MISSISSIPPI TAX INCENTIVE BULLSHIT IS...
GO! RUN IT IN! RUN IT IN, YOU IDIOT!
FUCK! NOW THAT'S GONNA BE A PENALTY.
--CAN FEED HIM IN A MINUTE, BUT FIRST YOU'RE GOING TO TELL ME WHY MY SANDWICH IS ON WHEAT BREAD WHEN I SAID RYE...
All that time he stayed.
The busiest man I'd ever known and he stayed there with me.
He didn't stop coming until I got better.
But by then I could keep myself busy, reading.

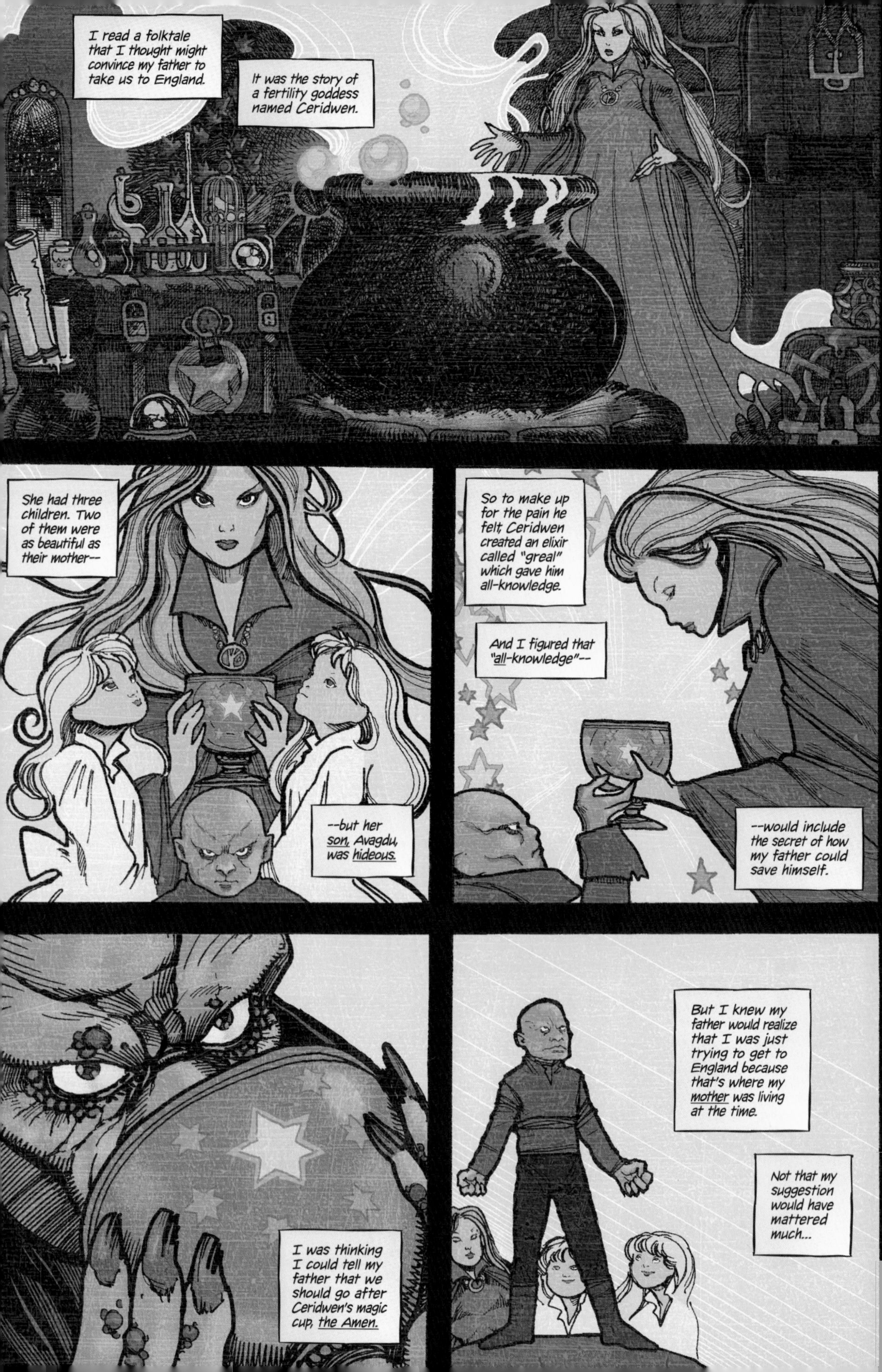
I read a folktale that I thought might convince my father to take us to England.
It was the story of a fertility goddess named Ceridwen.
She had three children. Two of them were as beautiful as their mother--
--but her son, Avagdu, was hideous.
So to make up for the pain he felt, Ceridwen created an elixir called "greal" which gave him all-knowledge.
And I figured that "all-knowledge"--
--would include the secret of how my father could save himself.
I was thinking I could tell my father that we should go after Ceridwen's magic cup, the Amen.
But I knew my father would realize that I was just trying to get to England because that's where my mother was living at the time.
Not that my suggestion would have mattered much...

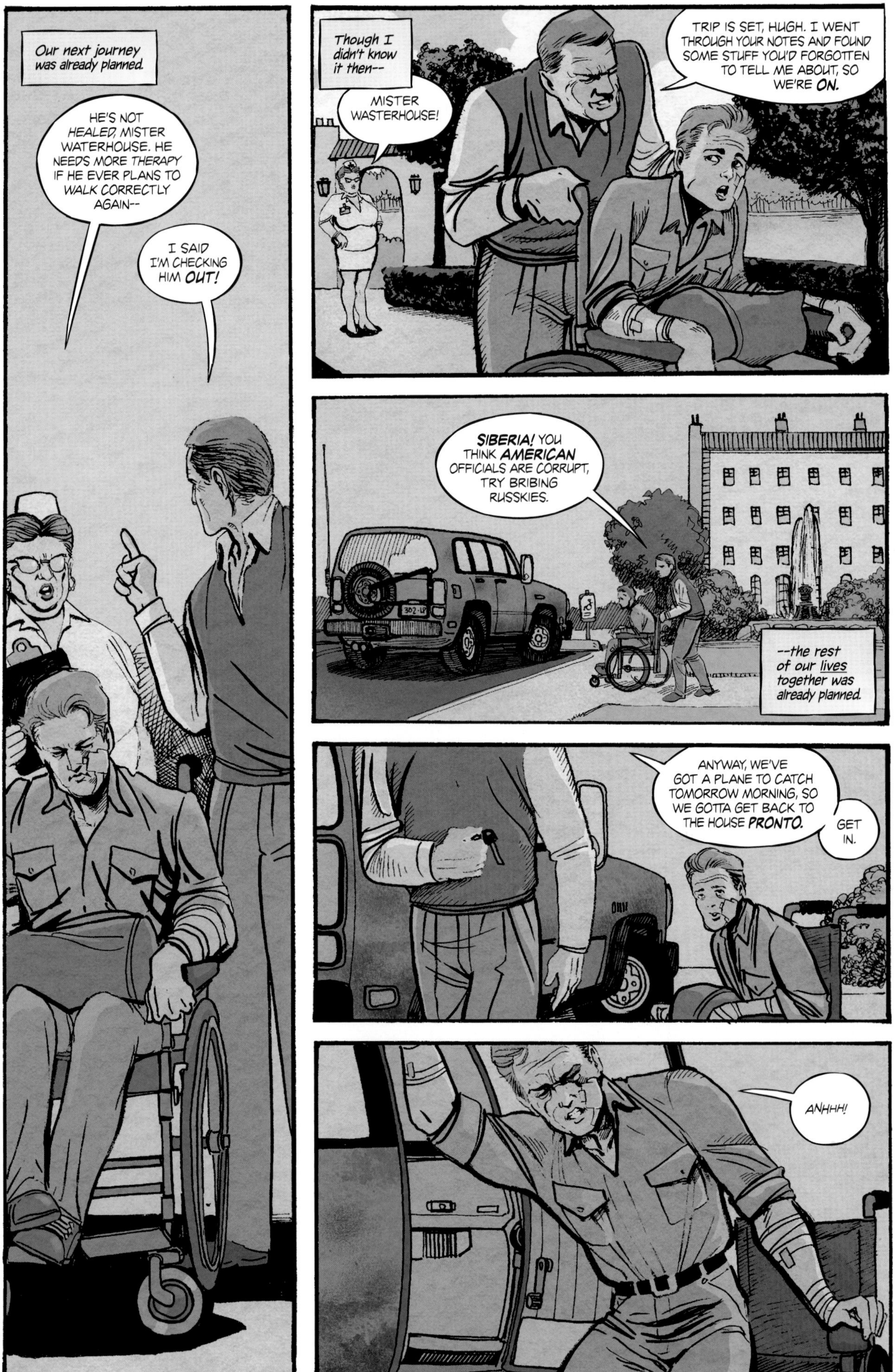
Our next journey was already planned.
HE'S NOT HEALED, MISTER WATERHOUSE. HE NEEDS MORE THERAPY IF HE EVER PLANS TO WALK CORRECTLY AGAIN--
I SAID I'M CHECKING HIM OUT!
Though I didn't know it then--
MISTER WASTERHOUSE!
TRIP IS SET, HUGH. I WENT THROUGH YOUR NOTES AND FOUND SOME STUFF YOU'D FORGOTTEN TO TELL ME ABOUT, SO WE'RE ON.
SIBERIA! YOU THINK AMERICAN OFFICIALS ARE CORRUPT, TRY BRIBING RUSSKIES.
--the rest of our lives together was already planned.
ANYWAY, WE'VE GOT A PLANE TO CATCH TOMORROW MORNING, SO WE GOTTA GET BACK TO THE HOUSE PRONTO.
GET IN.
ANHHH!

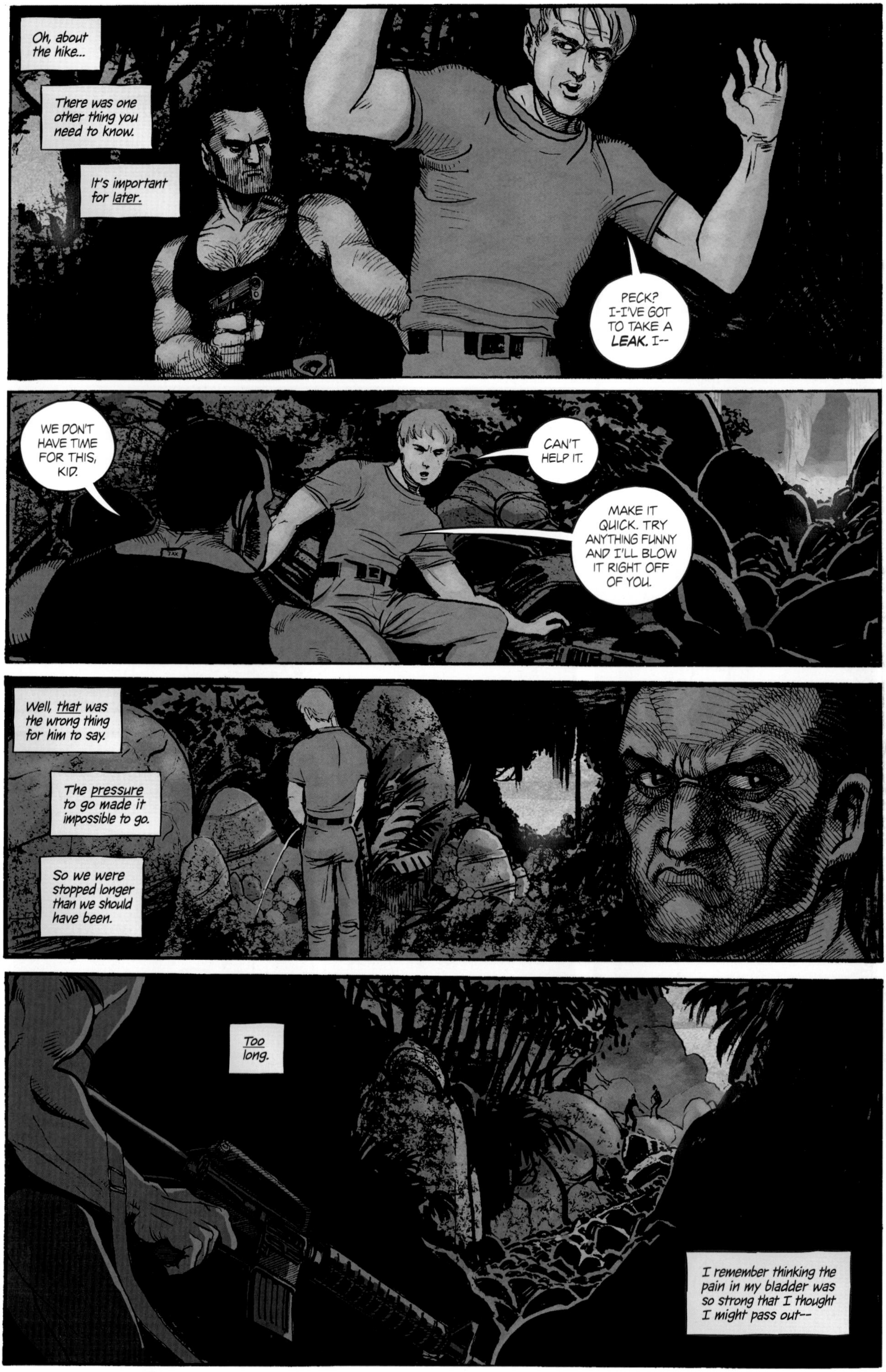

Oh, about the hike...
There was one other thing you need to know.
It's important for later.
PECK? I-I'VE GOT TO TAKE A LEAK. I--
WE DON'T HAVE TIME FOR THIS, KID.
CAN'T HELP IT.
MAKE IT QUICK. TRY ANYTHING FUNNY AND I'LL BLOW IT RIGHT OFF OF YOU.
Well, that was the wrong thing for him to say.
The pressure to go made it impossible to go.
So we were stopped longer than we should have been.
Too long.
I remember thinking the pain in my bladder was so strong that I thought I might pass out--

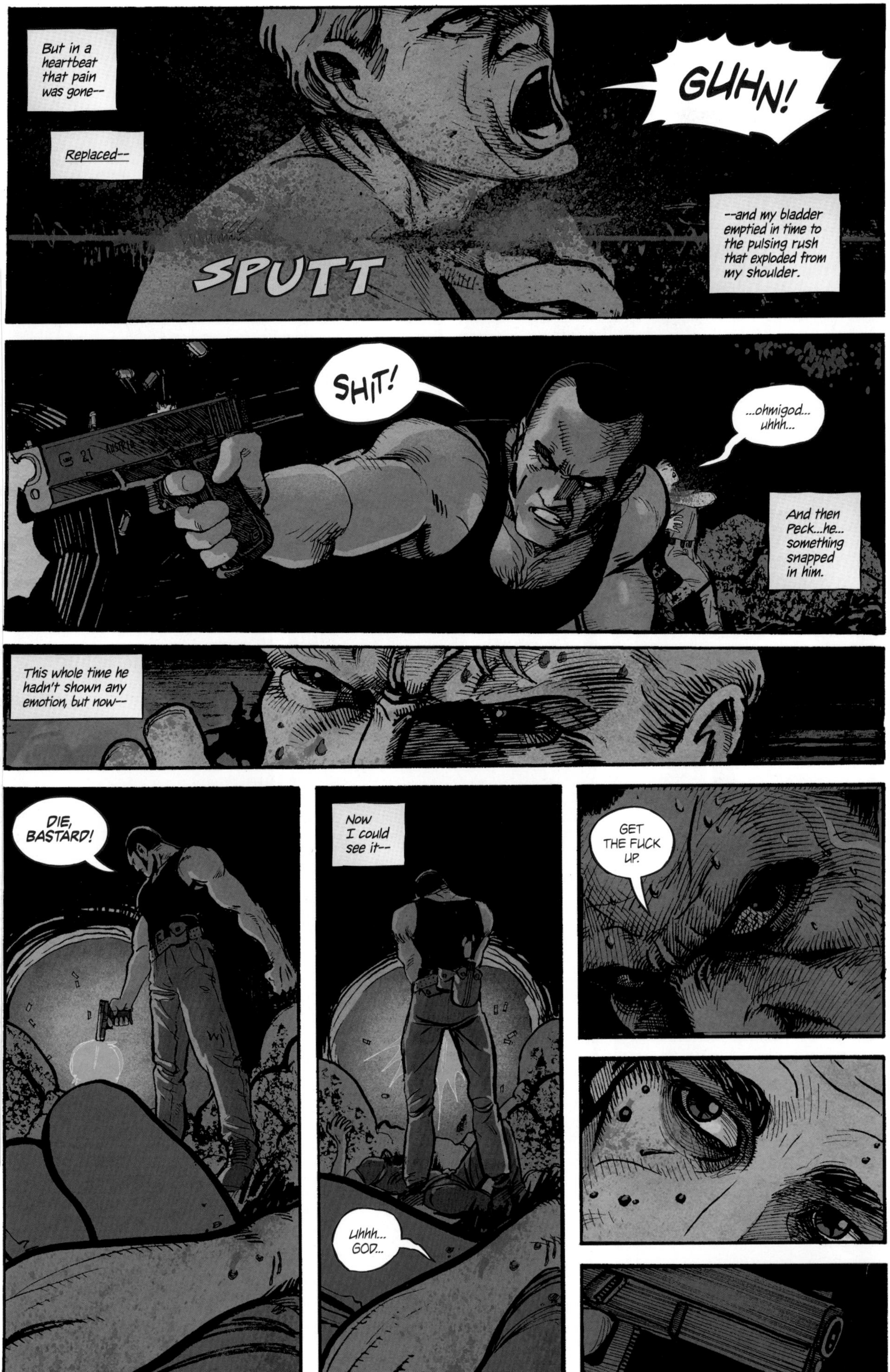
But in a heartbeat that pain was gone--
Replaced--
GUHN!
SPUTT
--and my bladder emptied in time to the pulsing rush that exploded from my shoulder.
SHIT!
...ohmigod... uhhh...
And then Peck...he... something snapped in him.
This whole time he hadn't shown any emotion, but now--
DIE, BASTARD!
Now I could see it--
Uhhh... GOD...
GET THE FUCK UP.

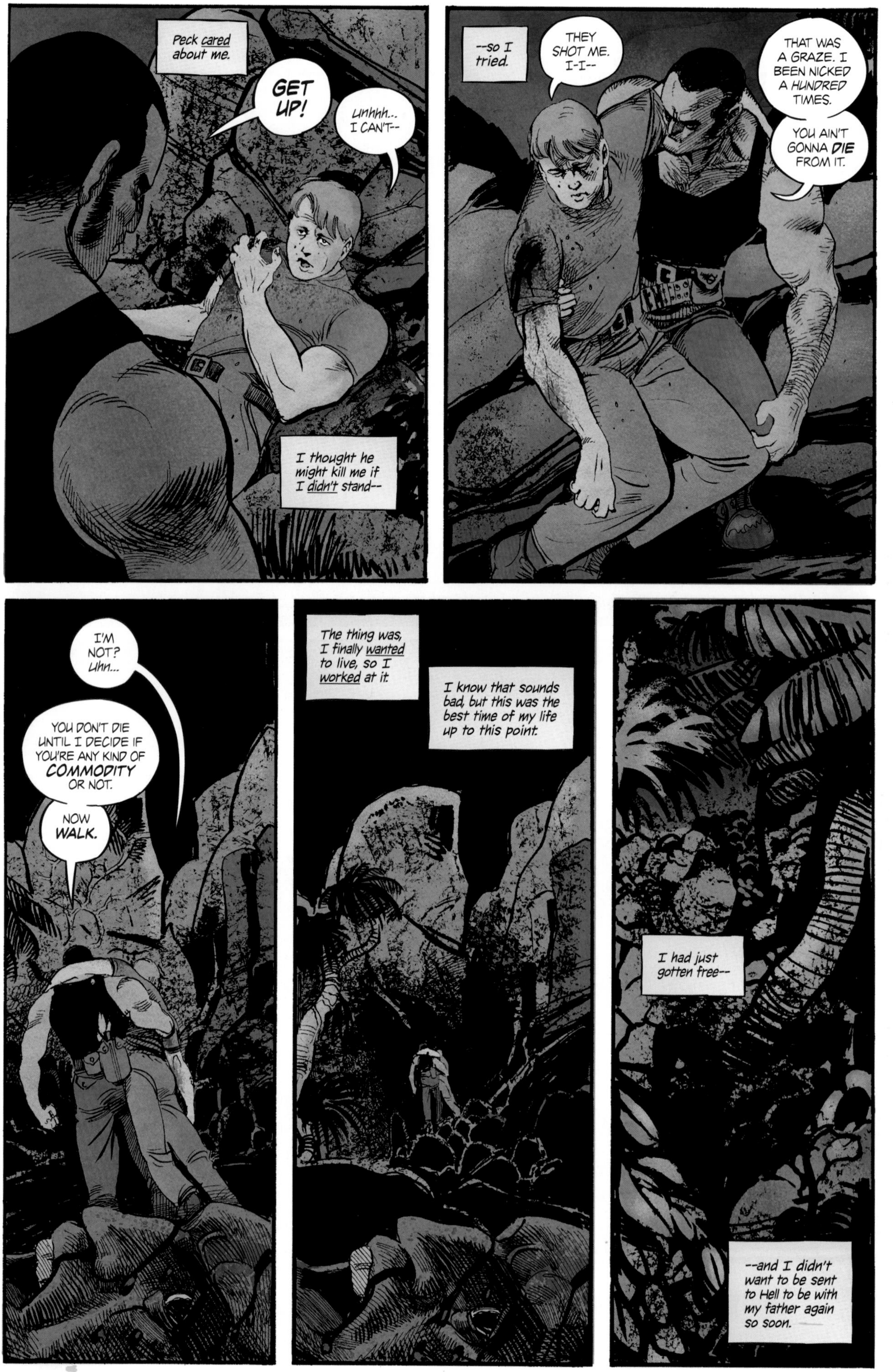
Peck cared about me.
GET UP!
Uhhh... I CAN'T--
I thought he might kill me if I didn't stand--
--so I tried.
THEY SHOT ME. I-I--
THAT WAS A GRAZE. I BEEN NICKED A HUNDRED TIMES.
YOU AIN'T GONNA DIE FROM IT.
I'M NOT? Uhn...
YOU DON'T DIE UNTIL I DECIDE IF YOU'RE ANY KIND OF COMMODITY OR NOT.
NOW WALK.
The thing was, I finally wanted to live, so I worked at it.
I know that sounds bad, but this was the best time of my life up to this point.
I had just gotten free--
--and I didn't want to be sent to Hell to be with my father again so soon.

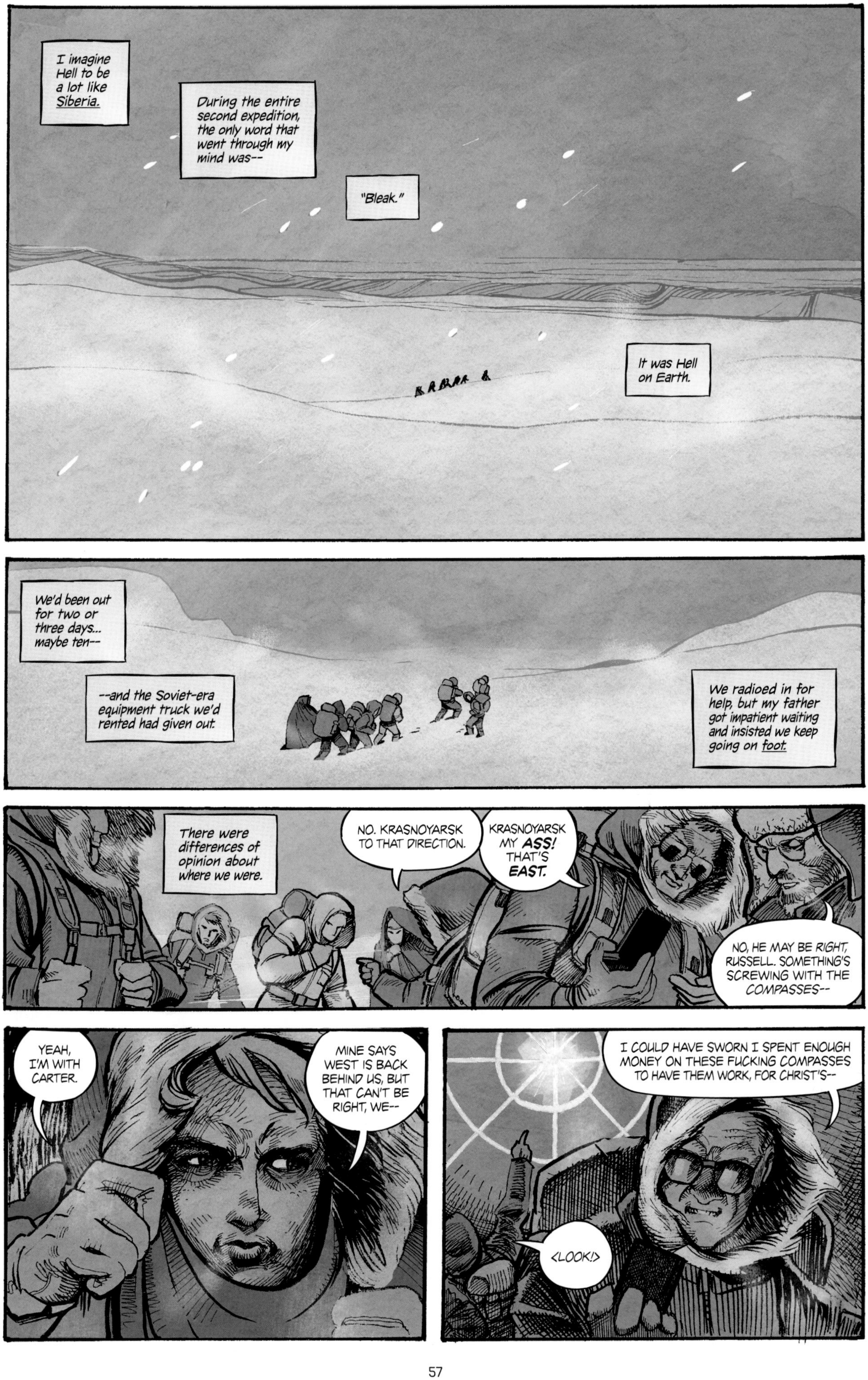
I imagine Hell to be a lot like Siberia.
During the entire second expedition, the only word that went through my mind was--
"Bleak."
It was Hell on Earth.
We'd been out for two or three days... maybe ten--
--and the Soviet-era equipment truck we'd rented had given out.
We radioed in for help, but my father got impatient waiting and insisted we keep going on foot.
There were differences of opinion about where we were.
NO. KRASNOYARSK TO THAT DIRECTION.
KRASNOYARSK MY ASS! THAT'S EAST.
NO, HE MAY BE RIGHT, RUSSELL. SOMETHING'S SCREWING WITH THE COMPASSES--
YEAH, I'M WITH CARTER.
MINE SAYS WEST IS BACK BEHIND US, BUT THAT CAN'T BE RIGHT, WE--
I COULD HAVE SWORN I SPENT ENOUGH MONEY ON THESE FUCKING COMPASSES TO HAVE THEM WORK, FOR CHRIST'S--
<LOOK!>

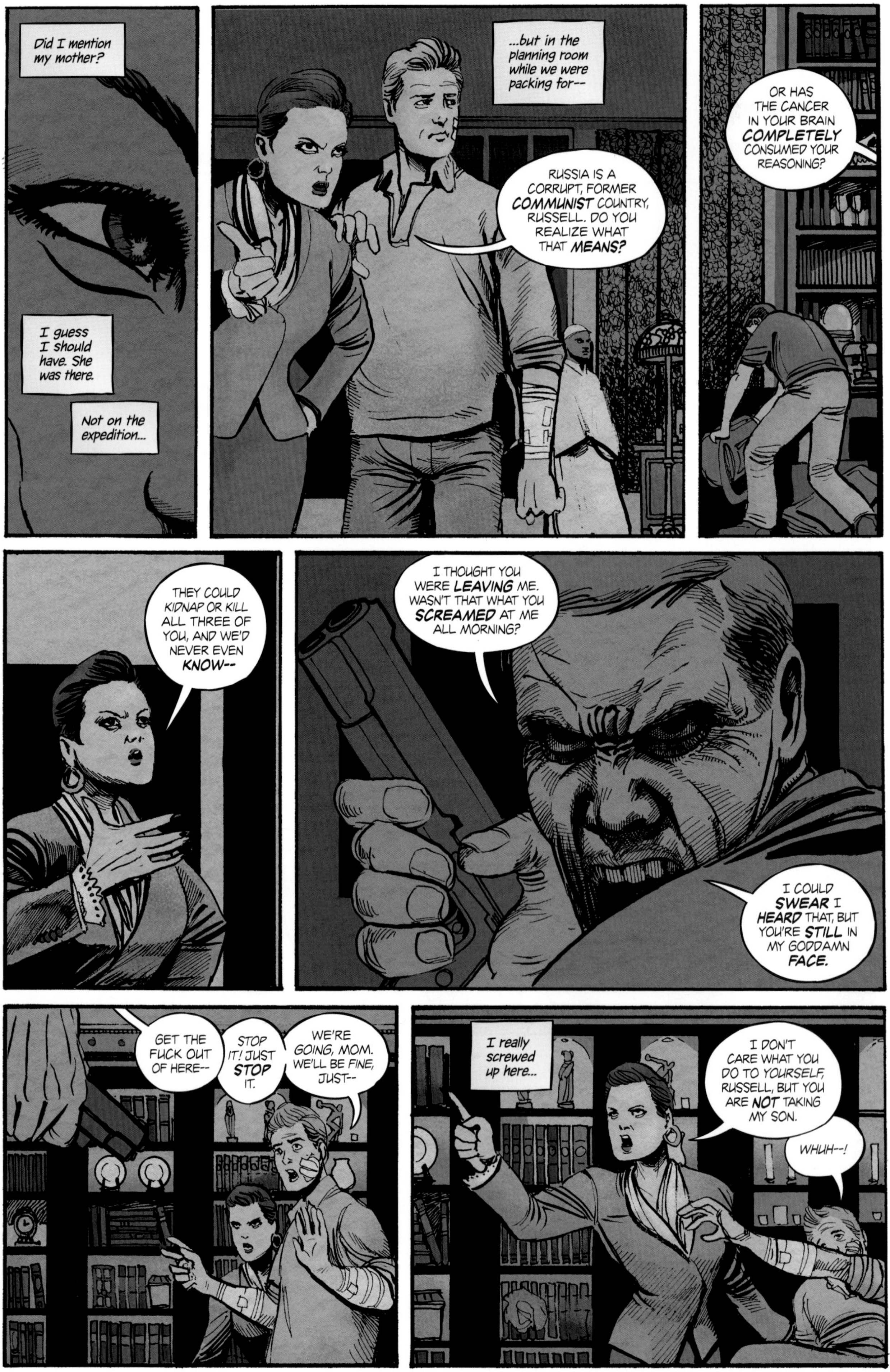
Did I mention my mother?
I guess I should have. She was there.
Not on the expedition...
...but in the planning room while we were packing for--
RUSSIA IS A CORRUPT, FORMER COMMUNIST COUNTRY, RUSSELL. DO YOU REALIZE WHAT THAT MEANS?
OR HAS THE CANCER IN YOUR BRAIN COMPLETELY CONSUMED YOUR REASONING?
THEY COULD KIDNAP OR KILL ALL THREE OF YOU, AND WE'D NEVER EVEN KNOW--
I THOUGHT YOU WERE LEAVING ME. WASN'T THAT WHAT YOU SCREAMED AT ME ALL MORNING?
I COULD SWEAR I HEARD THAT, BUT YOU'RE STILL IN MY GODDAMN FACE.
GET THE FUCK OUT OF HERE--
STOP IT! JUST STOP IT.
WE'RE GOING, MOM. WE'LL BE FINE, JUST--
I really screwed up here...
I DON'T CARE WHAT YOU DO TO YOURSELF, RUSSELL, BUT YOU ARE NOT TAKING MY SON.
WHUH--!

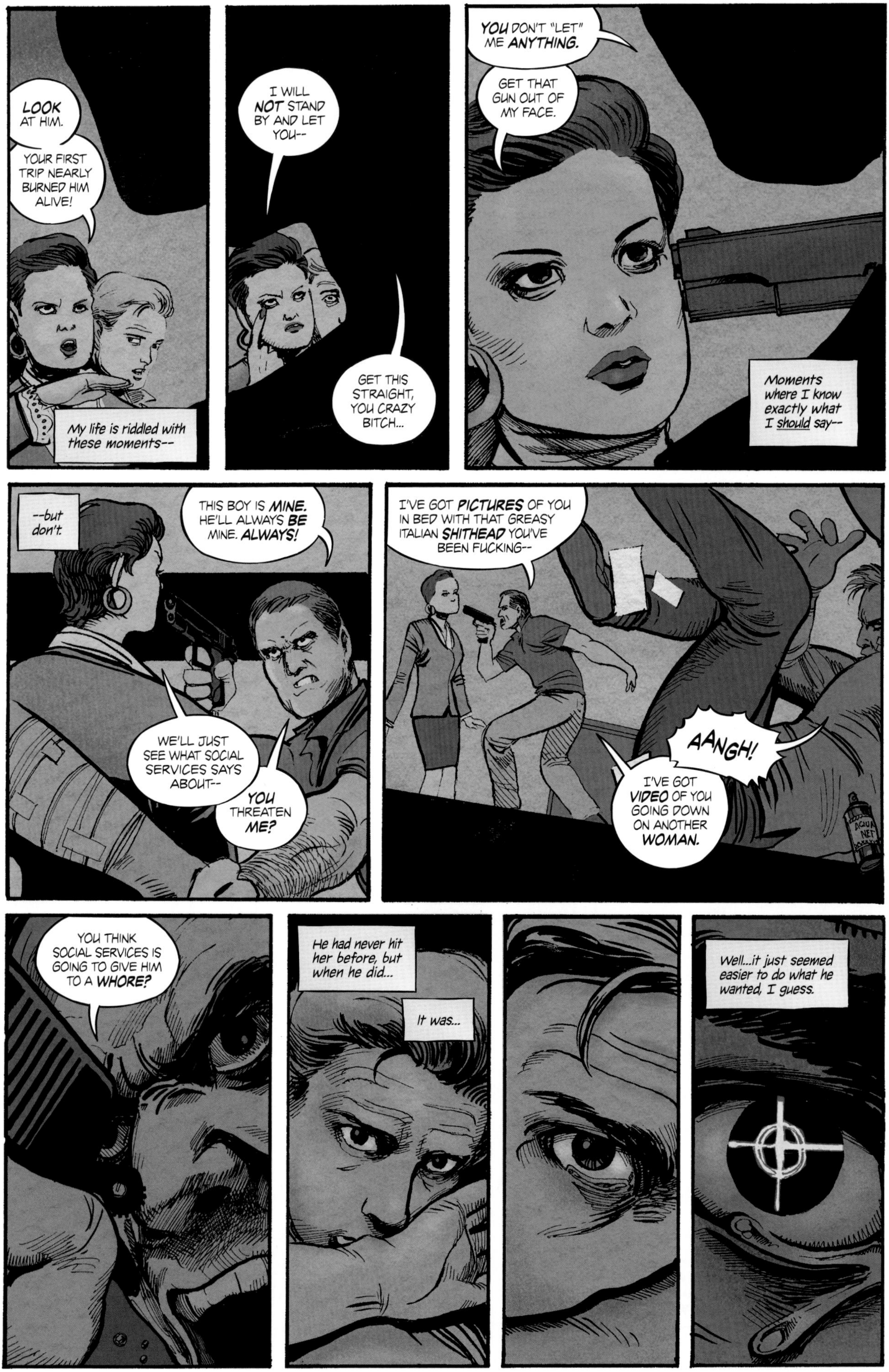
LOOK AT HIM.
YOUR FIRST TRIP NEARLY BURNED HIM ALIVE!
My life is riddled with these moments--
I WILL NOT STAND BY AND LET YOU--
GET THIS STRAIGHT, YOU CRAZY BITCH...
YOU DON'T "LET" ME ANYTHING.
GET THAT GUN OUT OF MY FACE.
Moments where I know exactly what I should say--
--but don't.
THIS BOY IS MINE. HE'LL ALWAYS BE MINE. ALWAYS!
WE'LL JUST SEE WHAT SOCIAL SERVICES SAYS ABOUT--
YOU THREATEN ME?
I'VE GOT PICTURES OF YOU IN BED WITH THAT GREASY ITALIAN SHITHEAD YOU'VE BEEN FUCKING--
AANGH!
I'VE GOT VIDEO OF YOU GOING DOWN ON ANOTHER WOMAN.
YOU THINK SOCIAL SERVICES IS GOING TO GIVE HIM TO A WHORE?
He had never hit her before, but when he did...
It was...
Well...it just seemed easier to do what he wanted, I guess.

So anyway, _Siberia_.

We were confused about where to go when a light appeared in the sky.

WHAT THE HELL--?

I was pretty sure it wasn't the second coming.

Though for a moment I wished it was.

AAAAAAH!

I thought typical teenage things like...

"I hope the world just ends," and--

--and "I'd rather be dead than do this any more..."

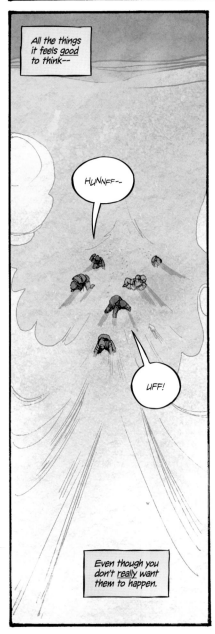

All the things it feels _good_ to think--

HUNNFF--

UFF!

Even though you don't _really_ want them to happen.

WAS THAT A _UFO?_

UFOs DON'T _EXIST_, CARTER. THAT WAS A _MIG._

FRIGGIN' GOVERNMENT PROBABLY REALIZED WHAT I'M ABOUT TO FIND AND WANTS TO _STOP_ ME NOW THAT I--

I'd seen him walk like that before--

DAD...?

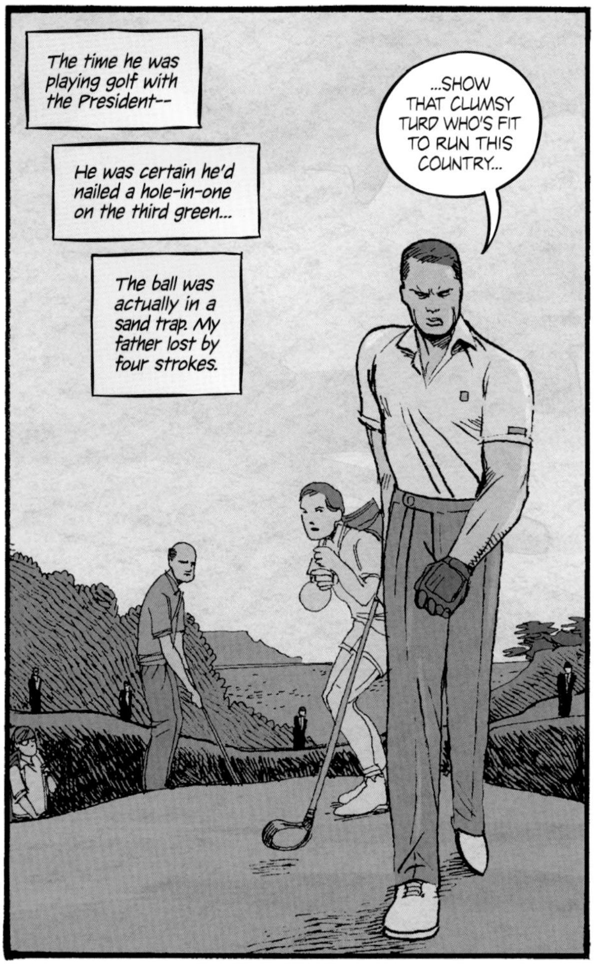
The time he was playing golf with the President--
He was certain he'd nailed a hole-in-one on the third green...
The ball was actually in a sand trap. My father lost by four strokes.
...SHOW THAT CLUMSY TURD WHO'S FIT TO RUN THIS COUNTRY...

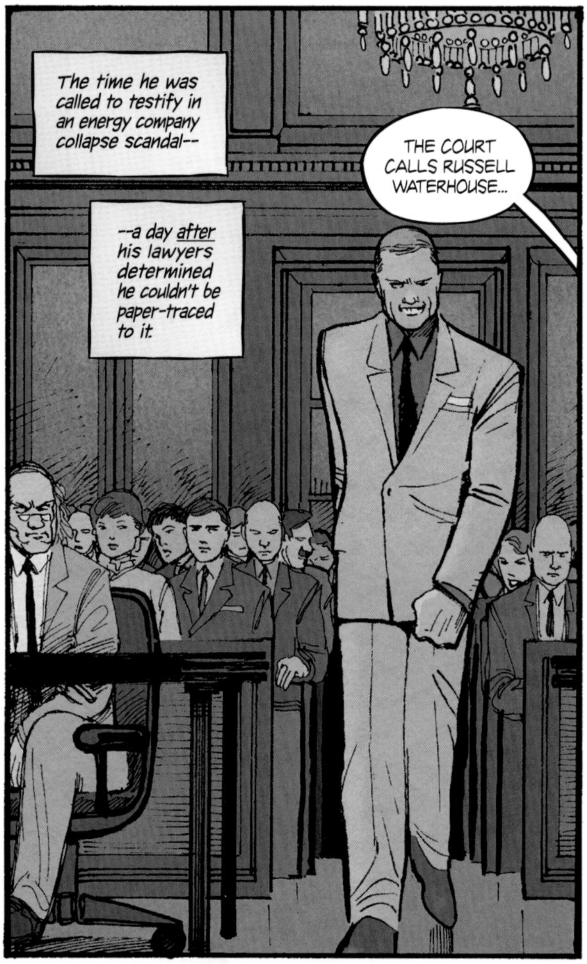
The time he was called to testify in an energy company collapse scandal--
--a day after his lawyers determined he couldn't be paper-traced to it.
THE COURT CALLS RUSSELL WATERHOUSE...

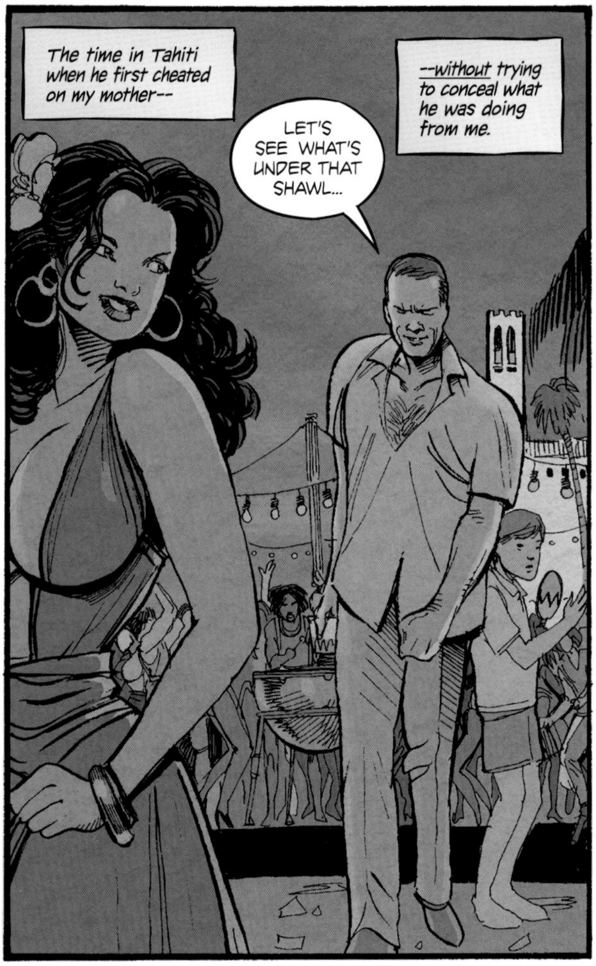
The time in Tahiti when he first cheated on my mother--
--without trying to conceal what he was doing from me.
LET'S SEE WHAT'S UNDER THAT SHAWL...

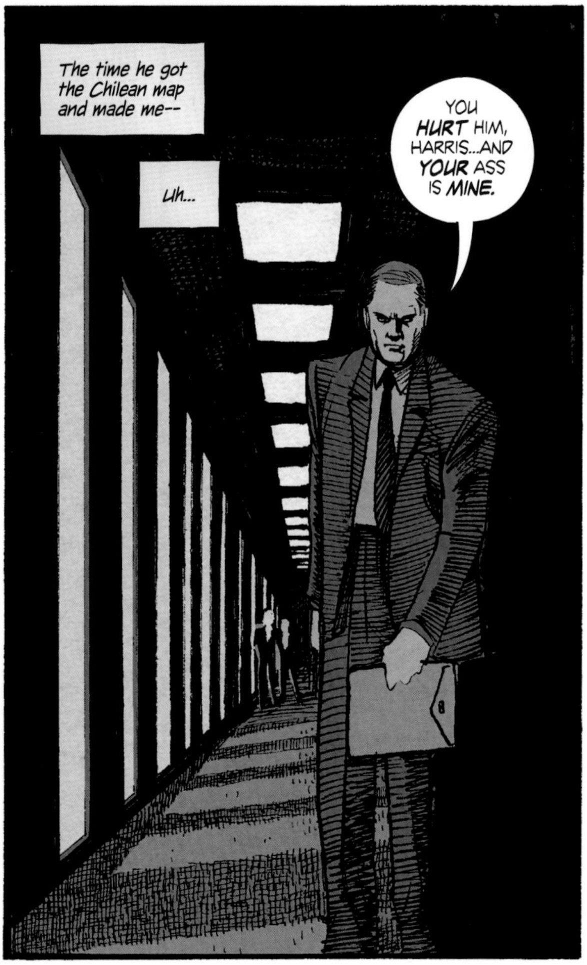
The time he got the Chilean map and made me--
uh...
YOU HURT HIM, HARRIS...AND YOUR ASS IS MINE.

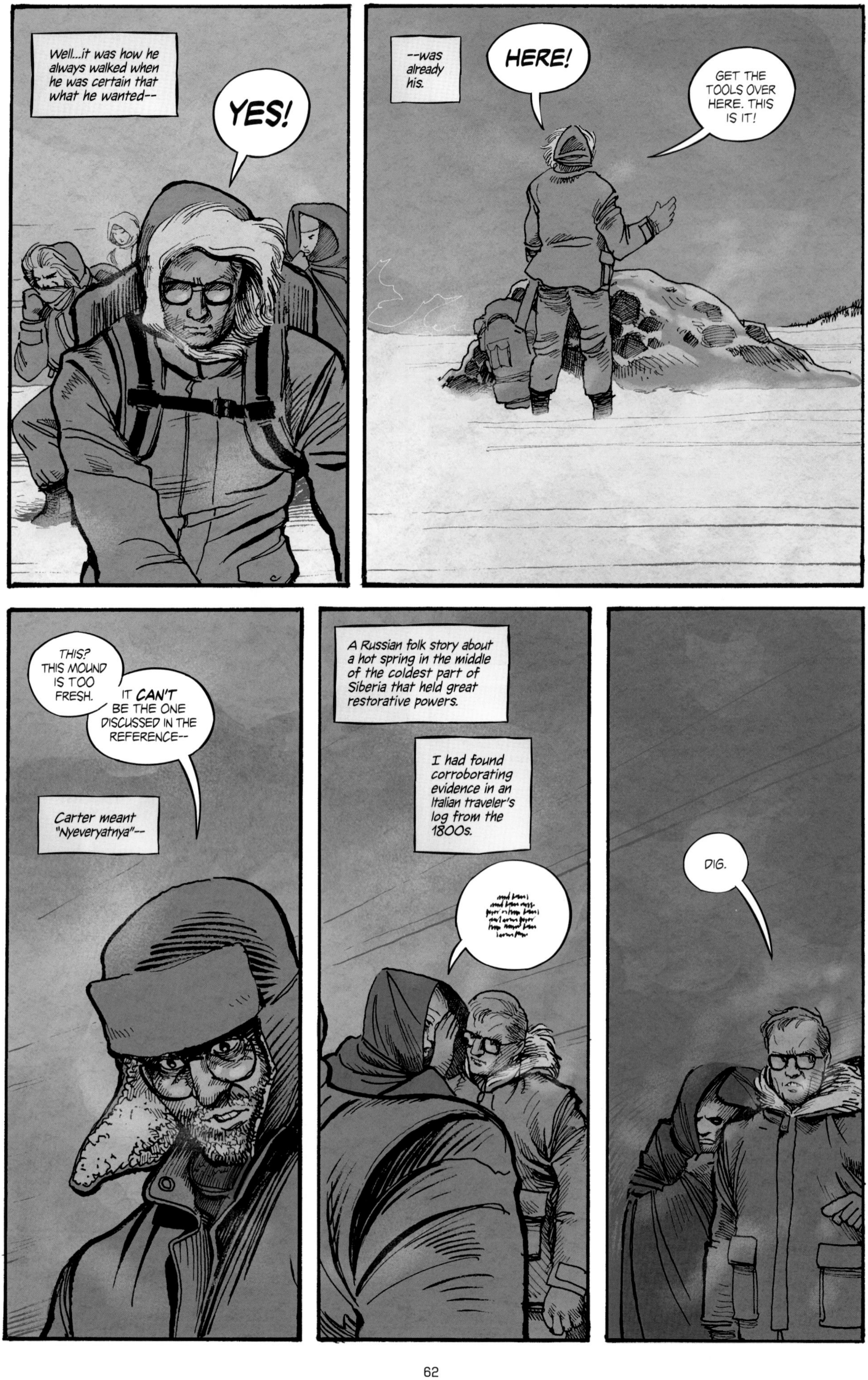
Well...it was how he always walked when he was certain that what he wanted--
YES!
--was already his.
HERE!
GET THE TOOLS OVER HERE. THIS IS IT!
THIS? THIS MOUND IS TOO FRESH.
IT CAN'T BE THE ONE DISCUSSED IN THE REFERENCE--
Carter meant "Nyeveryatnya"--
A Russian folk story about a hot spring in the middle of the coldest part of Siberia that held great restorative powers.
I had found corroborating evidence in an Italian traveler's log from the 1800s.
DIG.

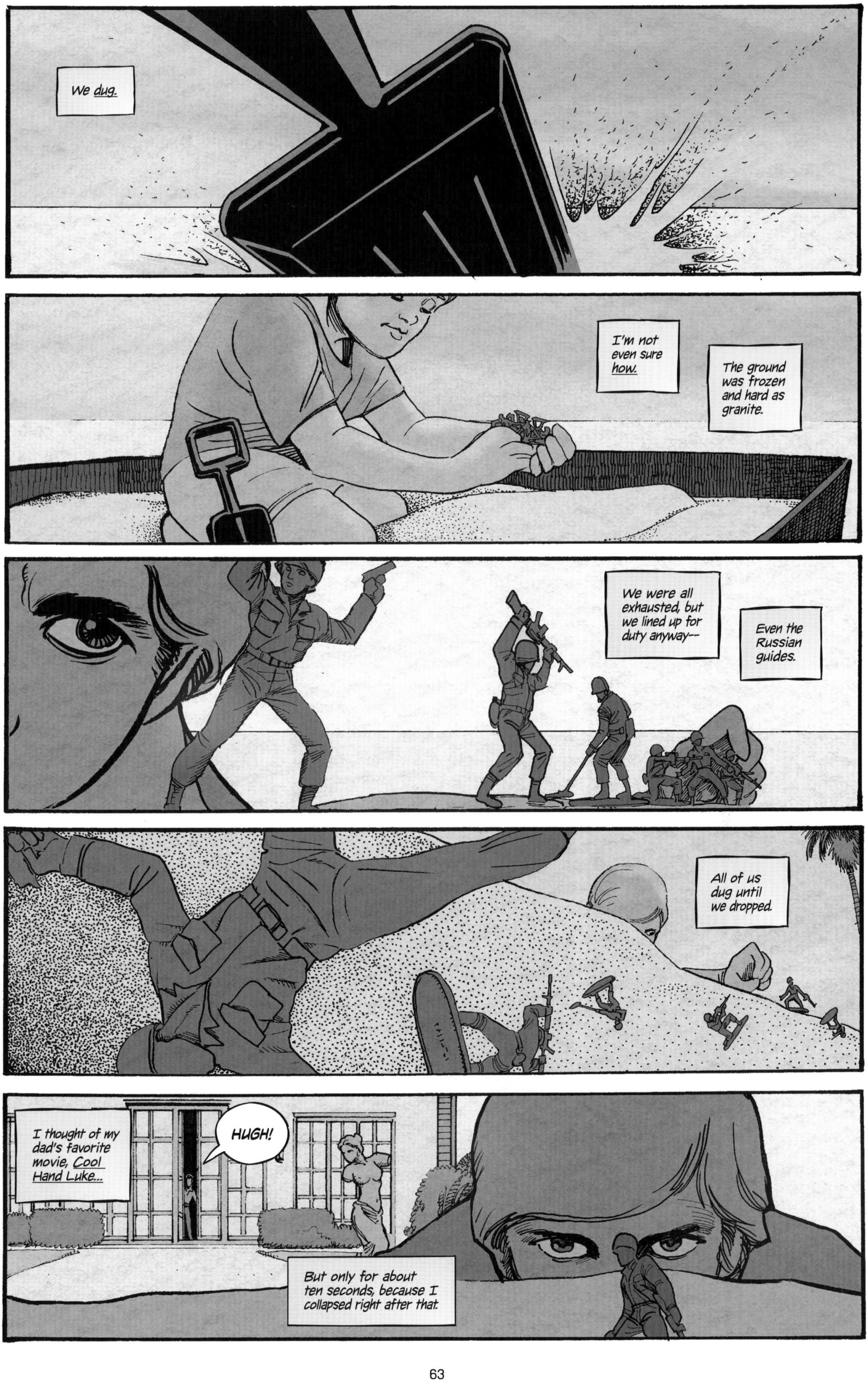
We dug.
I'm not even sure how.
The ground was frozen and hard as granite.
We were all exhausted, but we lined up for duty anyway--
Even the Russian guides.
All of us dug until we dropped.
I thought of my dad's favorite movie, Cool Hand Luke...
HUGH!
But only for about ten seconds, because I collapsed right after that.

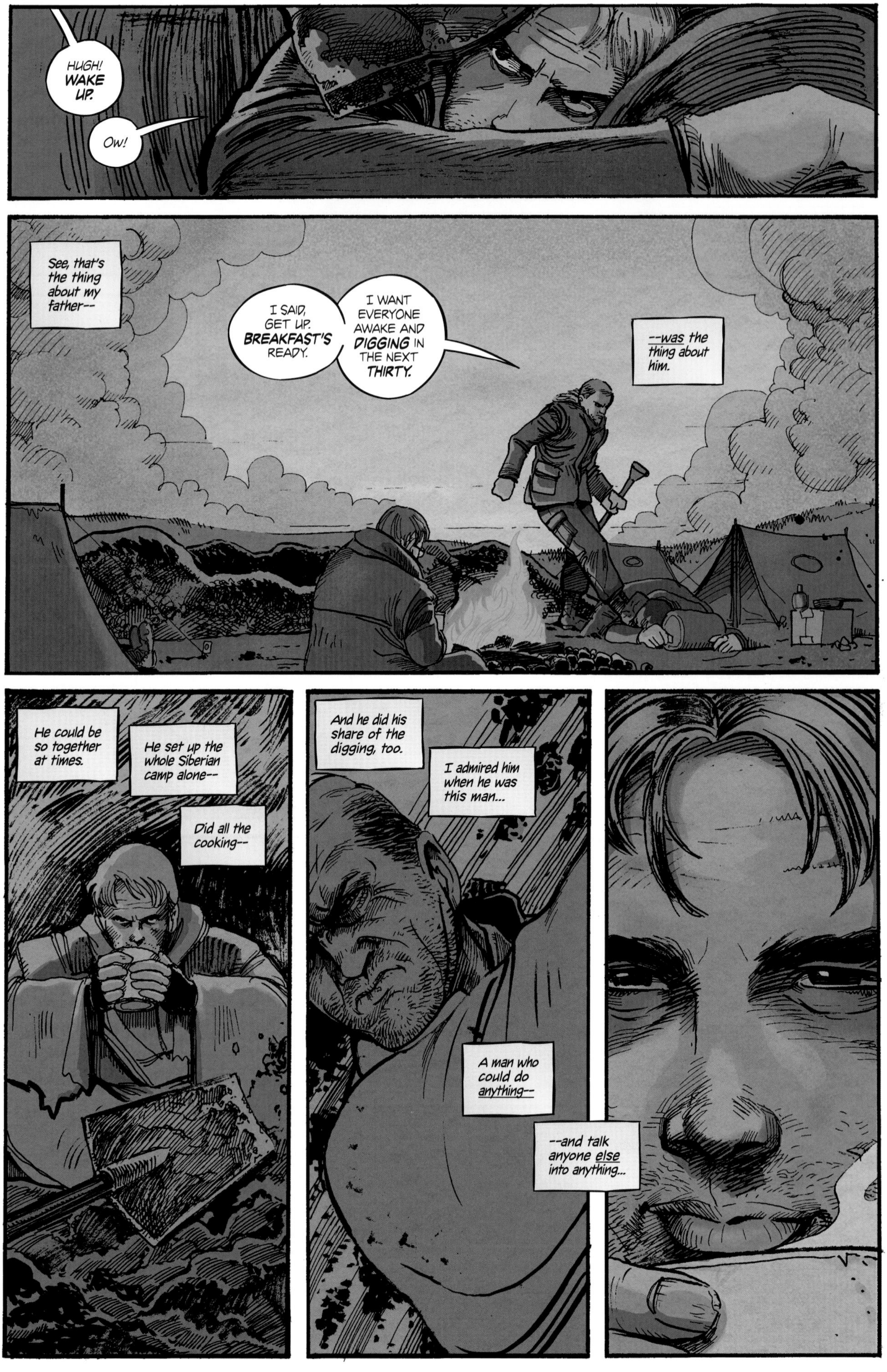
HUGH! WAKE UP.
Ow!
See, that's the thing about my father--
I SAID, GET UP. BREAKFAST'S READY.
I WANT EVERYONE AWAKE AND DIGGING IN THE NEXT THIRTY.
--was the thing about him.
He could be so together at times.
He set up the whole Siberian camp alone--
Did all the cooking--
And he did his share of the digging, too.
I admired him when he was this man...
A man who could do anything--
--and talk anyone else into anything...

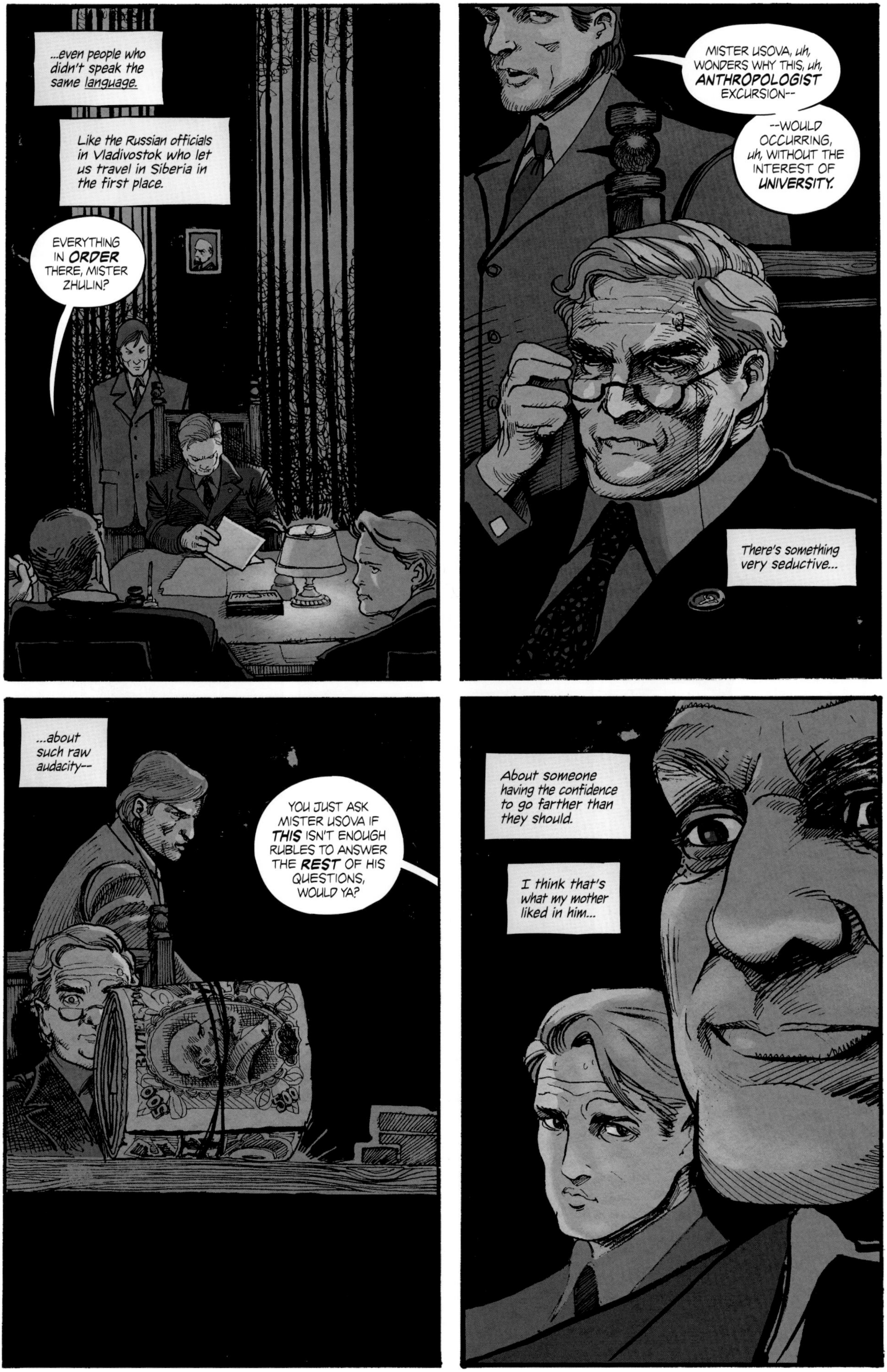
...even people who didn't speak the same language.
Like the Russian officials in Vladivostok who let us travel in Siberia in the first place.
EVERYTHING IN ORDER THERE, MISTER ZHULIN?
MISTER USOVA, uh, WONDERS WHY THIS, uh, ANTHROPOLOGIST EXCURSION--
--WOULD OCCURRING, uh, WITHOUT THE INTEREST OF UNIVERSITY.
There's something very seductive...
...about such raw audacity--
YOU JUST ASK MISTER USOVA IF THIS ISN'T ENOUGH RUBLES TO ANSWER THE REST OF HIS QUESTIONS, WOULD YA?
About someone having the confidence to go farther than they should.
I think that's what my mother liked in him...

...until she realized that it couldn't be turned off.

MISTER USOVA WOULD, *uh*, LIKE TO HAVE... *DINING* WITH YOU.

GOOD.

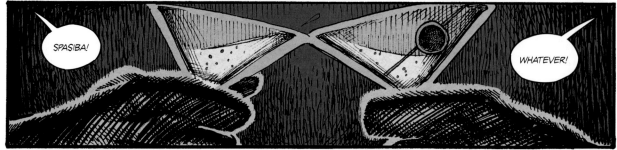

SPASIBA!

WHATEVER!

Getting involved with a person like that is a lot like getting a good drunk going--

MISTER USOVA, *uh*, SAYS YOU MUST HAVE *SIX* RUSSIAN, *uh*, *ESCORTS* WITH YOU AT ALL THE TIME.

YOU TELL FATTY TO MAKE IT *THREE* AND HE'S GOT A *DEAL!* HA!

MORE VODKA!

It's very appealing when you start in--

--but once you get there...

--TITS. YOU KNOW--

SPAZEEEEBA-BA-BA-BOOMS! *HA! HA!*

UNNHHH...

HA HA HA HA HA HA

...you swear you'll never go back again--

--even though deep in your heart you know you probably will.

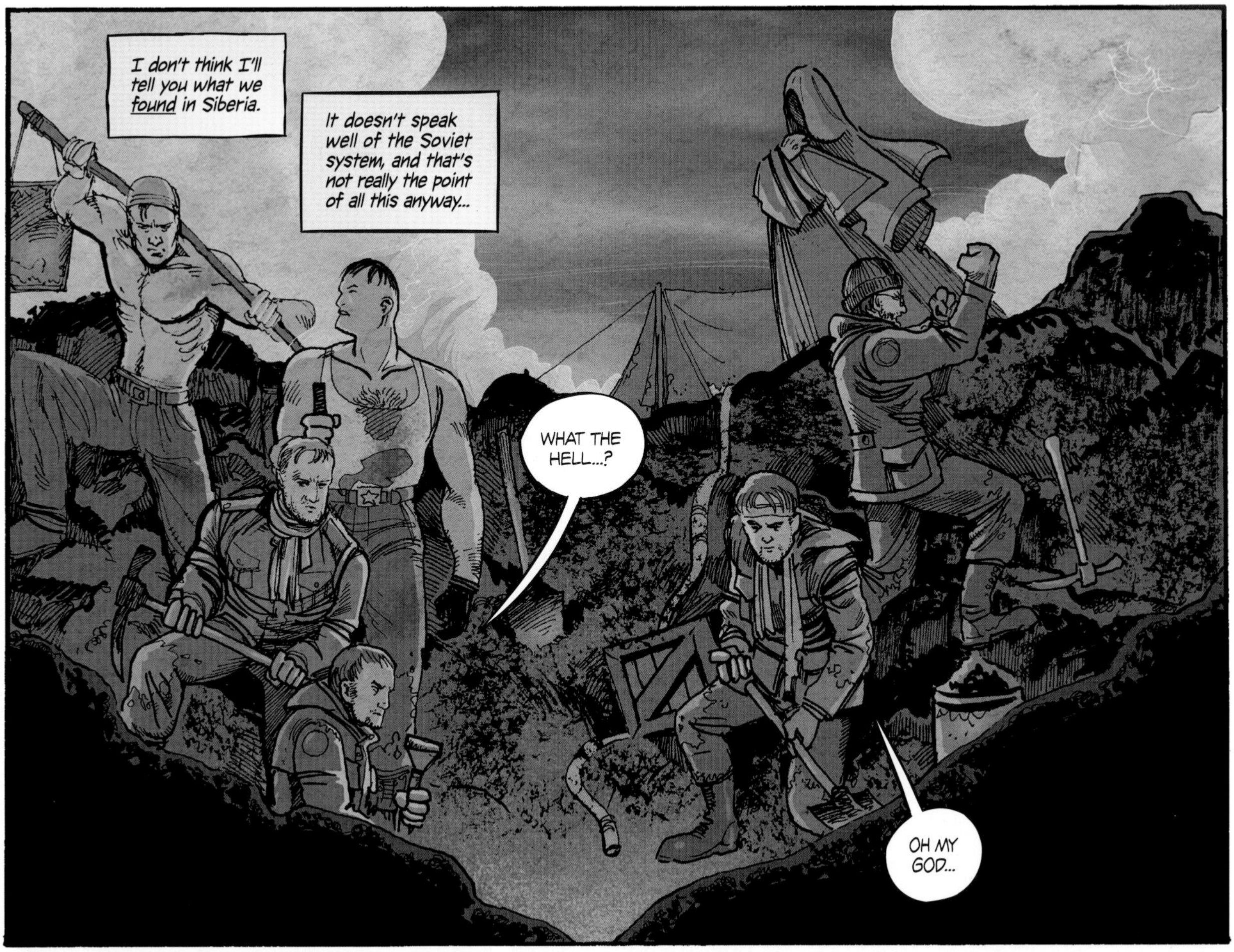
I don't think I'll tell you what we found in Siberia.
It doesn't speak well of the Soviet system, and that's not really the point of all this anyway...
WHAT THE HELL...?
OH MY GOD...

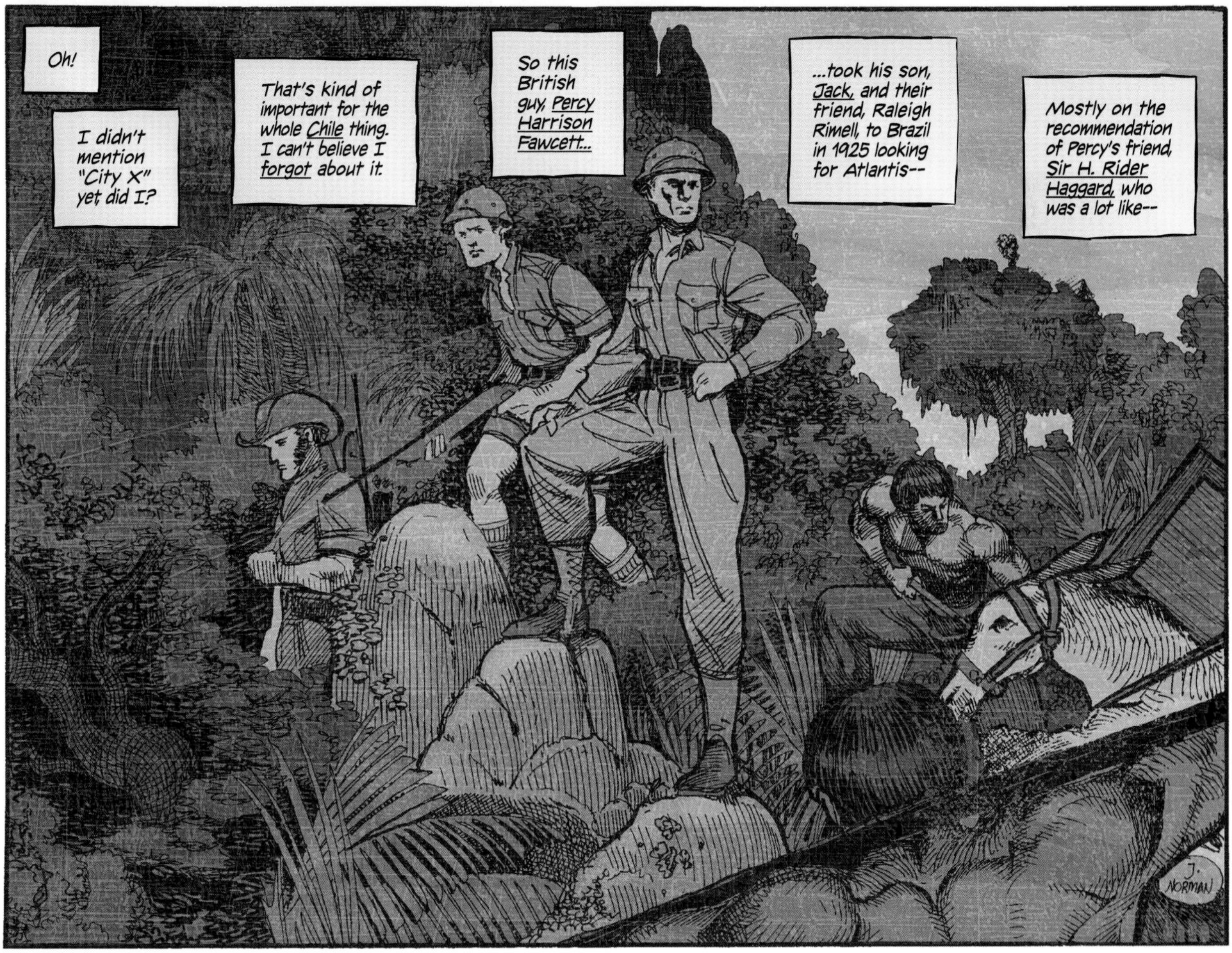
Oh!
I didn't mention "City X" yet, did I?
That's kind of important for the whole Chile thing. I can't believe I forgot about it.
So this British guy, Percy Harrison Fawcett...
...took his son, Jack, and their friend, Raleigh Rimell, to Brazil in 1925 looking for Atlantis--
Mostly on the recommendation of Percy's friend, Sir H. Rider Haggard, who was a lot like--
J. NORMAN

Peck--

YOU GOTTA HELP ME, KID, OR I'M GONNA HAVE TO **DUMP** YOU.

--who I guess I should finish up with before I get too into "City X", even though the city thing's more interesting.

I'M TRYING, PECK, BUT I--

I-- Unngh!

Don't worry. This **looked** *worse than it really* **was.**

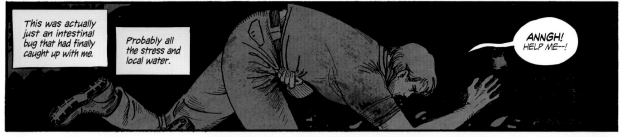

This was actually just an intestinal bug that had finally caught up with me.

Probably all the stress and local water.

ANNGH! HELP ME--!

AH, **SHIT!**

STOMACH'S SWELLING. **BACTERIA.**

I'M GONNA HAVE TO CUT IT TO LET OFF SOME OF THE PRESSURE--

CUT--?! **NO!**

It was when I fell that I saw him again...

68

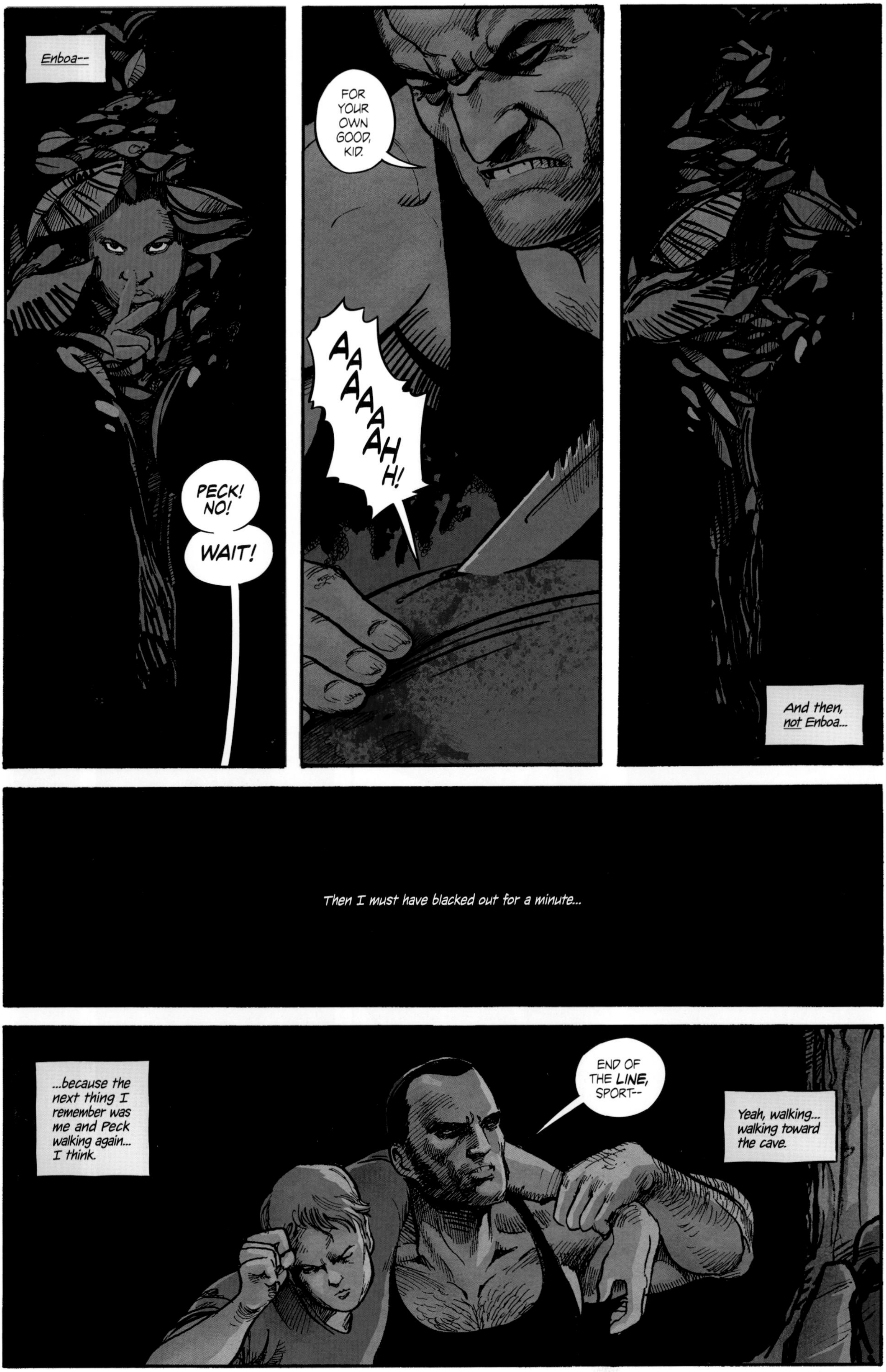
Enboa--
PECK! NO!
WAIT!
FOR YOUR OWN GOOD, KID.
AAAAAAH!
And then, not Enboa...
Then I must have blacked out for a minute...
...because the next thing I remember was me and Peck walking again... I think.
END OF THE LINE, SPORT--
Yeah, walking... walking toward the cave.

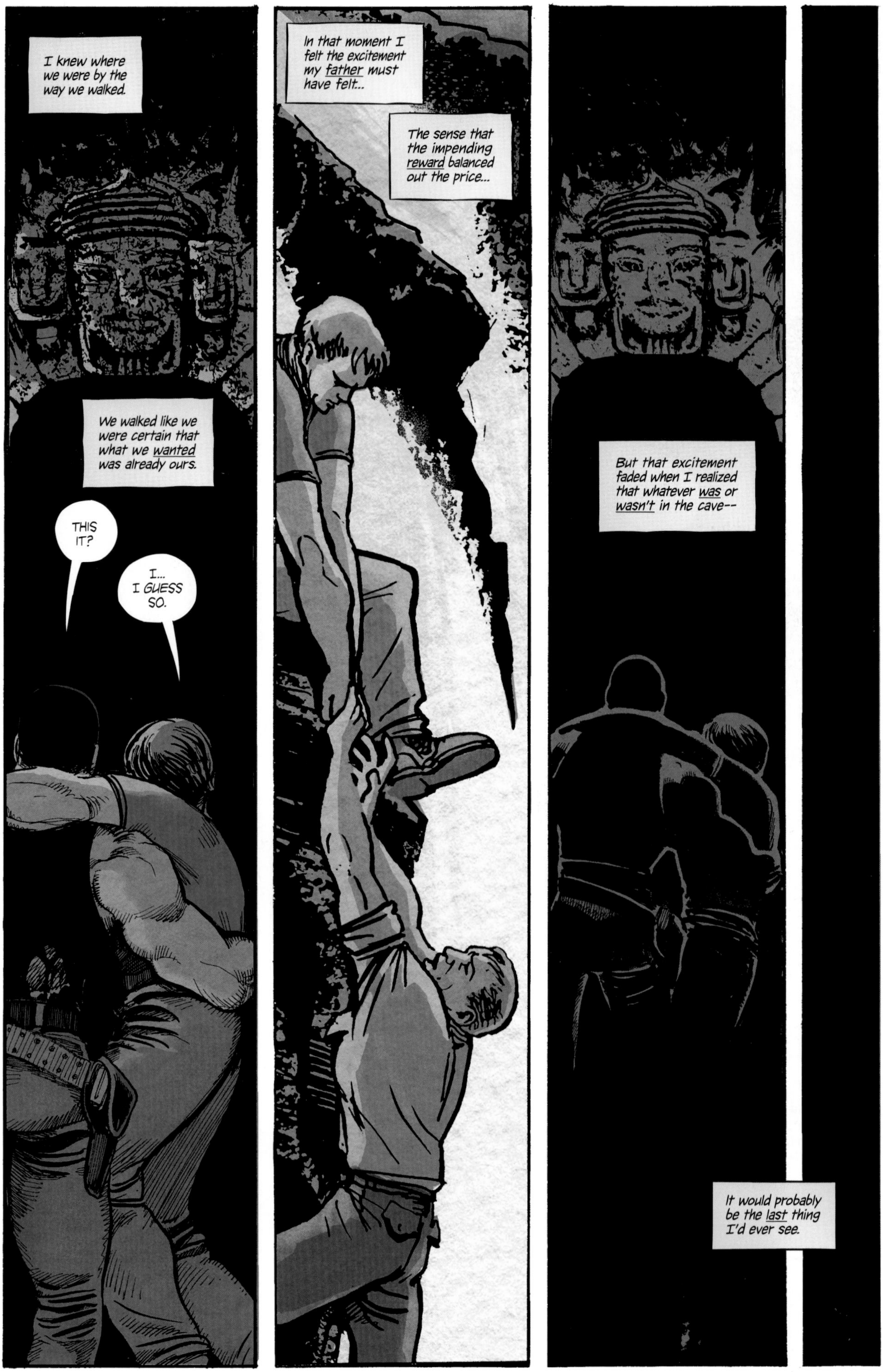

I knew where we were by the way we walked.
We walked like we were certain that what we wanted was already ours.
THIS IT?
I... I GUESS SO.
In that moment I felt the excitement my father must have felt...
The sense that the impending reward balanced out the price...
But that excitement faded when I realized that whatever was or wasn't in the cave--
It would probably be the last thing I'd ever see.

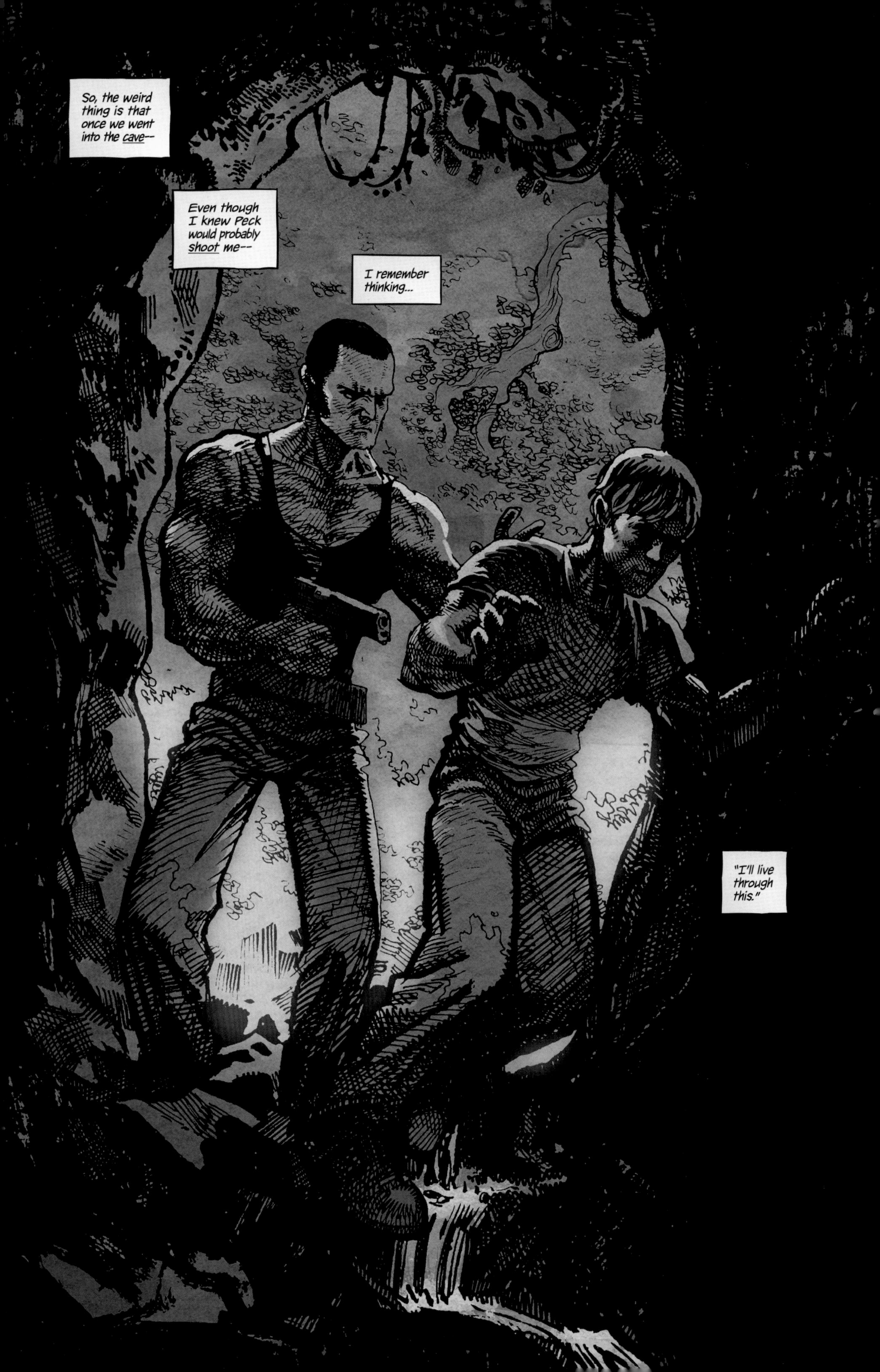
So, the weird thing is that once we went into the cave--
Even though I knew Peck would probably shoot me--
I remember thinking...
"I'll live through this."

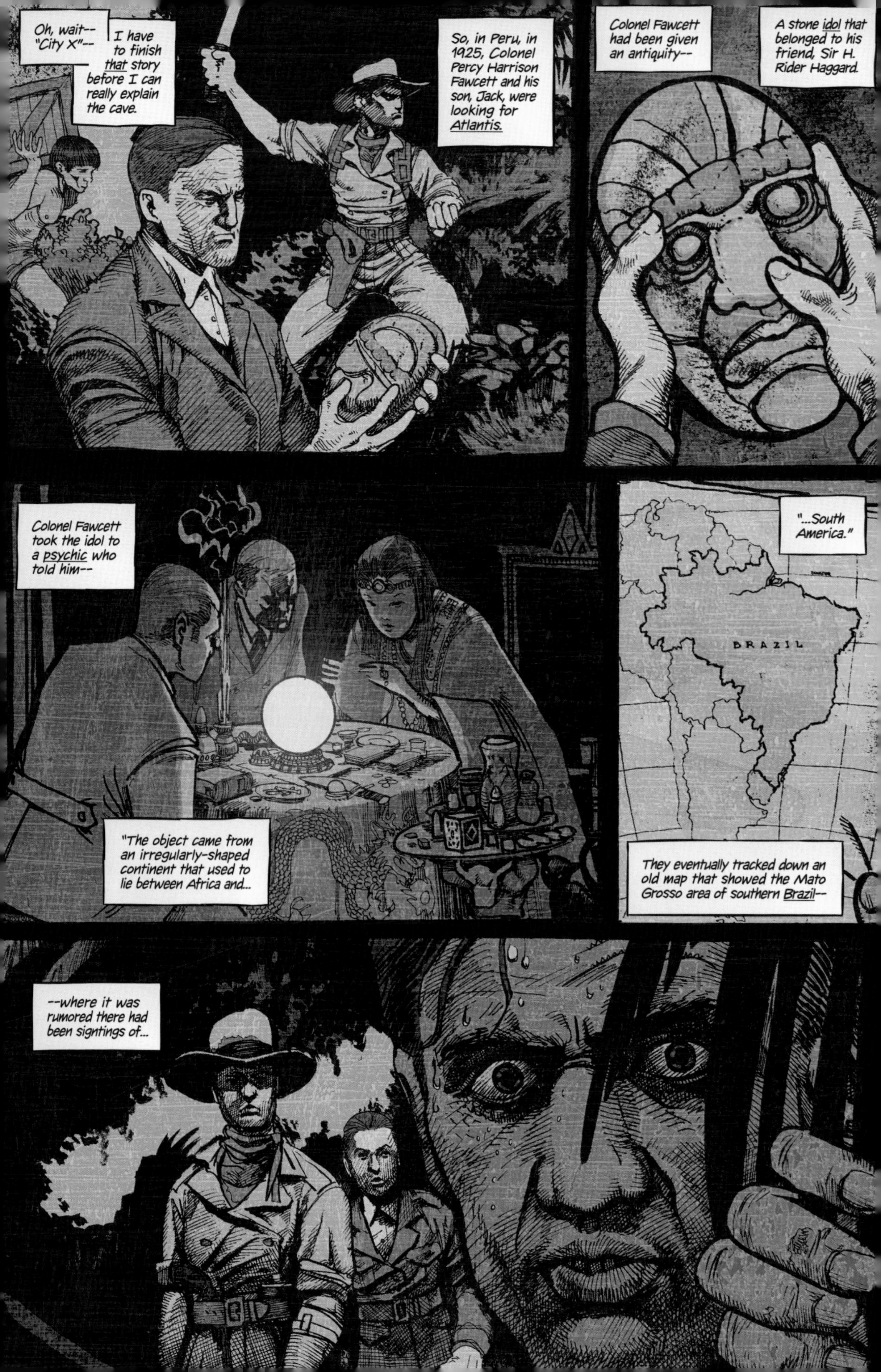

Oh, wait-- "City X"--
I have to finish that story before I can really explain the cave.
So, in Peru, in 1925, Colonel Percy Harrison Fawcett and his son, Jack, were looking for Atlantis.
Colonel Fawcett had been given an antiquity--
A stone idol that belonged to his friend, Sir H. Rider Haggard.
Colonel Fawcett took the idol to a psychic who told him--
"The object came from an irregularly-shaped continent that used to lie between Africa and...
"...South America."
BRAZIL
They eventually tracked down an old map that showed the Mato Grosso area of southern Brazil--
--where it was rumored there had been sightings of...

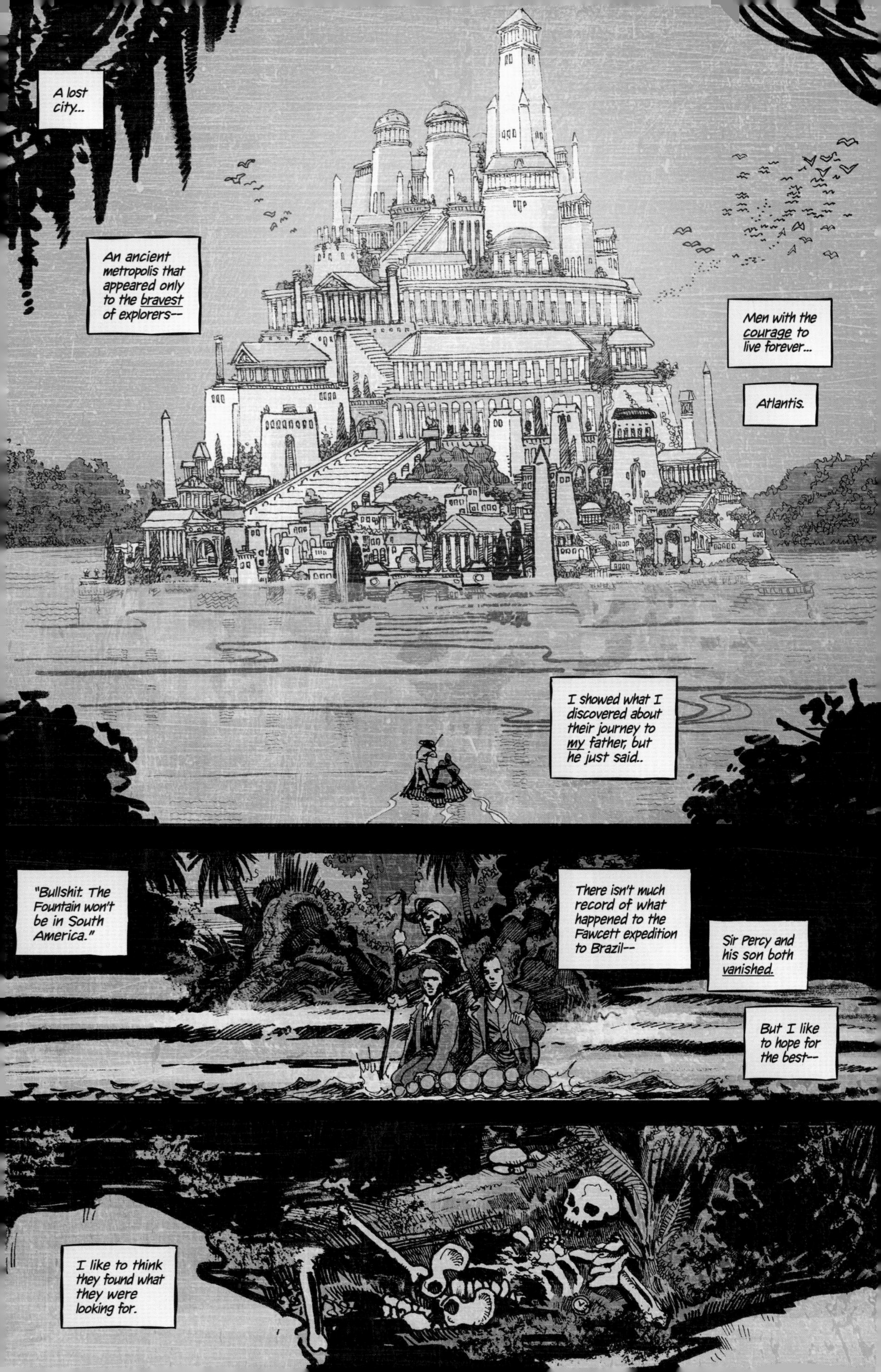
A lost city...
An ancient metropolis that appeared only to the bravest of explorers--
Men with the courage to live forever...
Atlantis.
I showed what I discovered about their journey to my father, but he just said..
"Bullshit. The Fountain won't be in South America."
There isn't much record of what happened to the Fawcett expedition to Brazil--
Sir Percy and his son both vanished.
But I like to hope for the best--
I like to think they found what they were looking for.

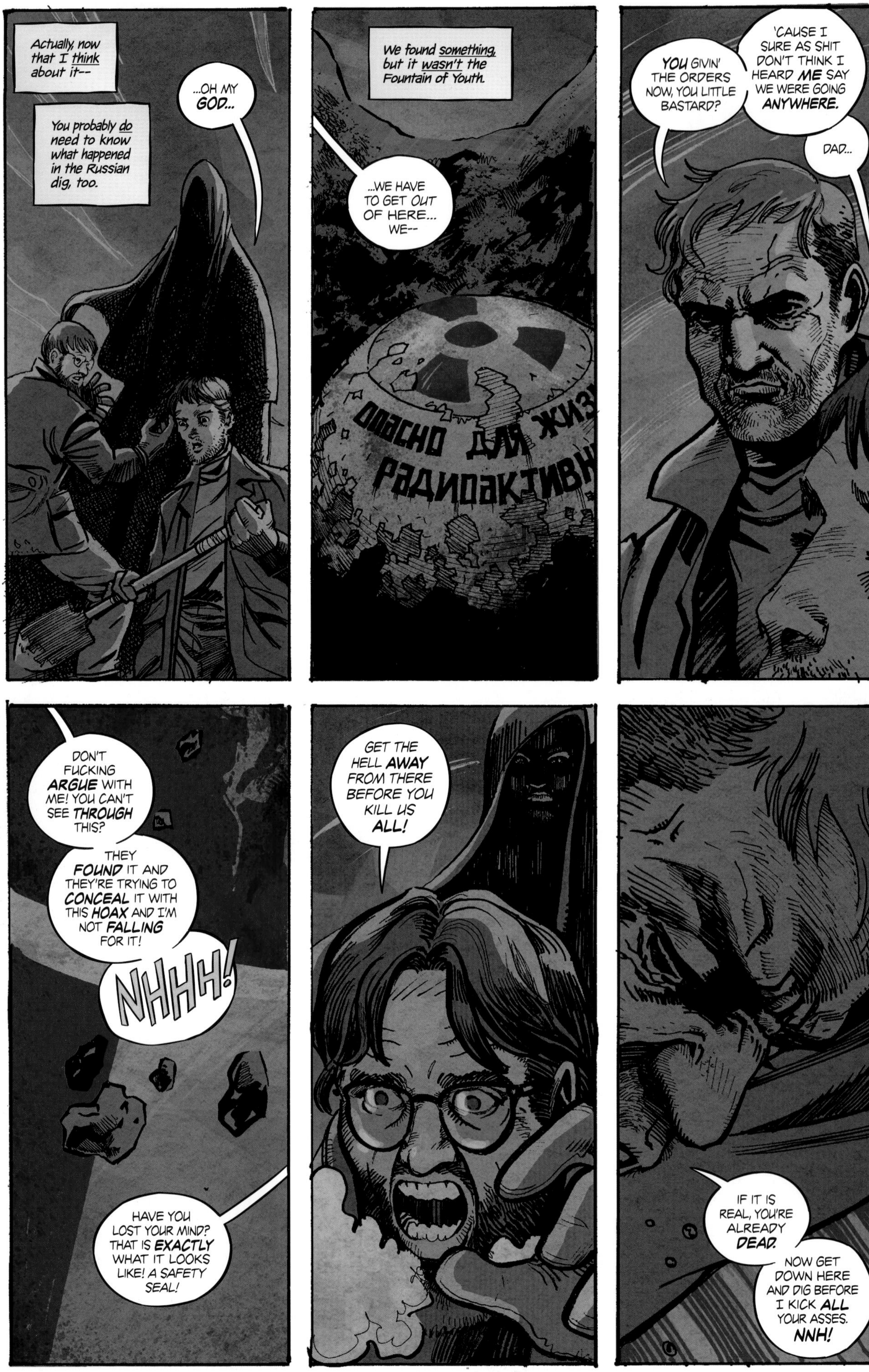
Actually, now that I think about it--
You probably do need to know what happened in the Russian dig, too.
...OH MY GOD...
We found something, but it wasn't the Fountain of Youth.
...WE HAVE TO GET OUT OF HERE... WE--
ОПАСНО ДЛЯ ЖИЗ
РАДИОАКТИВН
YOU GIVIN' THE ORDERS NOW, YOU LITTLE BASTARD?
'CAUSE I SURE AS SHIT DON'T THINK I HEARD ME SAY WE WERE GOING ANYWHERE.
DAD...
DON'T FUCKING ARGUE WITH ME! YOU CAN'T SEE THROUGH THIS?
THEY FOUND IT AND THEY'RE TRYING TO CONCEAL IT WITH THIS HOAX AND I'M NOT FALLING FOR IT!
NHHH!
HAVE YOU LOST YOUR MIND? THAT IS EXACTLY WHAT IT LOOKS LIKE! A SAFETY SEAL!
GET THE HELL AWAY FROM THERE BEFORE YOU KILL US ALL!
IF IT IS REAL, YOU'RE ALREADY DEAD.
NOW GET DOWN HERE AND DIG BEFORE I KICK ALL YOUR ASSES. NNH!

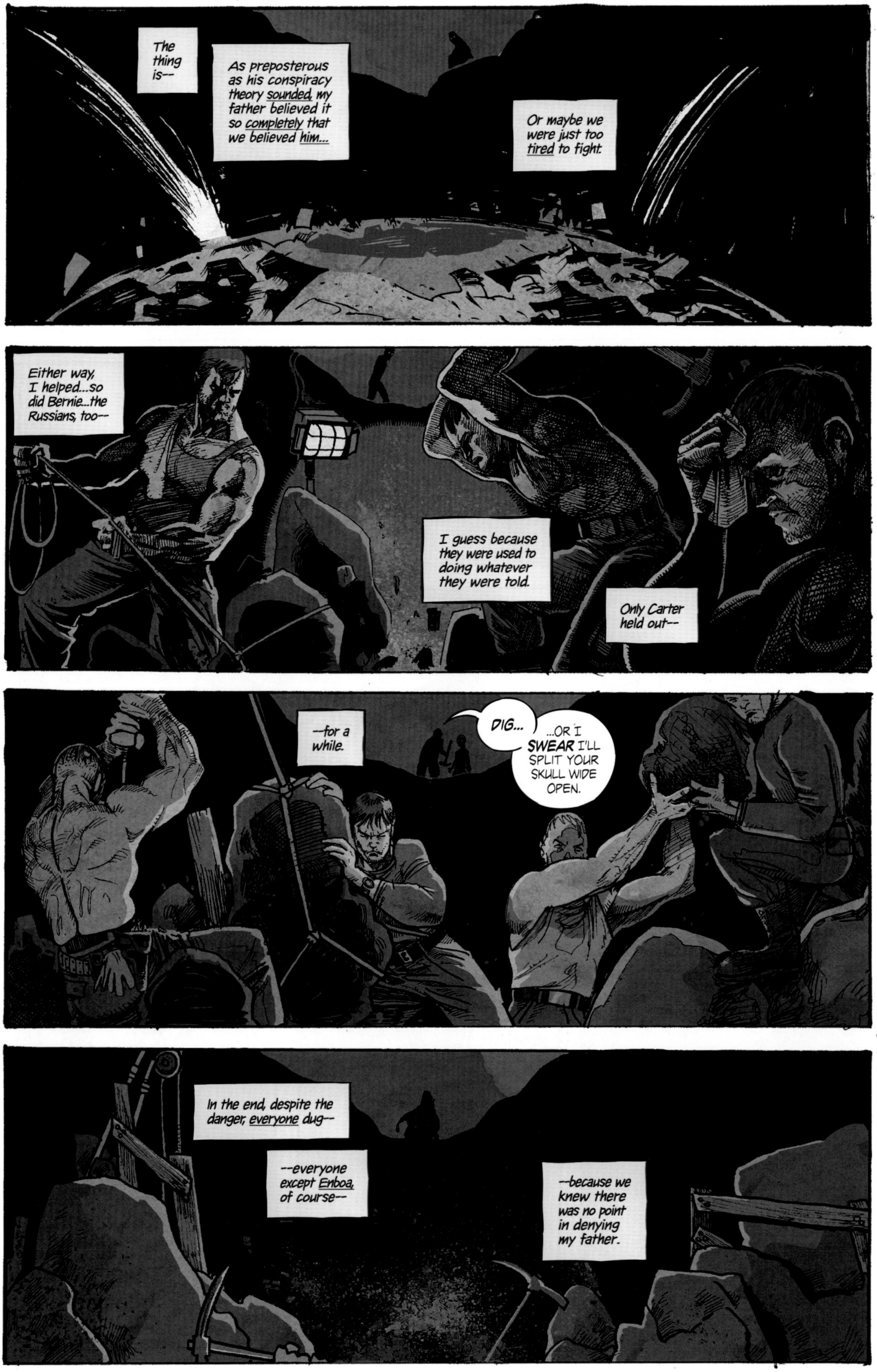
The thing is--
As preposterous as his conspiracy theory sounded, my father believed it so completely that we believed him...
Or maybe we were just too tired to fight.
Either way, I helped...so did Bernie...the Russians, too--
I guess because they were used to doing whatever they were told.
Only Carter held out--
--for a while.
DIG...
...OR I SWEAR I'LL SPLIT YOUR SKULL WIDE OPEN.
In the end, despite the danger, everyone dug--
--everyone except Enboa, of course--
--because we knew there was no point in denying my father.

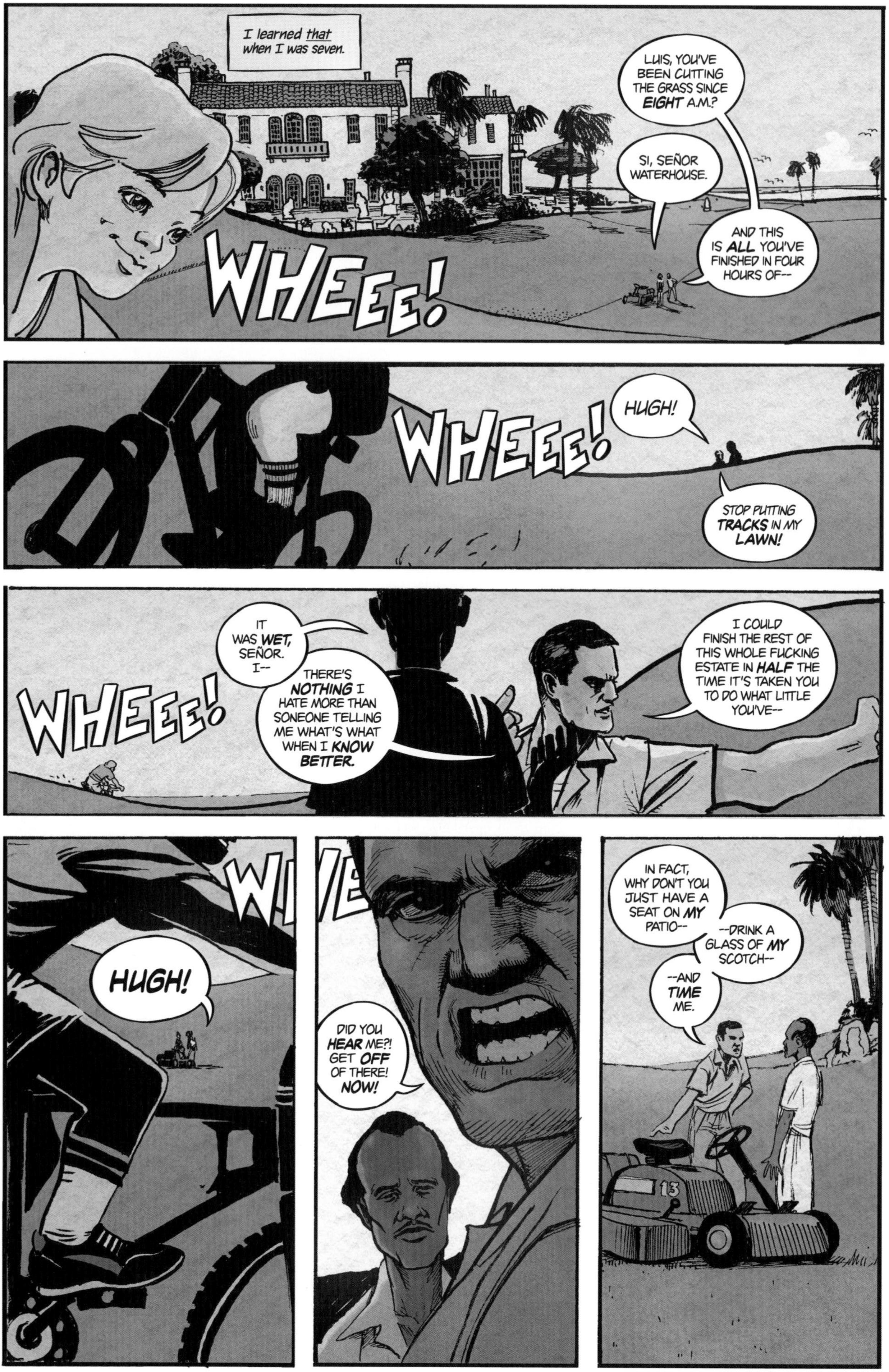
I learned that when I was seven.
LUIS, YOU'VE BEEN CUTTING THE GRASS SINCE EIGHT A.M.?
SI, SEÑOR WATERHOUSE.
AND THIS IS ALL YOU'VE FINISHED IN FOUR HOURS OF--
WHEEE!
WHEEE!
HUGH!
STOP PUTTING TRACKS IN MY LAWN!
WHEEE!
IT WAS WET, SEÑOR. I--
THERE'S NOTHING I HATE MORE THAN SONEONE TELLING ME WHAT'S WHAT WHEN I KNOW BETTER.
I COULD FINISH THE REST OF THIS WHOLE FUCKING ESTATE IN HALF THE TIME IT'S TAKEN YOU TO DO WHAT LITTLE YOU'VE--
HUGH!
DID YOU HEAR ME?! GET OFF OF THERE! NOW!
IN FACT, WHY DON'T YOU JUST HAVE A SEAT ON MY PATIO--
--DRINK A GLASS OF MY SCOTCH--
--AND TIME ME.

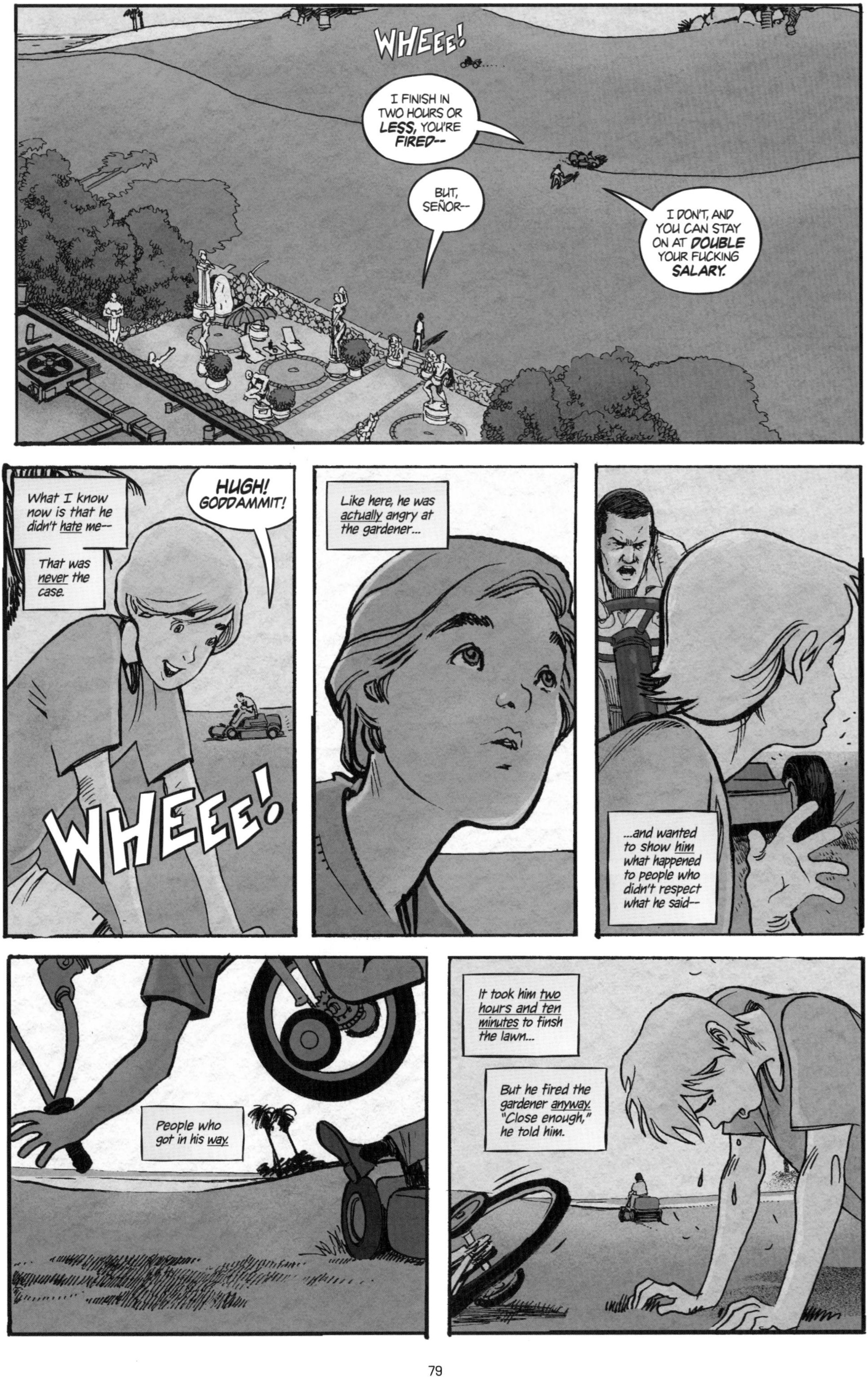
WHEEE!
I FINISH IN TWO HOURS OR LESS, YOU'RE FIRED--
BUT, SEÑOR--
I DON'T, AND YOU CAN STAY ON AT DOUBLE YOUR FUCKING SALARY.
What I know now is that he didn't hate me--
That was never the case.
HUGH! GODDAMMIT!
WHEEE!
Like here, he was actually angry at the gardener...
...and wanted to show him what happened to people who didn't respect what he said--
People who got in his way.
It took him two hours and ten minutes to finsh the lawn...
But he fired the gardener anyway. "Close enough," he told him.

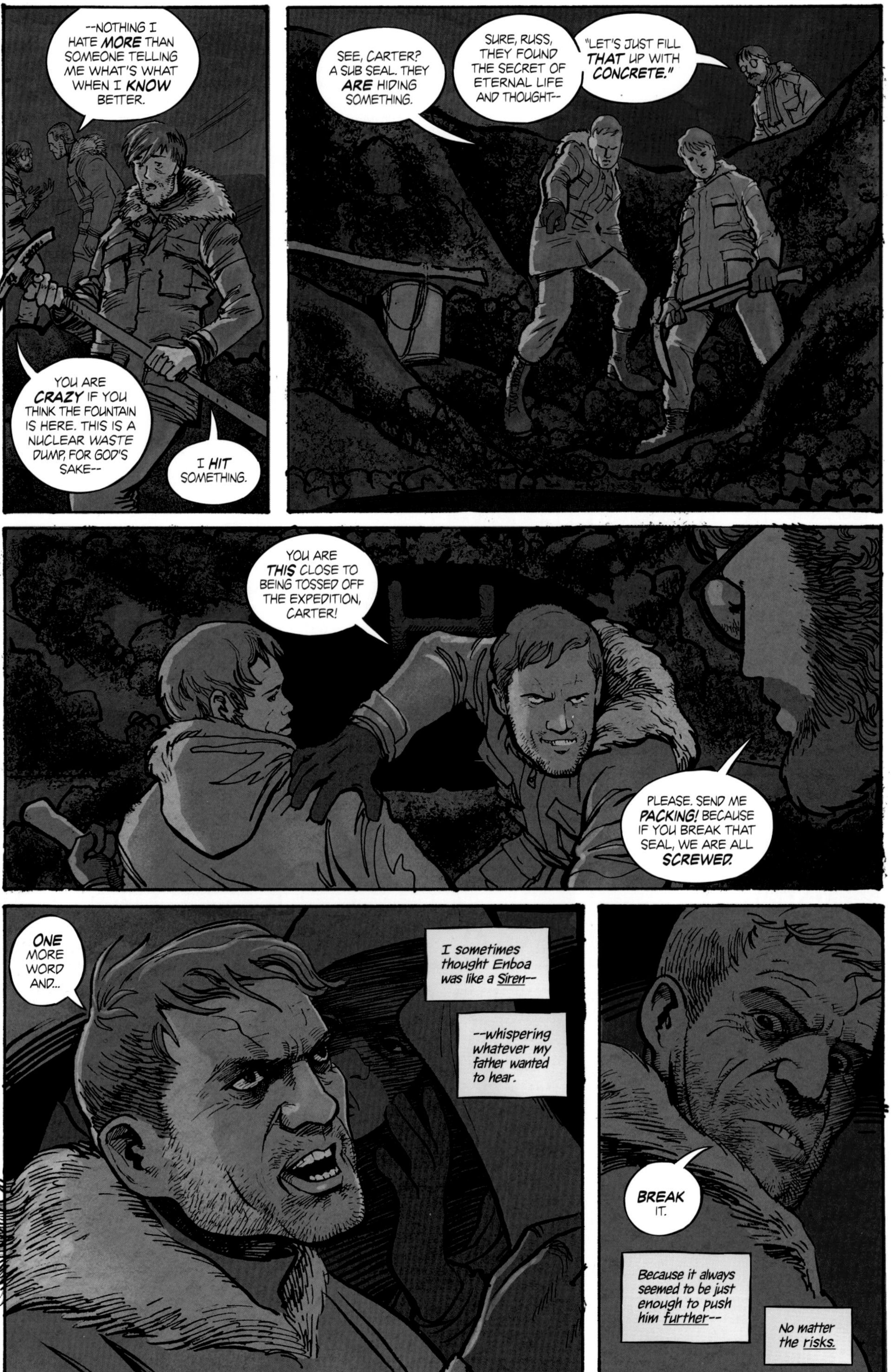
--NOTHING I HATE MORE THAN SOMEONE TELLING ME WHAT'S WHAT WHEN I KNOW BETTER.
YOU ARE CRAZY IF YOU THINK THE FOUNTAIN IS HERE. THIS IS A NUCLEAR WASTE DUMP, FOR GOD'S SAKE--
I HIT SOMETHING.
SEE, CARTER? A SUB SEAL. THEY ARE HIDING SOMETHING.
SURE, RUSS, THEY FOUND THE SECRET OF ETERNAL LIFE AND THOUGHT--
"LET'S JUST FILL THAT UP WITH CONCRETE."
YOU ARE THIS CLOSE TO BEING TOSSED OFF THE EXPEDITION, CARTER!
PLEASE. SEND ME PACKING! BECAUSE IF YOU BREAK THAT SEAL, WE ARE ALL SCREWED.
ONE MORE WORD AND...
I sometimes thought Enboa was like a Siren--
--whispering whatever my father wanted to hear.
BREAK IT.
Because it always seemed to be just enough to push him further--
No matter the risks.

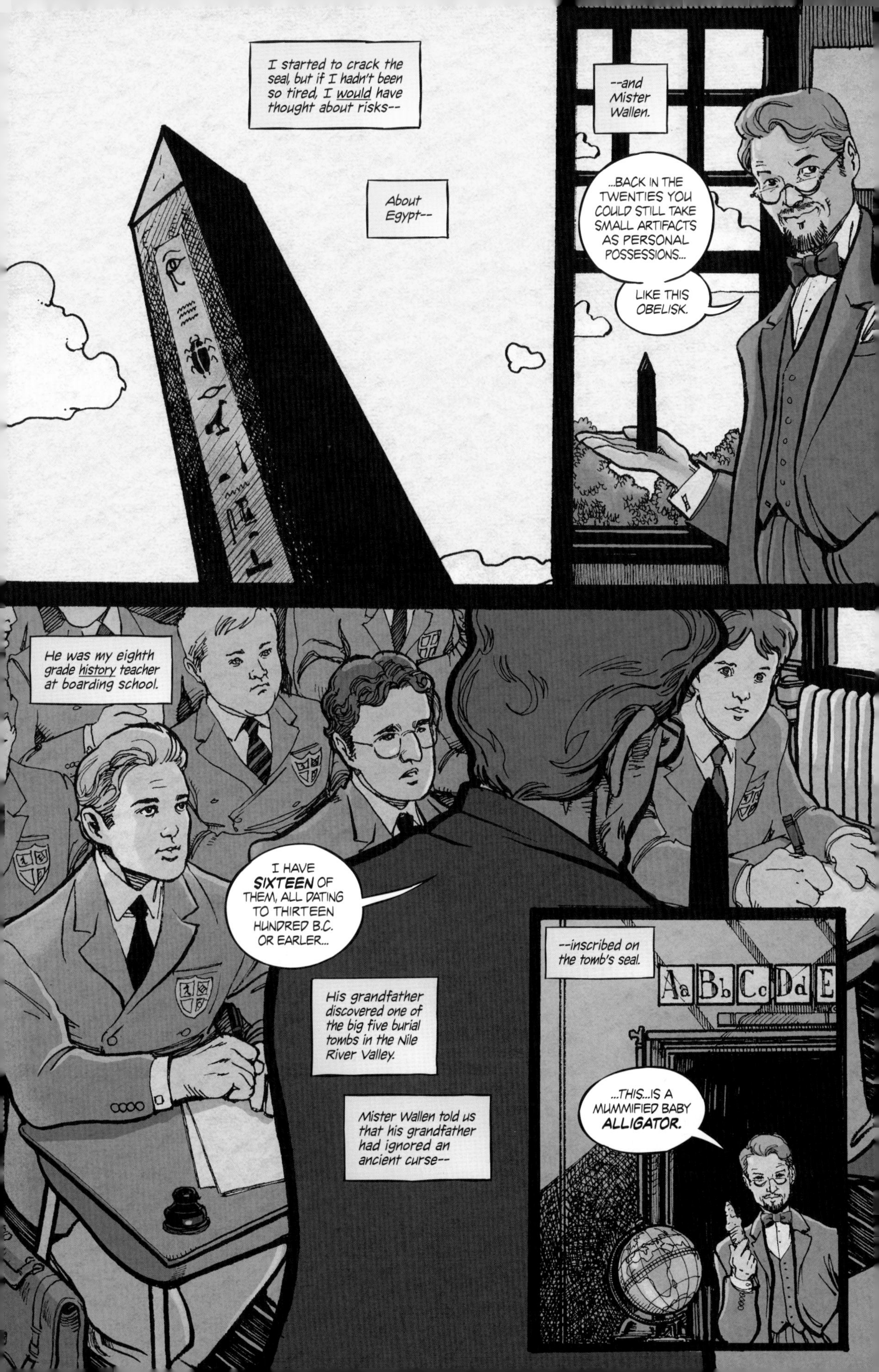
I started to crack the seal, but if I hadn't been so tired, I would have thought about risks--
About Egypt--
--and Mister Wallen.
...BACK IN THE TWENTIES YOU COULD STILL TAKE SMALL ARTIFACTS AS PERSONAL POSSESSIONS...
LIKE THIS OBELISK.
He was my eighth grade history teacher at boarding school.
I HAVE SIXTEEN OF THEM, ALL DATING TO THIRTEEN HUNDRED B.C. OR EARLER...
His grandfather discovered one of the big five burial tombs in the Nile River Valley.
Mister Wallen told us that his grandfather had ignored an ancient curse--
--inscribed on the tomb's seal.
Aa Bb Cc Dd E
...THIS...IS A MUMMIFIED BABY ALLIGATOR.

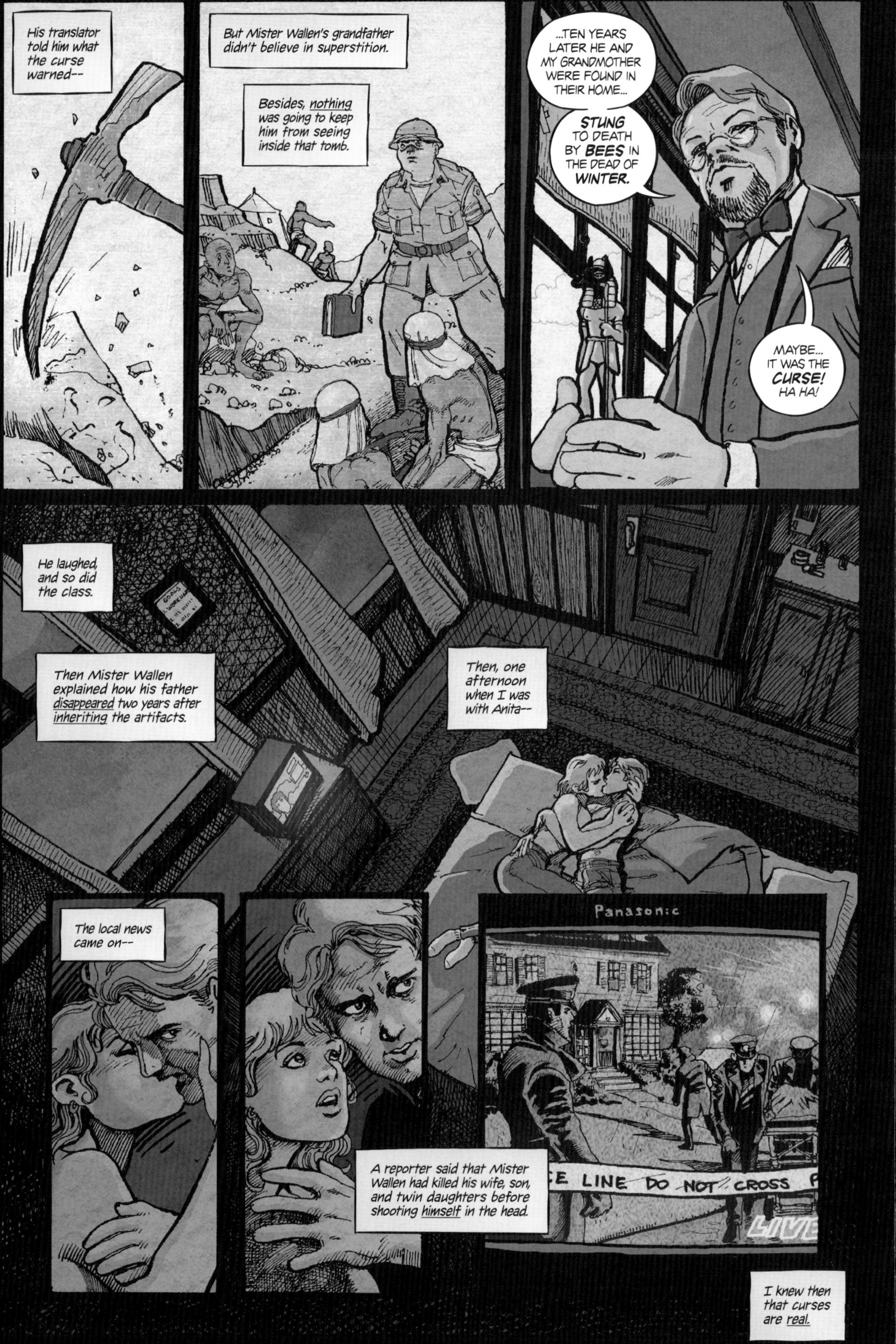

His translator told him what the curse warned--
But Mister Wallen's grandfather didn't believe in superstition.
Besides, nothing was going to keep him from seeing inside that tomb.
...TEN YEARS LATER HE AND MY GRANDMOTHER WERE FOUND IN THEIR HOME...
STUNG TO DEATH BY BEES IN THE DEAD OF WINTER.
MAYBE... IT WAS THE CURSE! HA HA!
He laughed, and so did the class.
Then Mister Wallen explained how his father disappeared two years after inheriting the artifacts.
Then, one afternoon when I was with Anita--
The local news came on--
Panasonic
A reporter said that Mister Wallen had killed his wife, son, and twin daughters before shooting himself in the head.
E LINE DO NOT CROSS
LIVE
I knew then that curses are real.

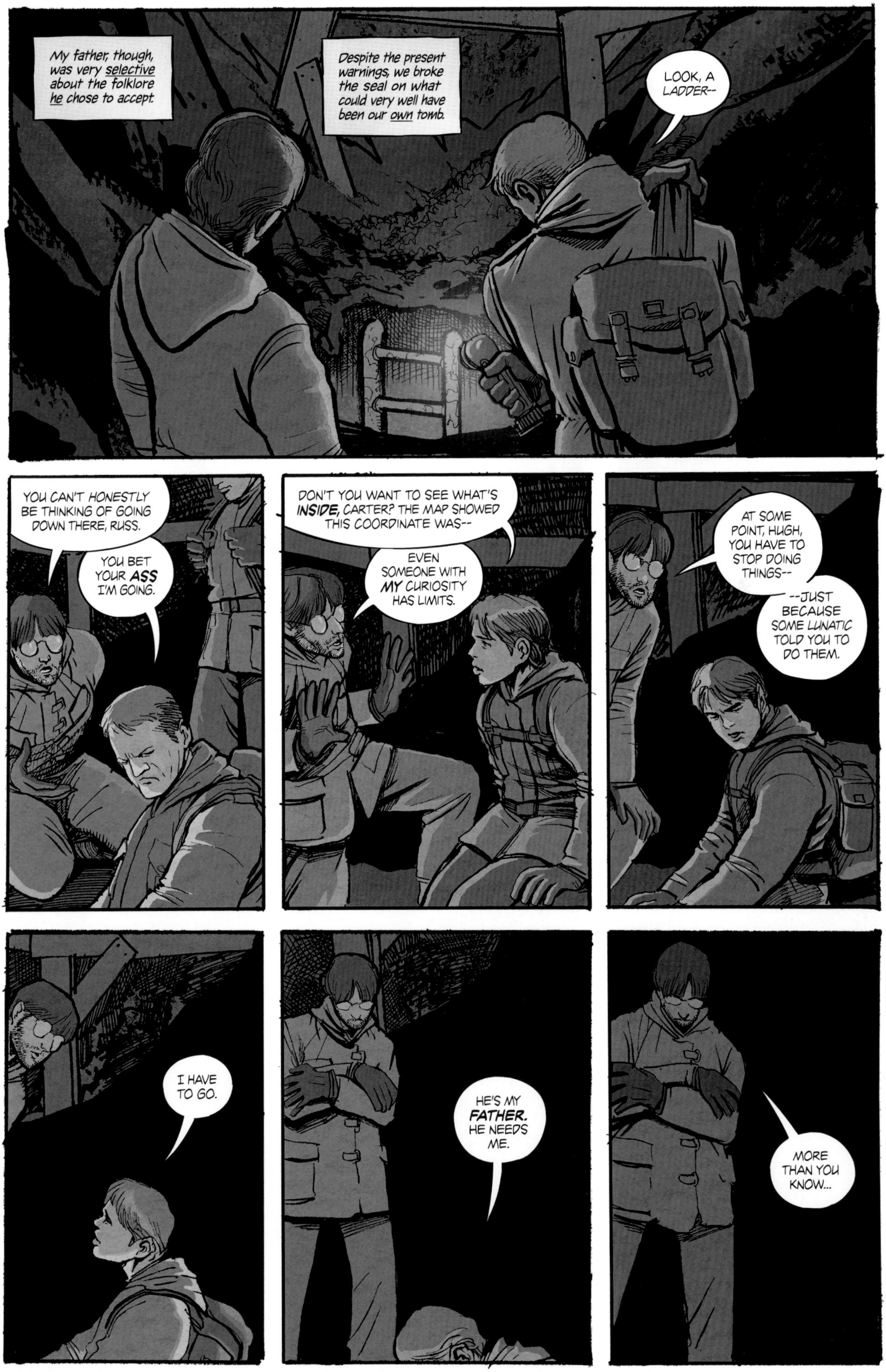
My father, though, was very selective about the folklore he chose to accept.
Despite the present warnings, we broke the seal on what could very well have been our own tomb.
LOOK, A LADDER--
YOU CAN'T HONESTLY BE THINKING OF GOING DOWN THERE, RUSS.
YOU BET YOUR ASS I'M GOING.
DON'T YOU WANT TO SEE WHAT'S INSIDE, CARTER? THE MAP SHOWED THIS COORDINATE WAS--
EVEN SOMEONE WITH MY CURIOSITY HAS LIMITS.
AT SOME POINT, HUGH, YOU HAVE TO STOP DOING THINGS--
--JUST BECAUSE SOME LUNATIC TOLD YOU TO DO THEM.
I HAVE TO GO.
HE'S MY FATHER. HE NEEDS ME.
MORE THAN YOU KNOW...

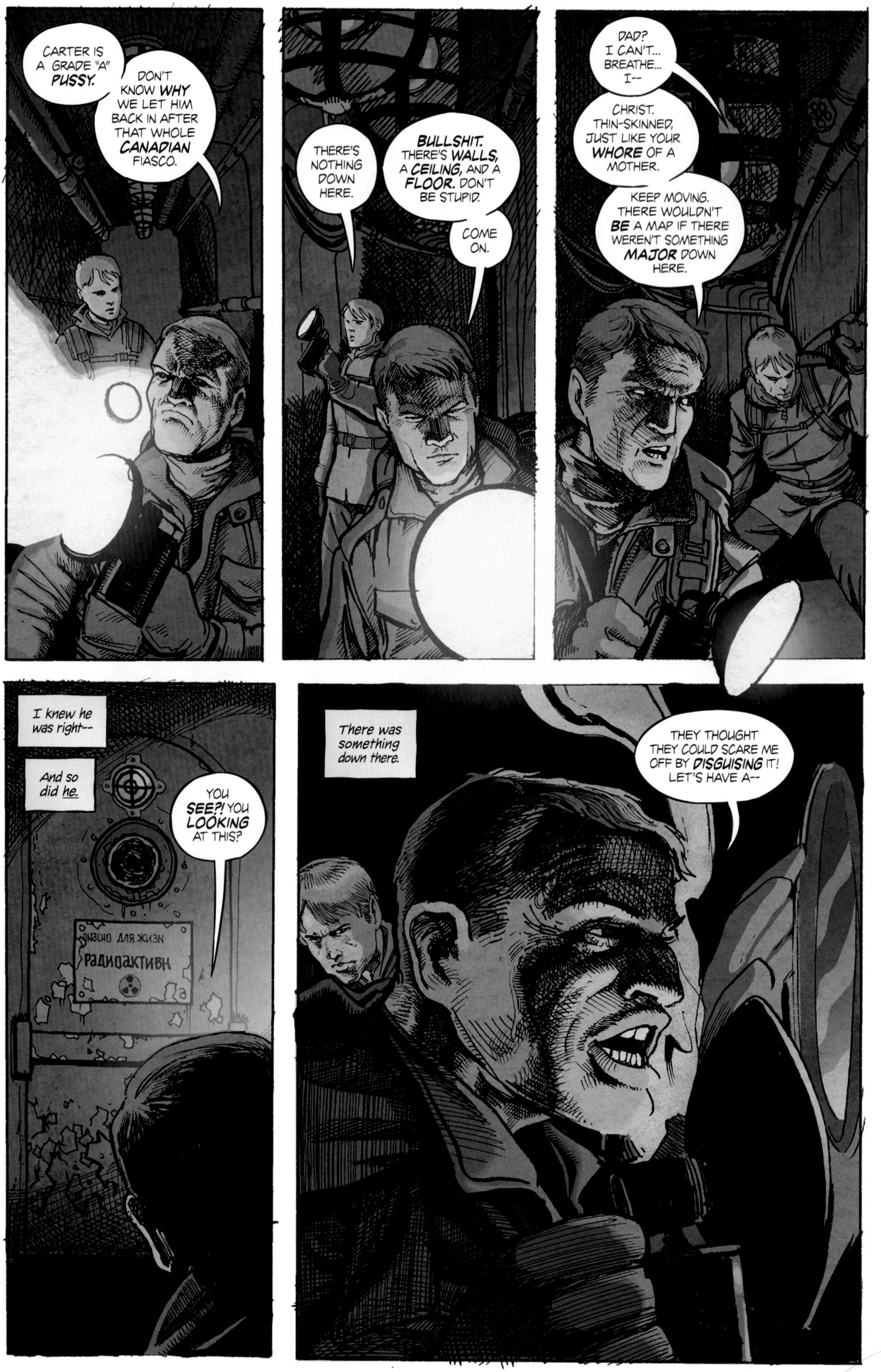
CARTER IS A GRADE "A" PUSSY.
DON'T KNOW WHY WE LET HIM BACK IN AFTER THAT WHOLE CANADIAN FIASCO.
THERE'S NOTHING DOWN HERE.
BULLSHIT. THERE'S WALLS, A CEILING, AND A FLOOR. DON'T BE STUPID.
COME ON.
DAD? I CAN'T... BREATHE... I--
CHRIST. THIN-SKINNED, JUST LIKE YOUR WHORE OF A MOTHER.
KEEP MOVING. THERE WOULDN'T BE A MAP IF THERE WEREN'T SOMETHING MAJOR DOWN HERE.
I knew he was right--
And so did he.
YOU SEE?! YOU LOOKING AT THIS?
ПАСНО ДЛЯ ЖИЗН
РАДИОАКТИВН
There was something down there.
THEY THOUGHT THEY COULD SCARE ME OFF BY DISGUISING IT! LET'S HAVE A--

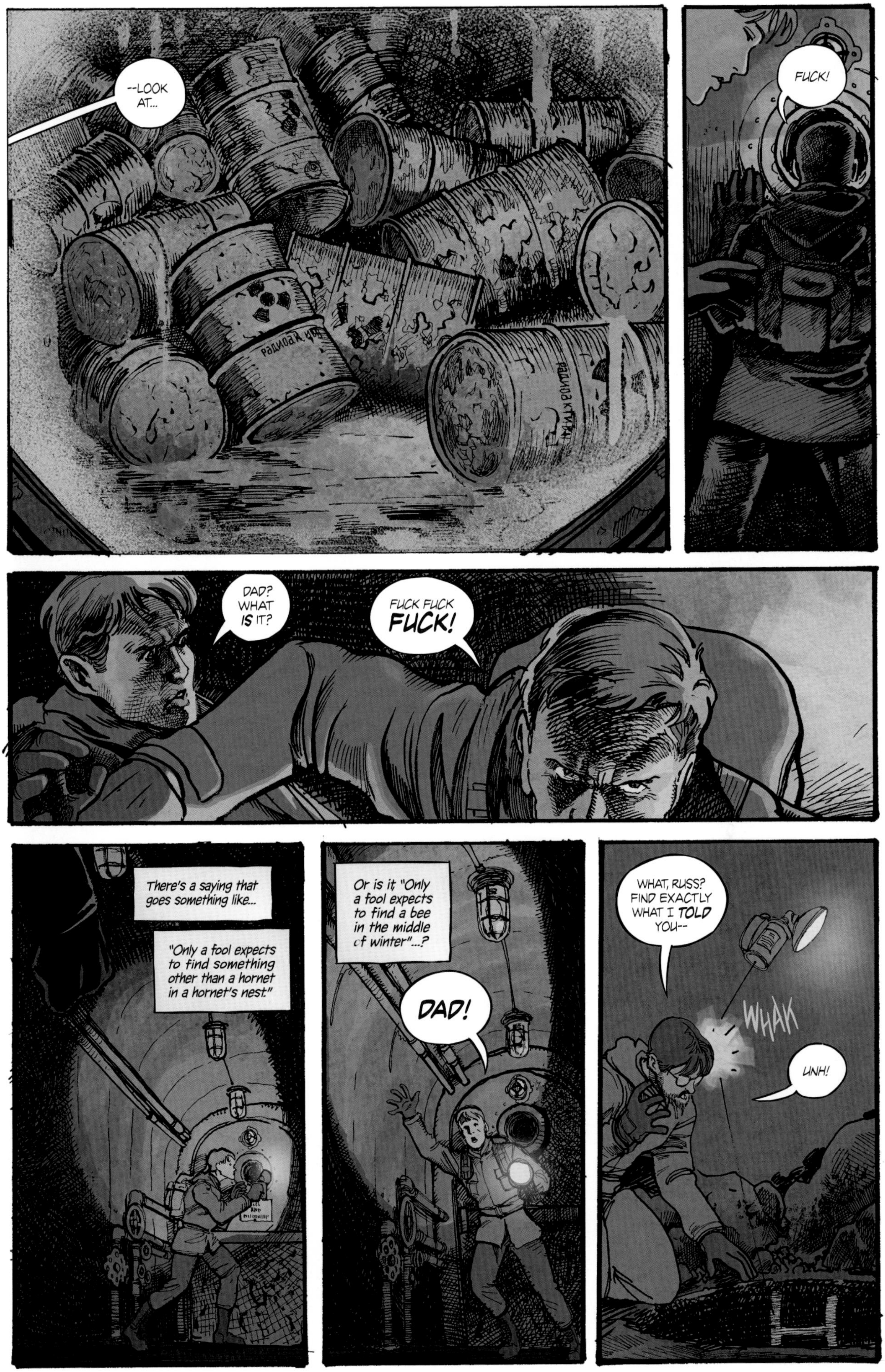
--LOOK AT...
FUCK!
DAD? WHAT IS IT?
FUCK FUCK FUCK!
There's a saying that goes something like...
"Only a fool expects to find something other than a hornet in a hornet's nest."
Or is it "Only a fool expects to find a bee in the middle of winter"...?
DAD!
WHAT, RUSS? FIND EXACTLY WHAT I TOLD YOU--
WHAK
UNH!

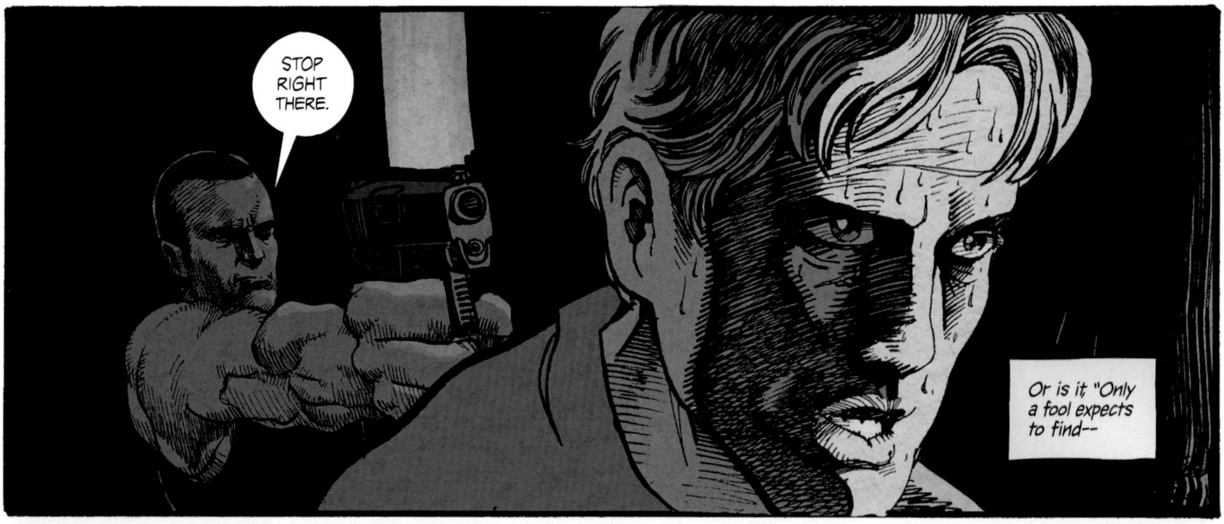
STOP RIGHT THERE.
Or is it "Only a fool expects to find--
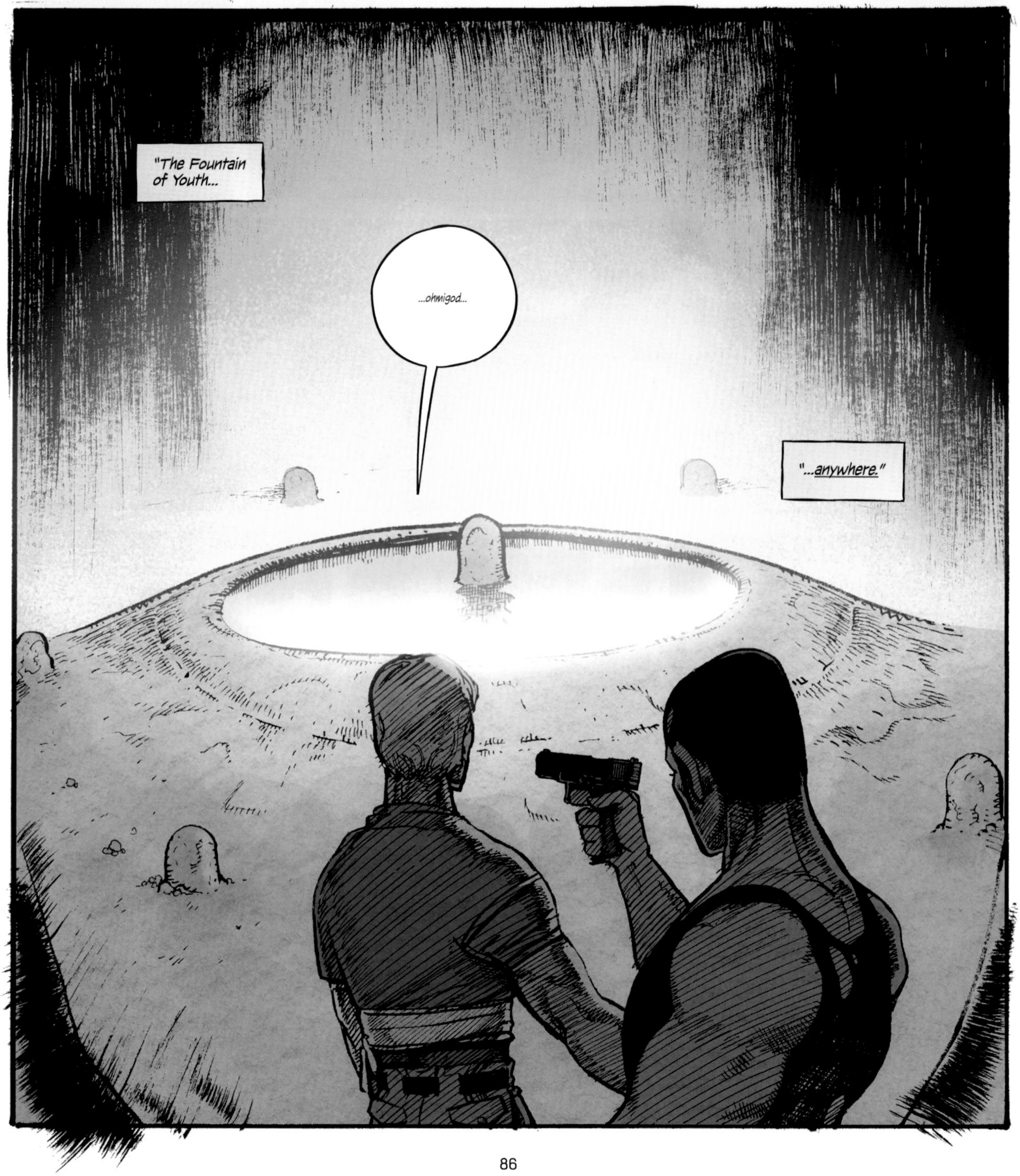
"The Fountain of Youth...
...ohmigod...
"...anywhere."

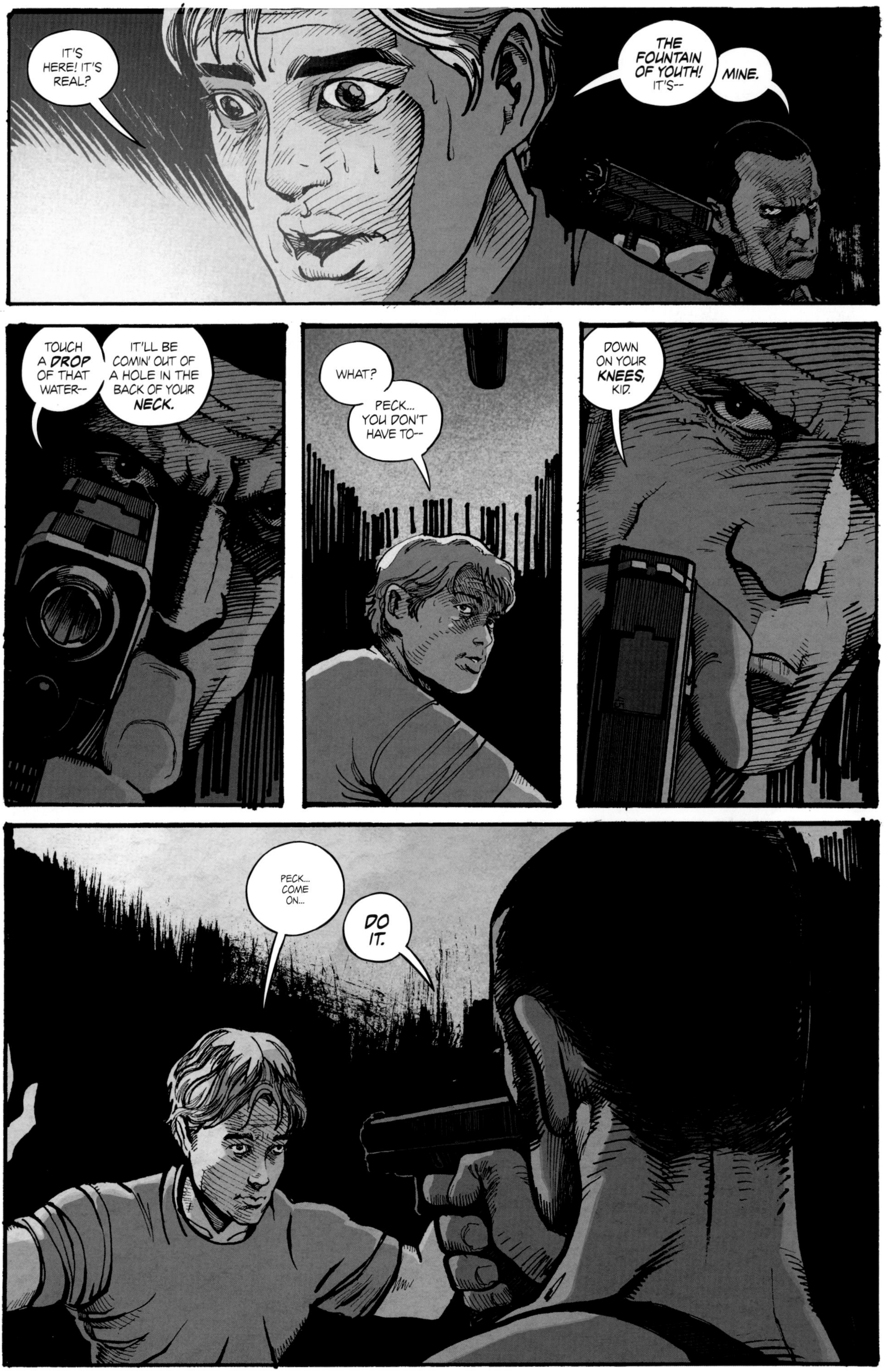
IT'S HERE! IT'S REAL?
THE FOUNTAIN OF YOUTH! IT'S--
MINE.
TOUCH A DROP OF THAT WATER--
IT'LL BE COMIN' OUT OF A HOLE IN THE BACK OF YOUR NECK.
WHAT?
PECK... YOU DON'T HAVE TO--
DOWN ON YOUR KNEES, KID.
PECK... COME ON...
DO IT.

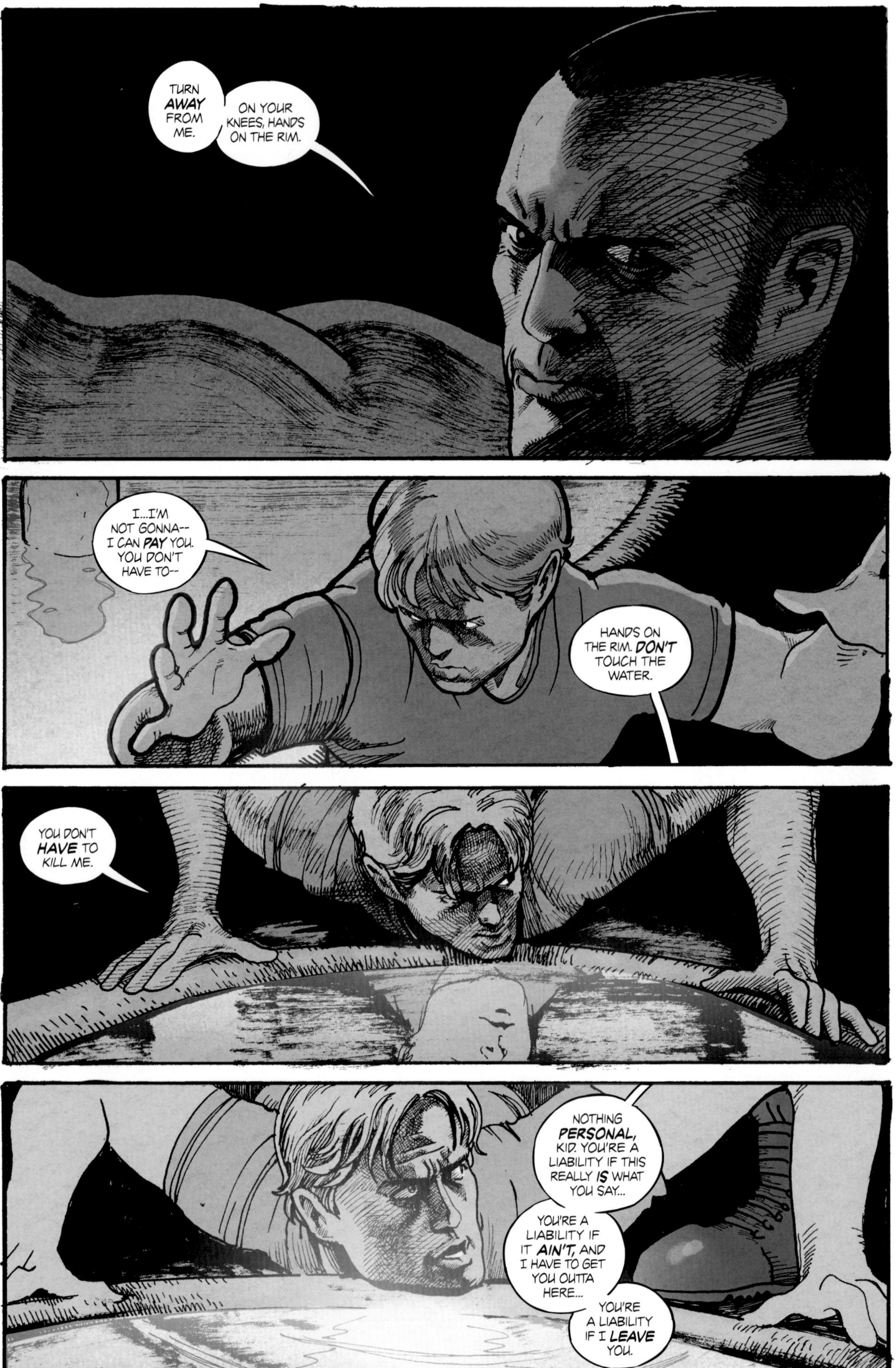
TURN AWAY FROM ME.
ON YOUR KNEES, HANDS ON THE RIM.
I...I'M NOT GONNA-- I CAN PAY YOU. YOU DON'T HAVE TO--
HANDS ON THE RIM. DON'T TOUCH THE WATER.
YOU DON'T HAVE TO KILL ME.
NOTHING PERSONAL, KID. YOU'RE A LIABILITY IF THIS REALLY IS WHAT YOU SAY...
YOU'RE A LIABILITY IF IT AIN'T, AND I HAVE TO GET YOU OUTTA HERE...
YOU'RE A LIABILITY IF I LEAVE YOU.

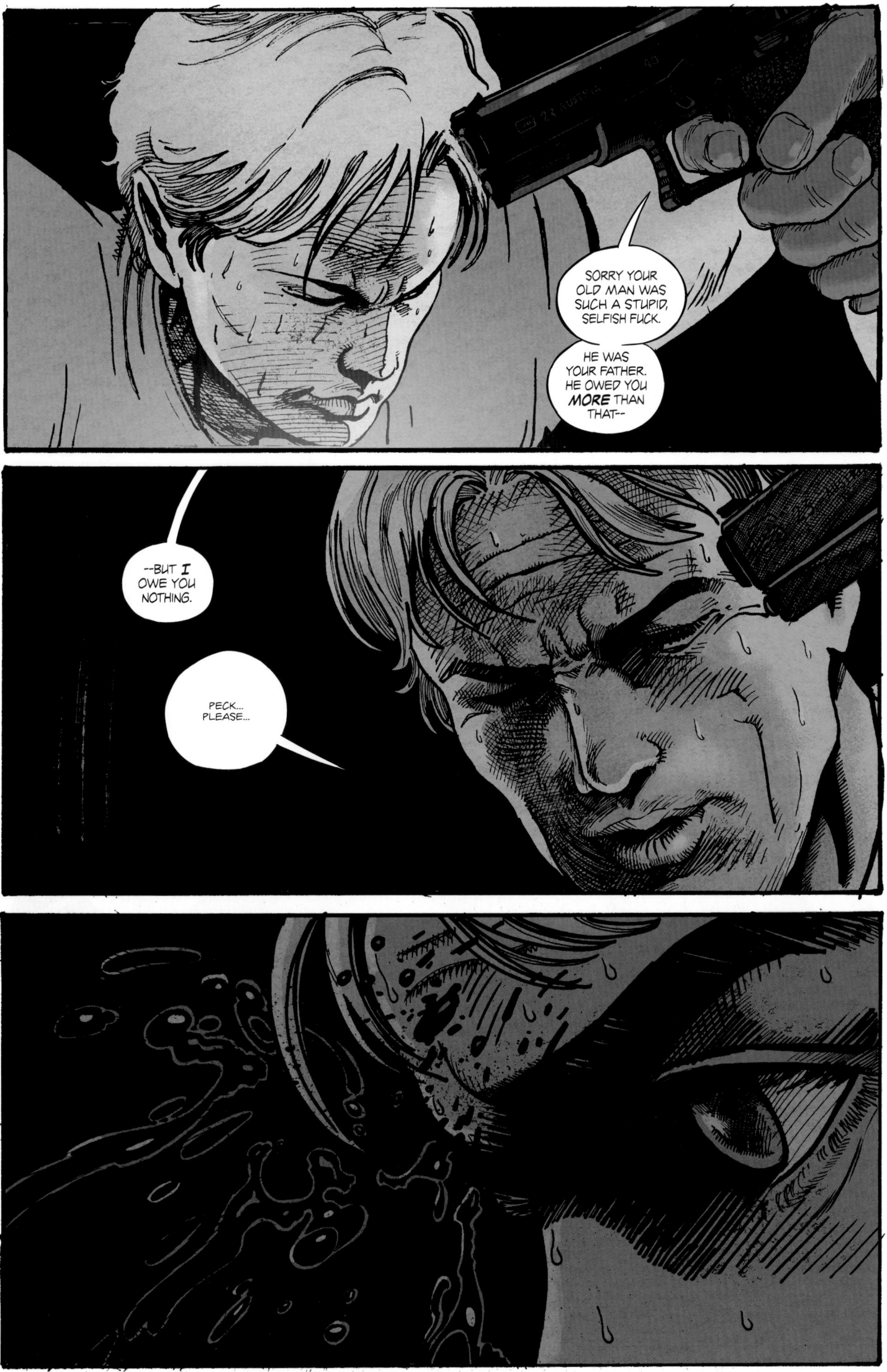
SORRY YOUR OLD MAN WAS SUCH A STUPID, SELFISH FUCK.
HE WAS YOUR FATHER. HE OWED YOU *MORE* THAN THAT--
--BUT *I* OWE YOU NOTHING.
PECK... PLEASE...

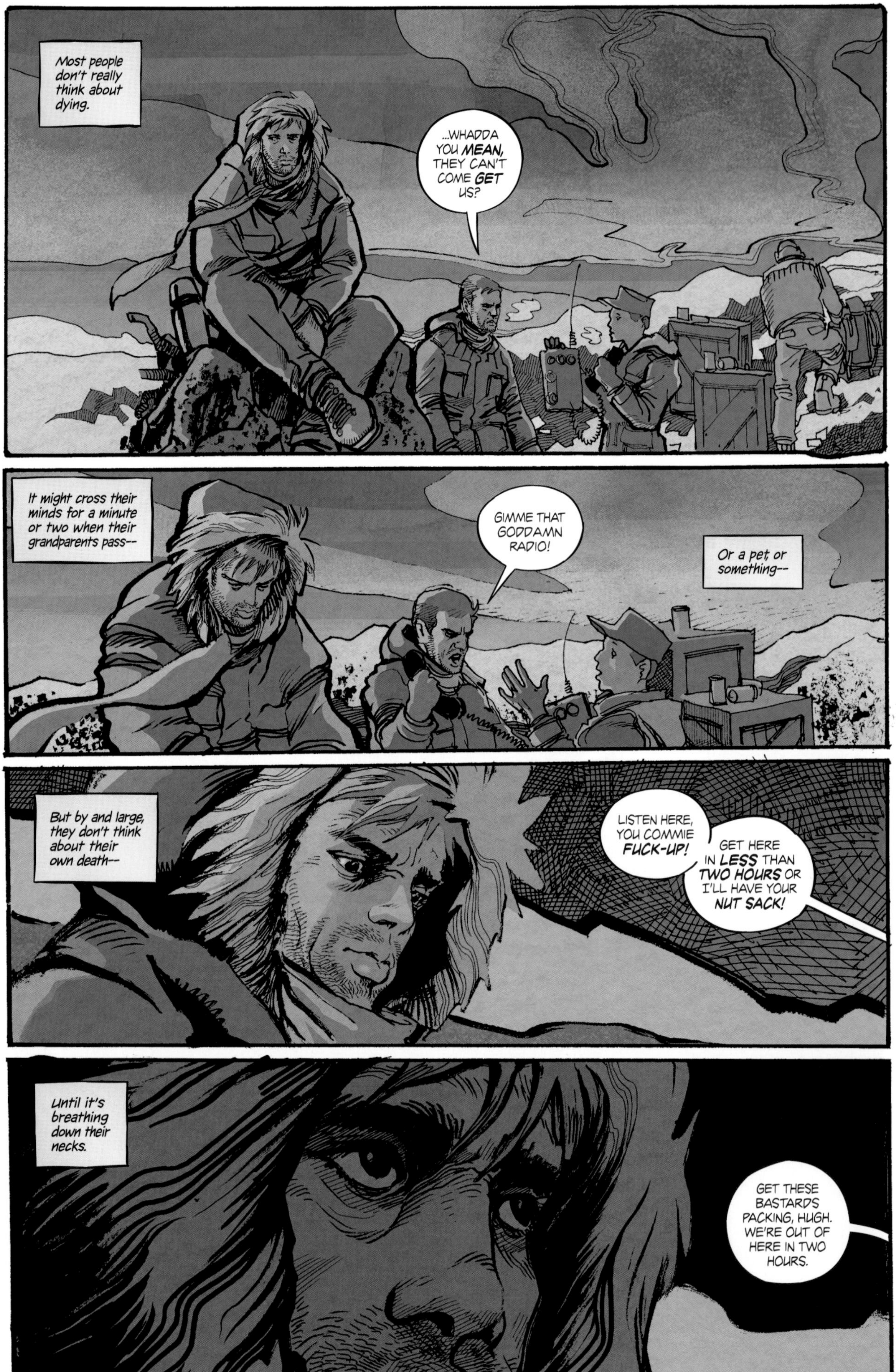
Most people don't really think about dying.
...WHADDA YOU MEAN, THEY CAN'T COME GET US?
It might cross their minds for a minute or two when their grandparents pass--
GIMME THAT GODDAMN RADIO!
Or a pet, or something--
But by and large, they don't think about their own death--
LISTEN HERE, YOU COMMIE FUCK-UP!
GET HERE IN LESS THAN TWO HOURS OR I'LL HAVE YOUR NUT SACK!
Until it's breathing down their necks.
GET THESE BASTARDS PACKING, HUGH. WE'RE OUT OF HERE IN TWO HOURS.

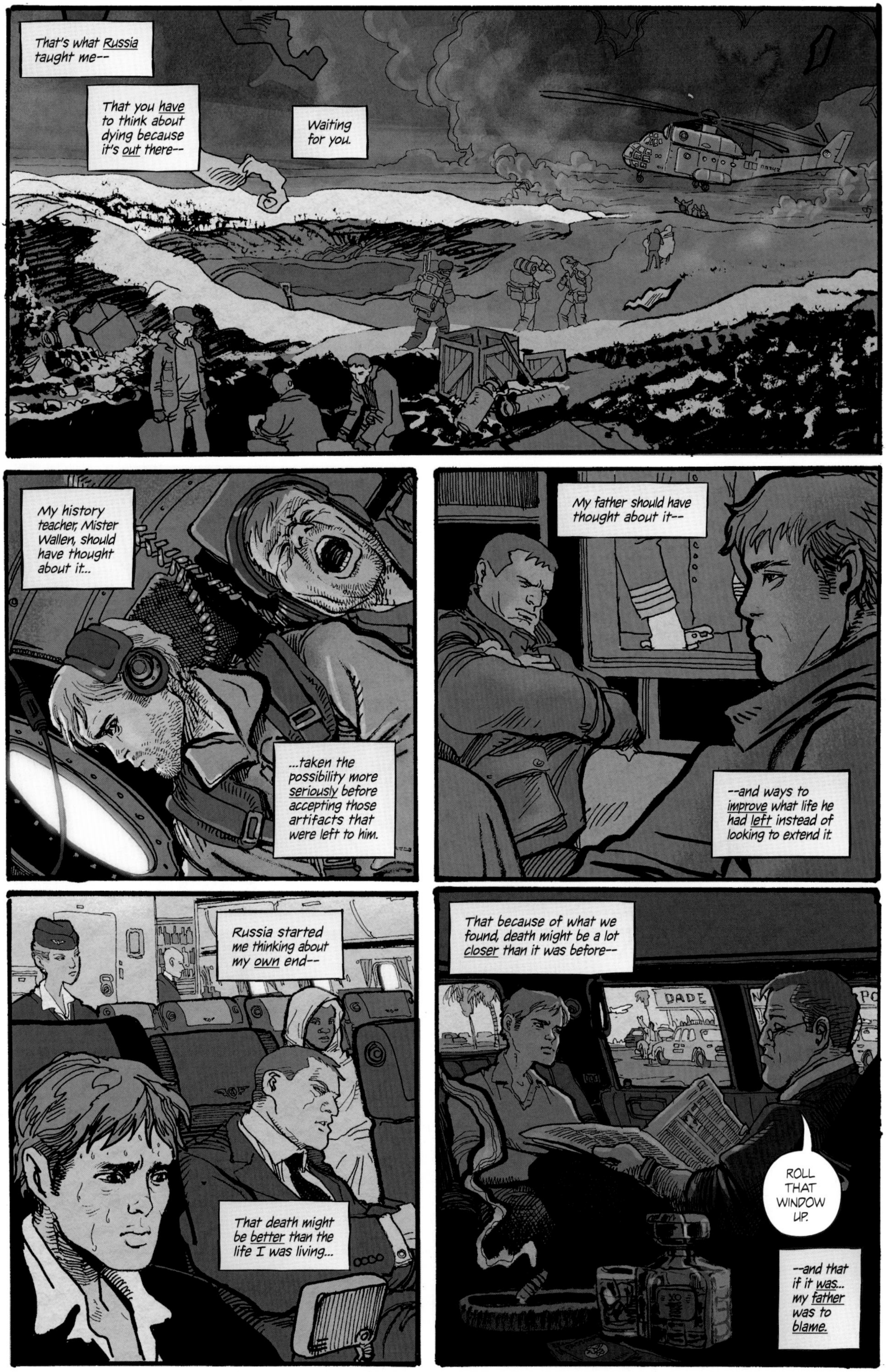
That's what Russia taught me--
That you have to think about dying because it's out there--
Waiting for you.
My history teacher, Mister Wallen, should have thought about it...
...taken the possibility more seriously before accepting those artifacts that were left to him.
My father should have thought about it--
--and ways to improve what life he had left instead of looking to extend it.
Russia started me thinking about my own end--
That death might be better than the life I was living...
That because of what we found, death might be a lot closer than it was before--
DADE
ROLL THAT WINDOW UP.
--and that if it was... my father was to blame.

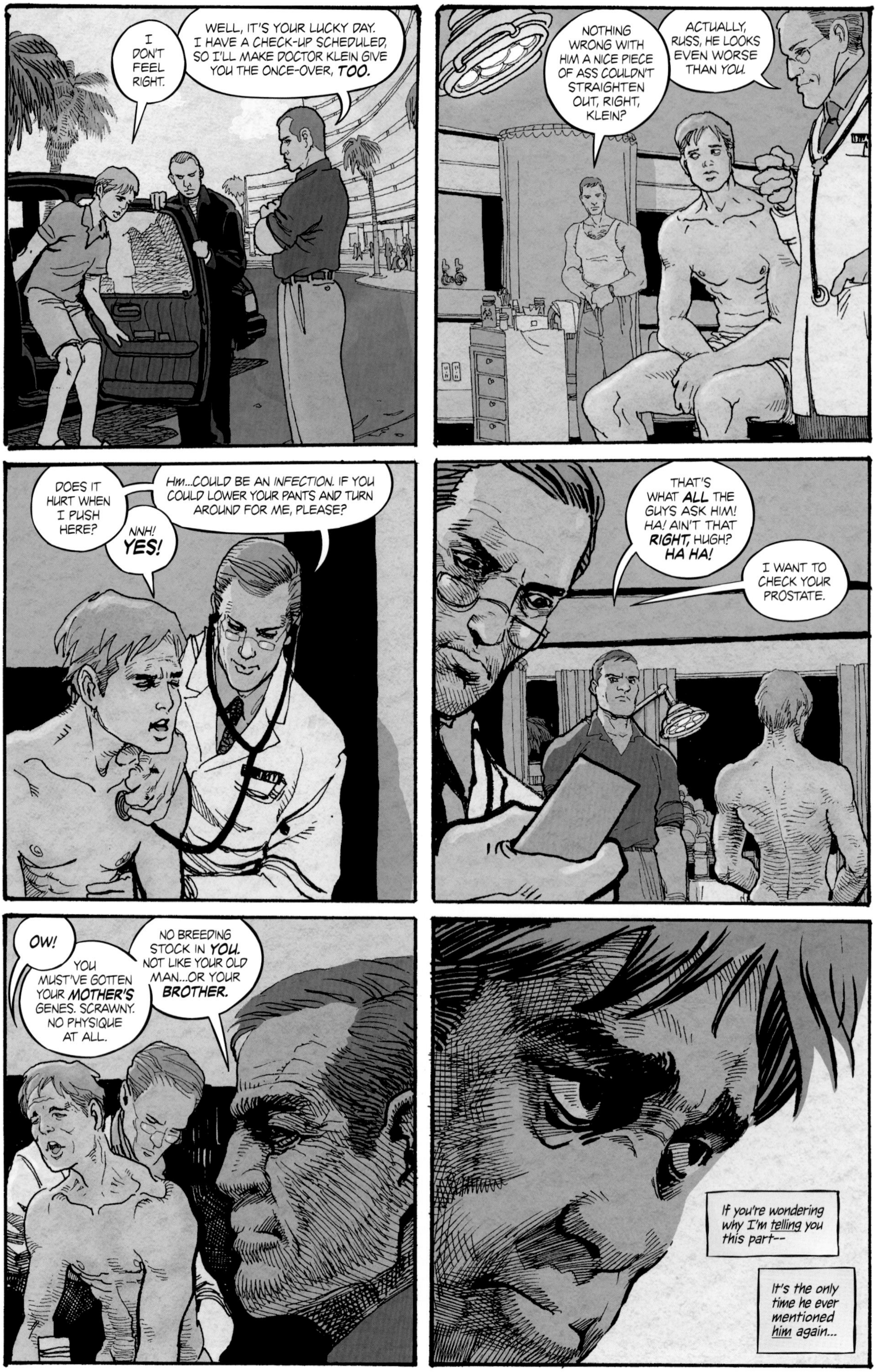
I DON'T FEEL RIGHT.
WELL, IT'S YOUR LUCKY DAY. I HAVE A CHECK-UP SCHEDULED, SO I'LL MAKE DOCTOR KLEIN GIVE YOU THE ONCE-OVER, TOO.
NOTHING WRONG WITH HIM A NICE PIECE OF ASS COULDN'T STRAIGHTEN OUT, RIGHT, KLEIN?
ACTUALLY, RUSS, HE LOOKS EVEN WORSE THAN YOU.
DOES IT HURT WHEN I PUSH HERE?
NNH! YES!
Hm...COULD BE AN INFECTION. IF YOU COULD LOWER YOUR PANTS AND TURN AROUND FOR ME, PLEASE?
THAT'S WHAT ALL THE GUYS ASK HIM! HA! AIN'T THAT RIGHT, HUGH? HA HA!
I WANT TO CHECK YOUR PROSTATE.
OW!
YOU MUST'VE GOTTEN YOUR MOTHER'S GENES. SCRAWNY. NO PHYSIQUE AT ALL.
NO BREEDING STOCK IN YOU. NOT LIKE YOUR OLD MAN...OR YOUR BROTHER.
If you're wondering why I'm telling you this part--
It's the only time he ever mentioned him again...

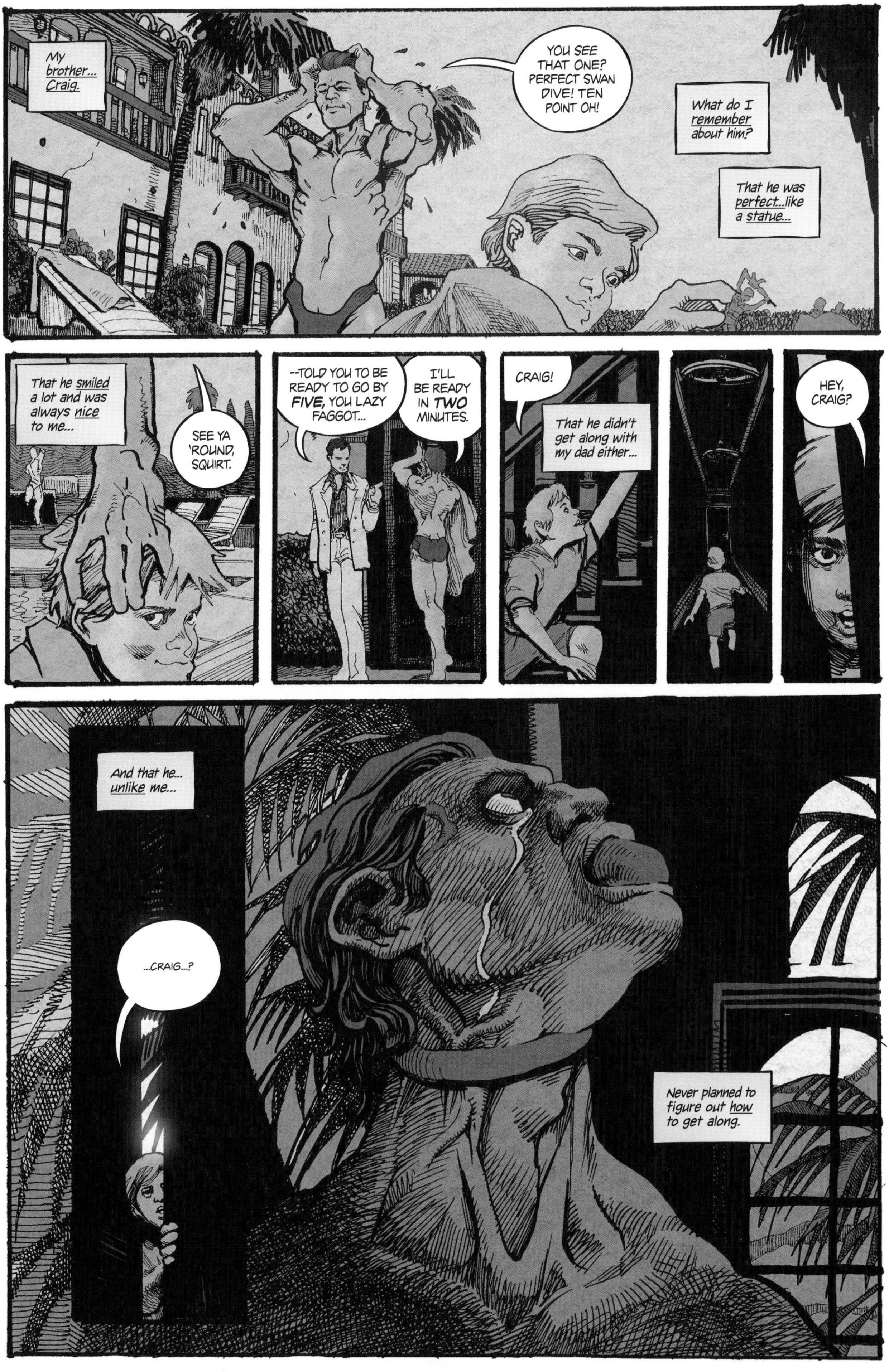

My brother... Craig.
YOU SEE THAT ONE? PERFECT SWAN DIVE! TEN POINT OH!
What do I remember about him?
That he was perfect...like a statue...
That he smiled a lot and was always nice to me...
SEE YA 'ROUND, SQUIRT.
--TOLD YOU TO BE READY TO GO BY FIVE, YOU LAZY FAGGOT...
I'LL BE READY IN TWO MINUTES.
CRAIG!
That he didn't get along with my dad either...
HEY, CRAIG?
And that he... unlike me...
...CRAIG...?
Never planned to figure out how to get along.

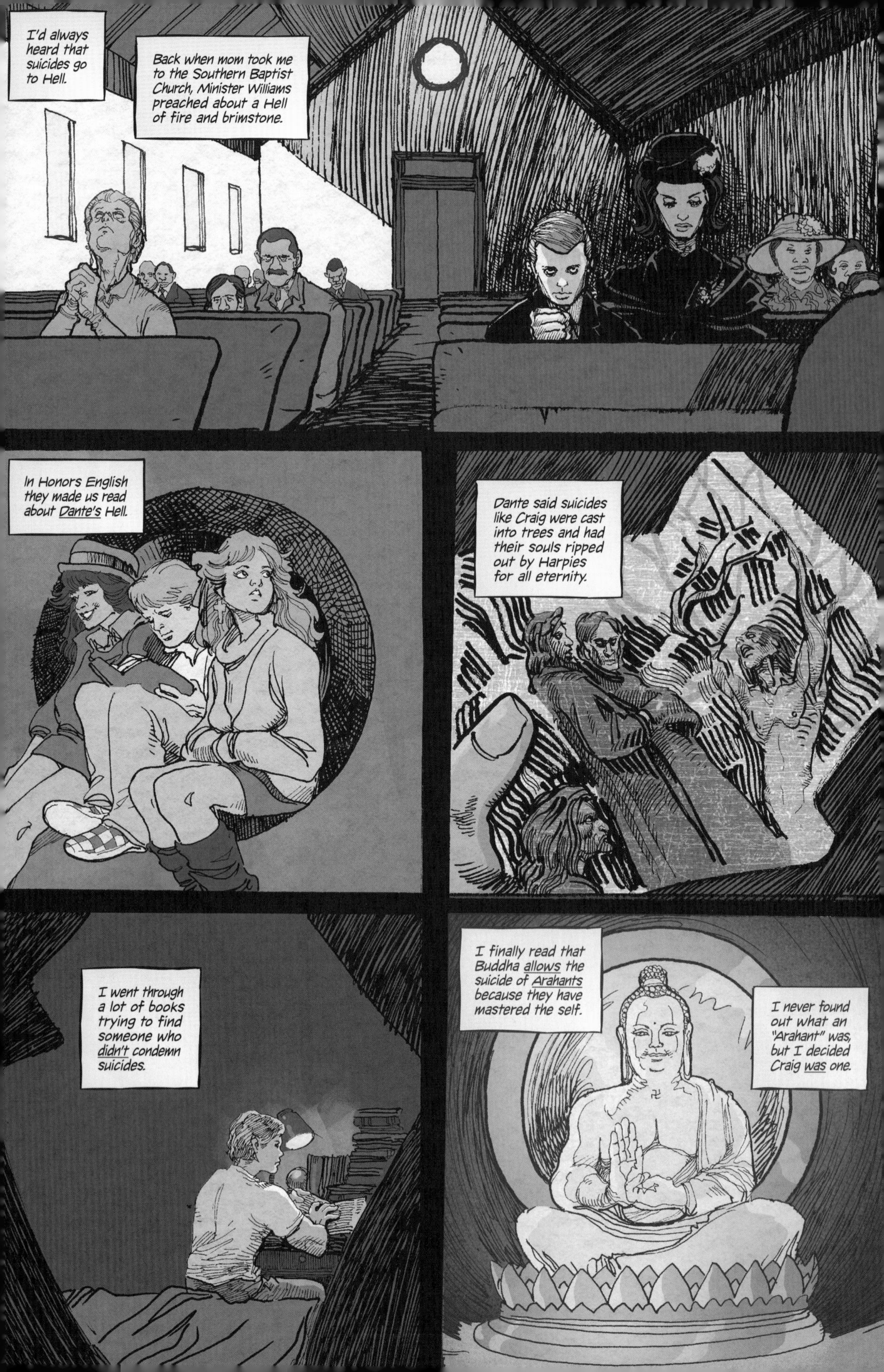
I'd always heard that suicides go to Hell.
Back when mom took me to the Southern Baptist Church, Minister Williams preached about a Hell of fire and brimstone.
In Honors English they made us read about Dante's Hell.
Dante said suicides like Craig were cast into trees and had their souls ripped out by Harpies for all eternity.
I went through a lot of books trying to find someone who didn't condemn suicides.
I finally read that Buddha allows the suicide of Arahants because they have mastered the self.
I never found out what an "Arahant" was, but I decided Craig was one.

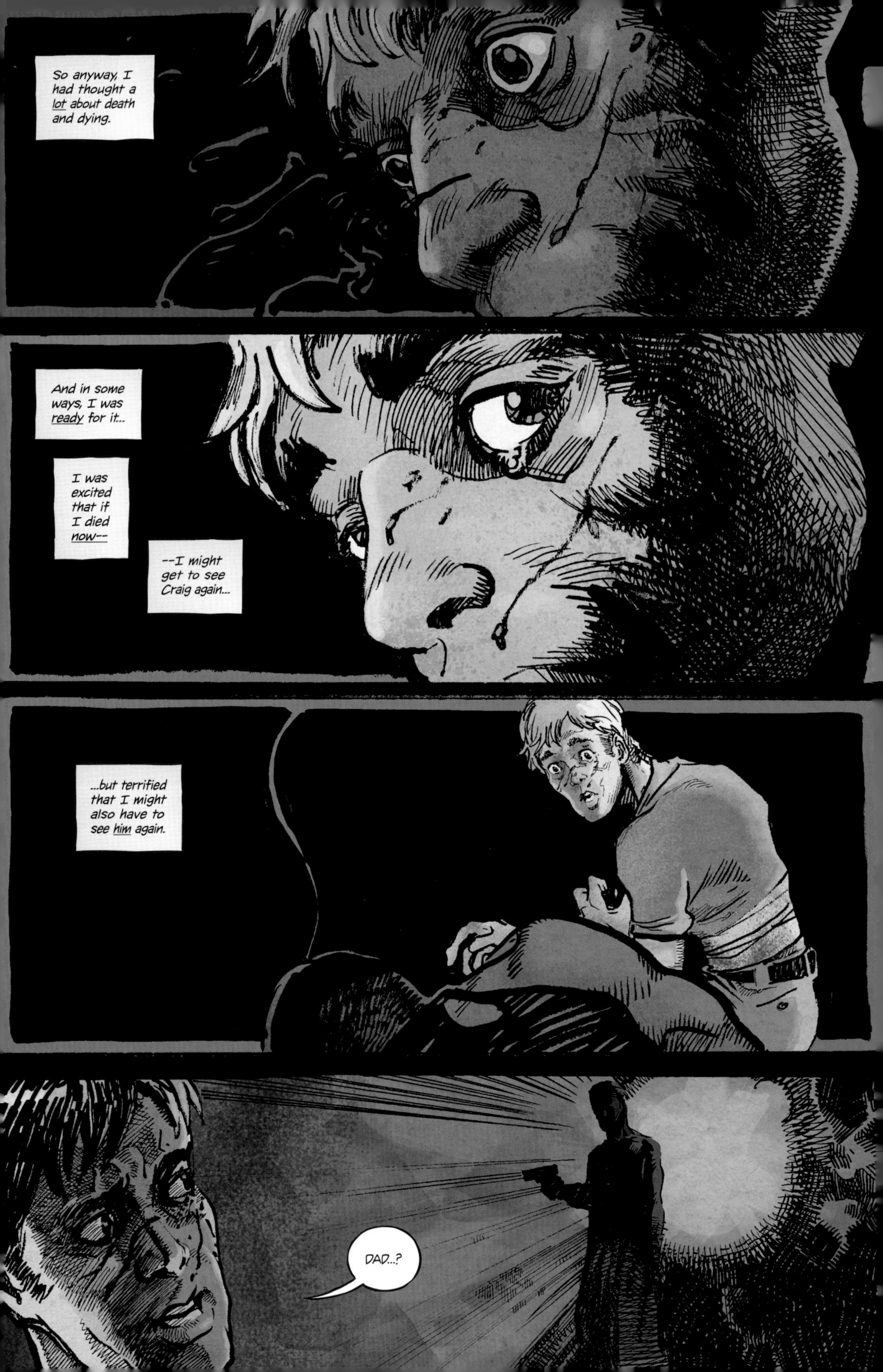
So anyway, I had thought a lot about death and dying.
And in some ways, I was ready for it...
I was excited that if I died now--
--I might get to see Craig again...
...but terrified that I might also have to see him again.
DAD...?

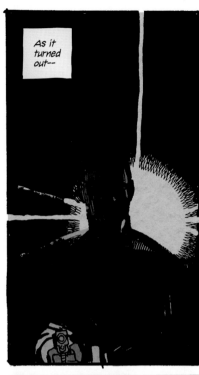

As it turned out--

This wasn't a day for _any_ of that.

I don't know how _Enboa_ found The Fountain on his own...

...but he did.

And for the first time _ever_--

He whispered something--

--to _me._

THIS IS YOUR DAY OF BIRTH.

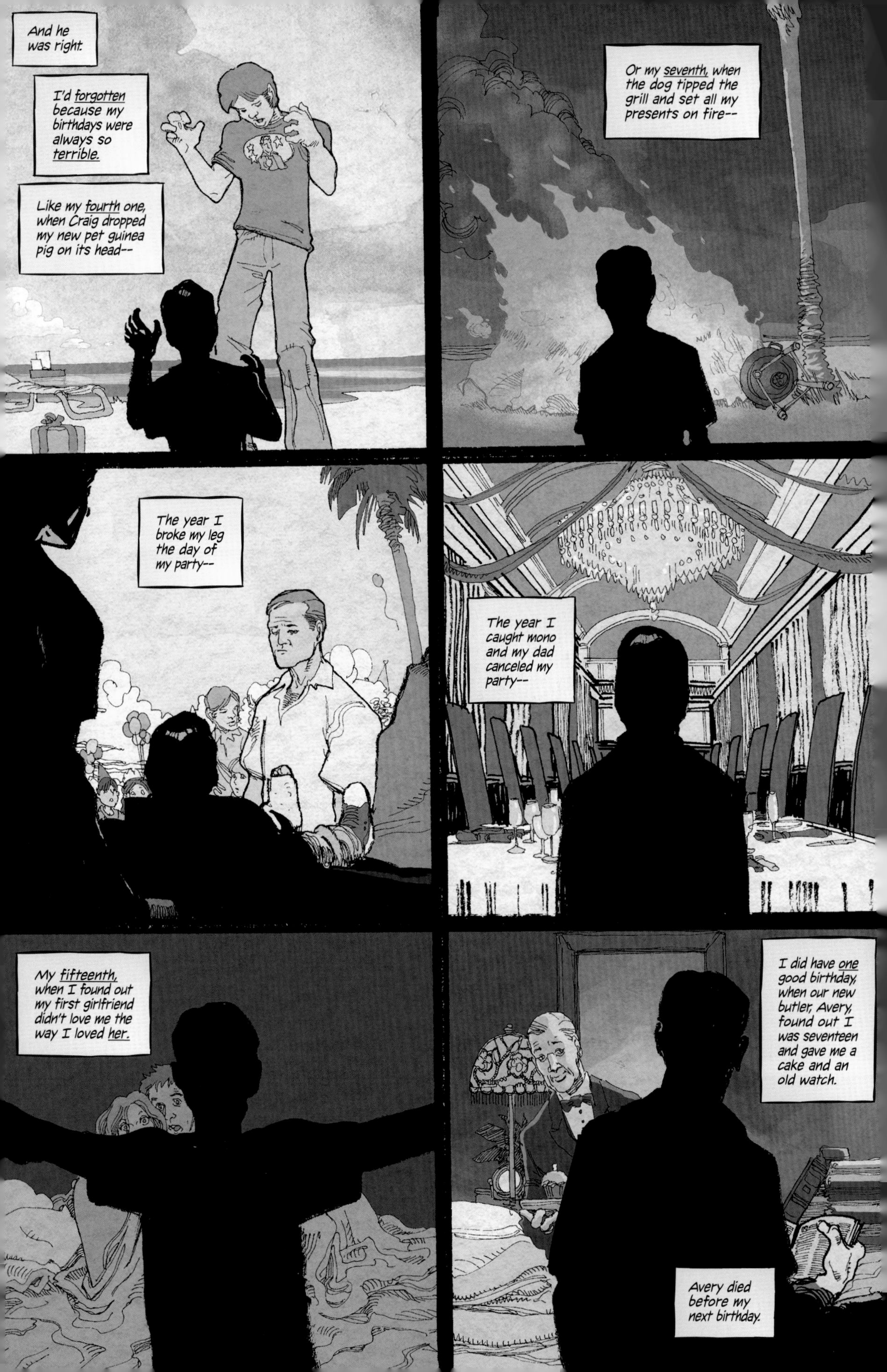
And he was right.
I'd forgotten because my birthdays were always so terrible.
Like my fourth one, when Craig dropped my new pet guinea pig on its head--
Or my seventh, when the dog tipped the grill and set all my presents on fire--
The year I broke my leg the day of my party--
The year I caught mono and my dad canceled my party--
My fifteenth, when I found out my first girlfriend didn't love me the way I loved her.
I did have one good birthday, when our new butler, Avery, found out I was seventeen and gave me a cake and an old watch.
Avery died before my next birthday.

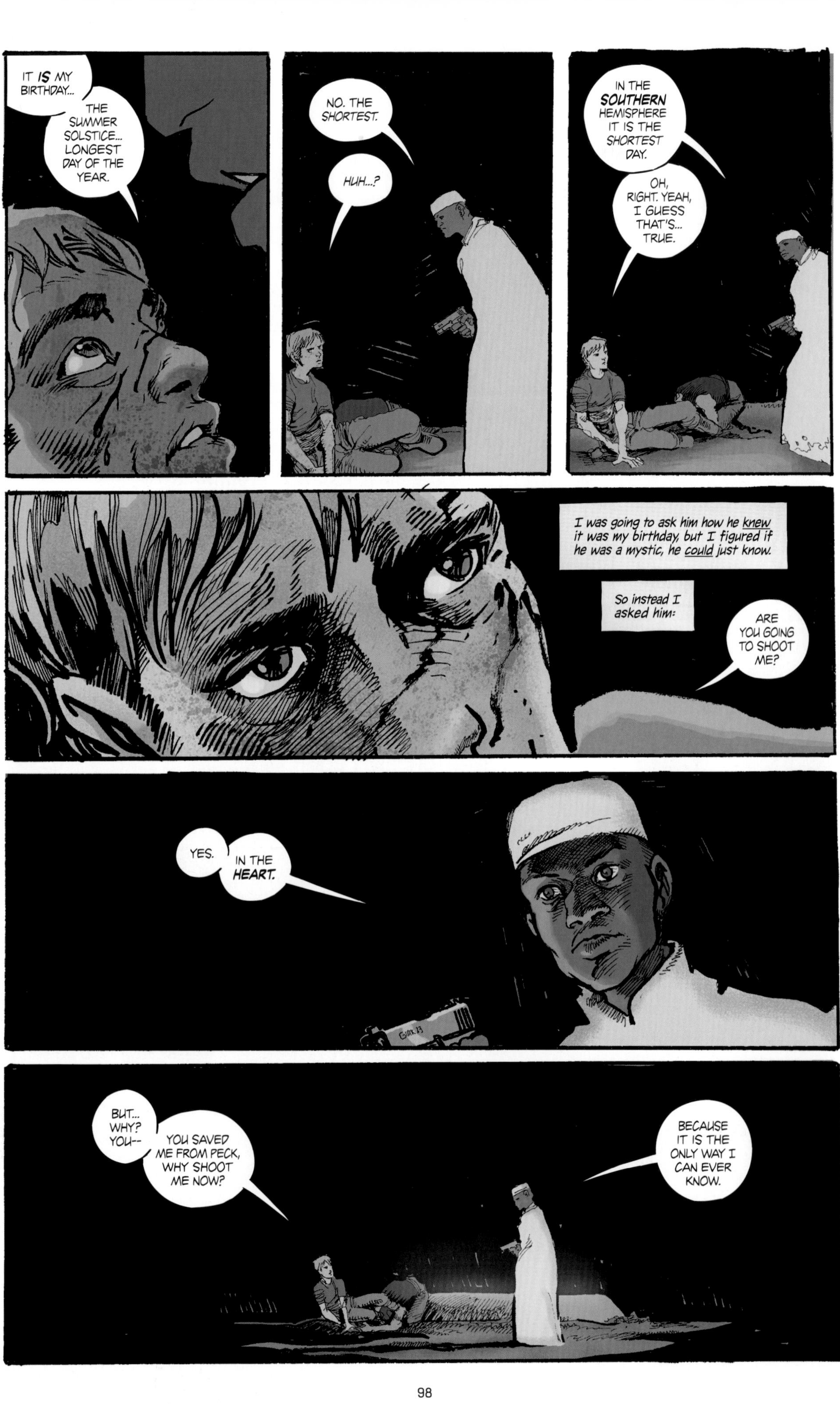
IT IS MY BIRTHDAY...
THE SUMMER SOLSTICE... LONGEST DAY OF THE YEAR.
NO. THE SHORTEST.
HUH...?
IN THE SOUTHERN HEMISPHERE IT IS THE SHORTEST DAY.
OH, RIGHT. YEAH, I GUESS THAT'S... TRUE.
I was going to ask him how he knew it was my birthday, but I figured if he was a mystic, he could just know.
So instead I asked him:
ARE YOU GOING TO SHOOT ME?
YES.
IN THE HEART.
BUT... WHY? YOU--
YOU SAVED ME FROM PECK, WHY SHOOT ME NOW?
BECAUSE IT IS THE ONLY WAY I CAN EVER KNOW.

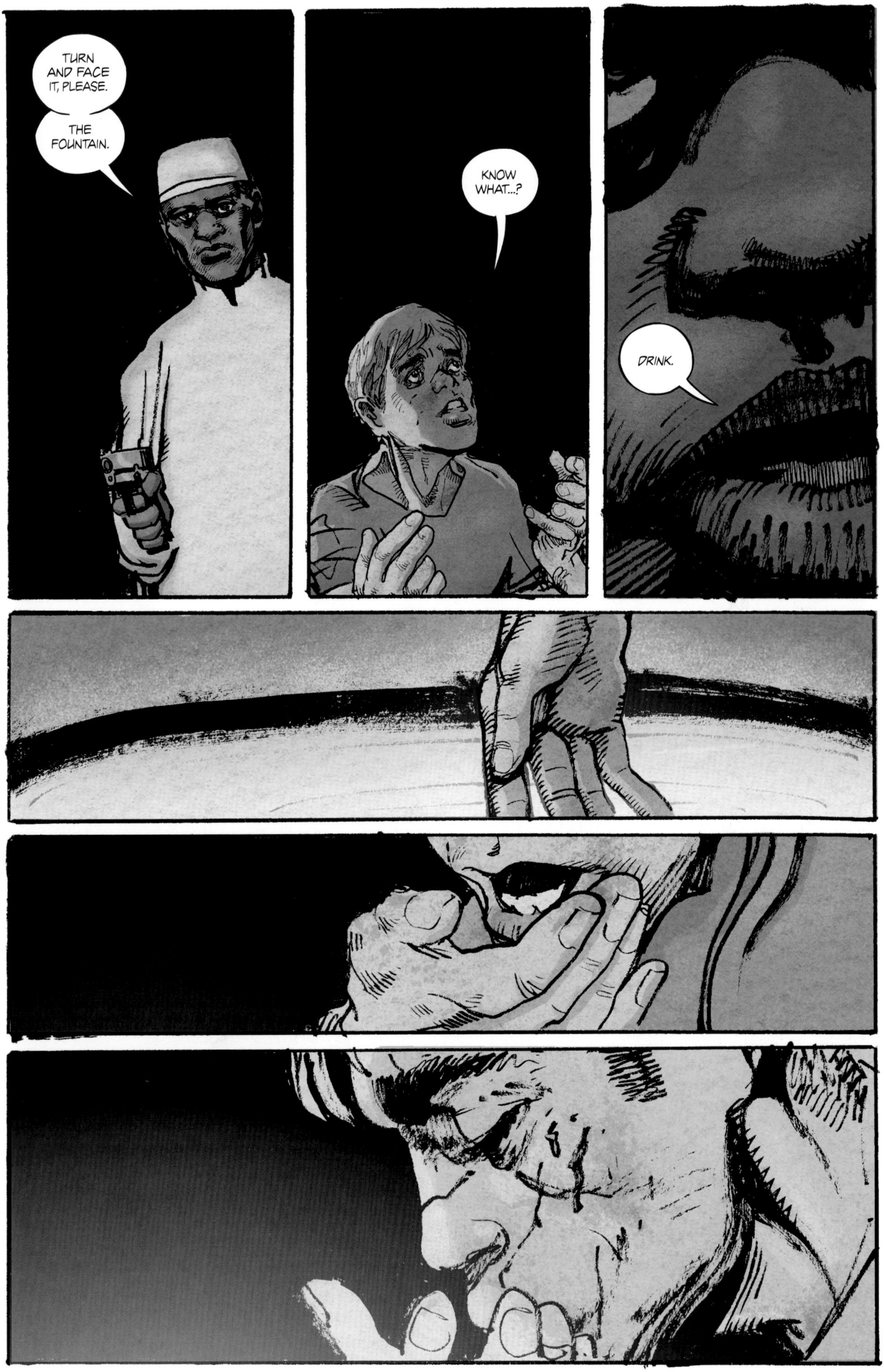
TURN AND FACE IT, PLEASE.
THE FOUNTAIN.
KNOW WHAT...?
DRINK.

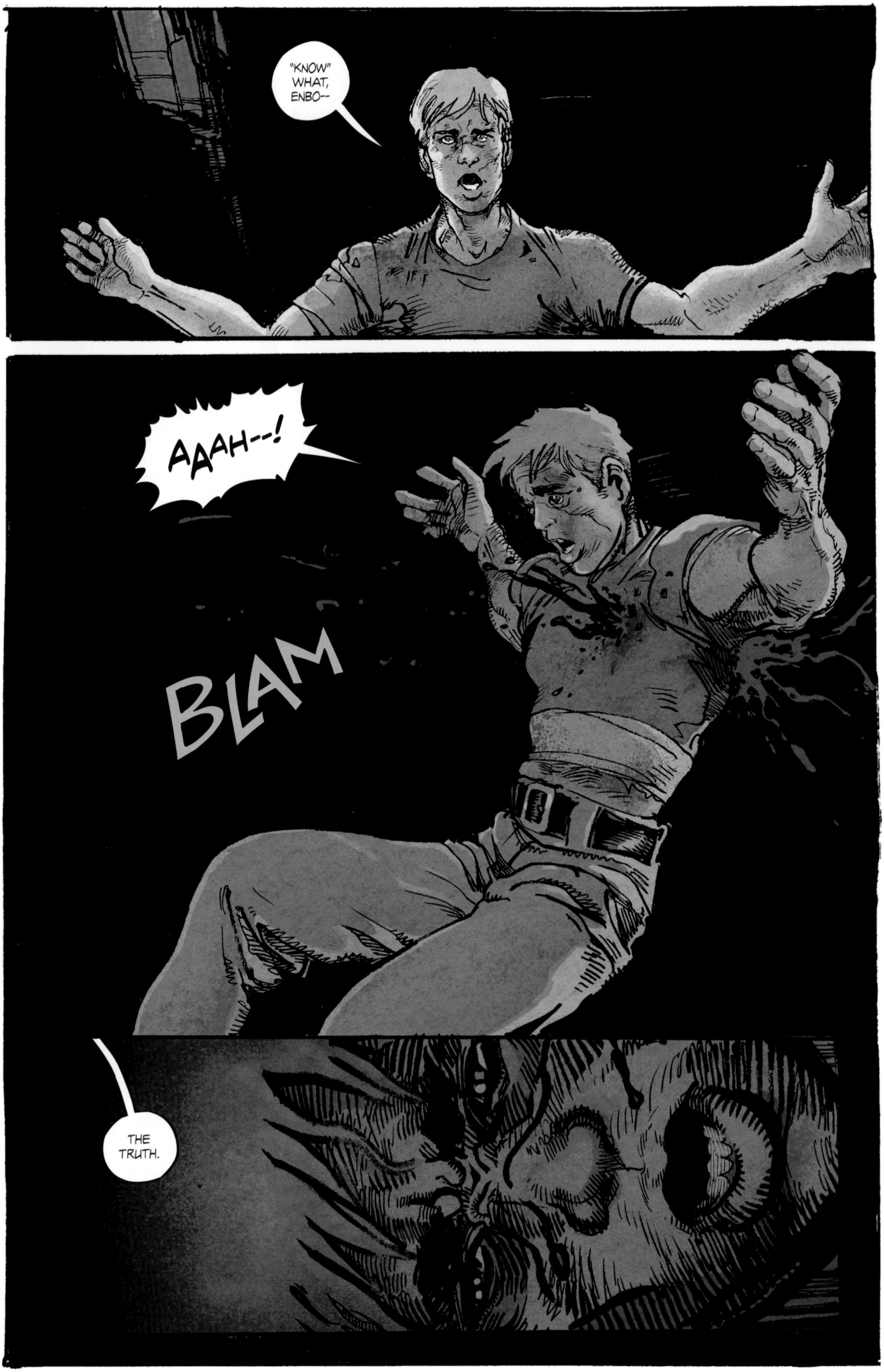
"KNOW" WHAT, ENBO--
AAAH--!
BLAM
THE TRUTH.

As I watched the blood pour out of my chest--

Enboa whispered one more thing to me--

--and then he was _gone..._

And I was _alone._

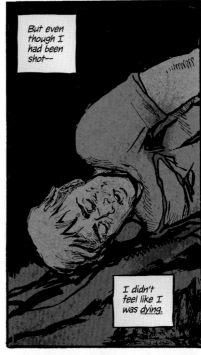

But even though I had been shot--

I didn't feel like I was _dying._

I felt...

Maybe for the first time ever...

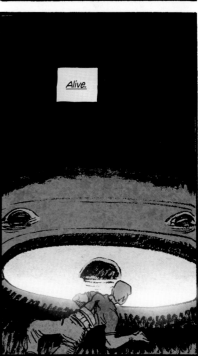

Alive.

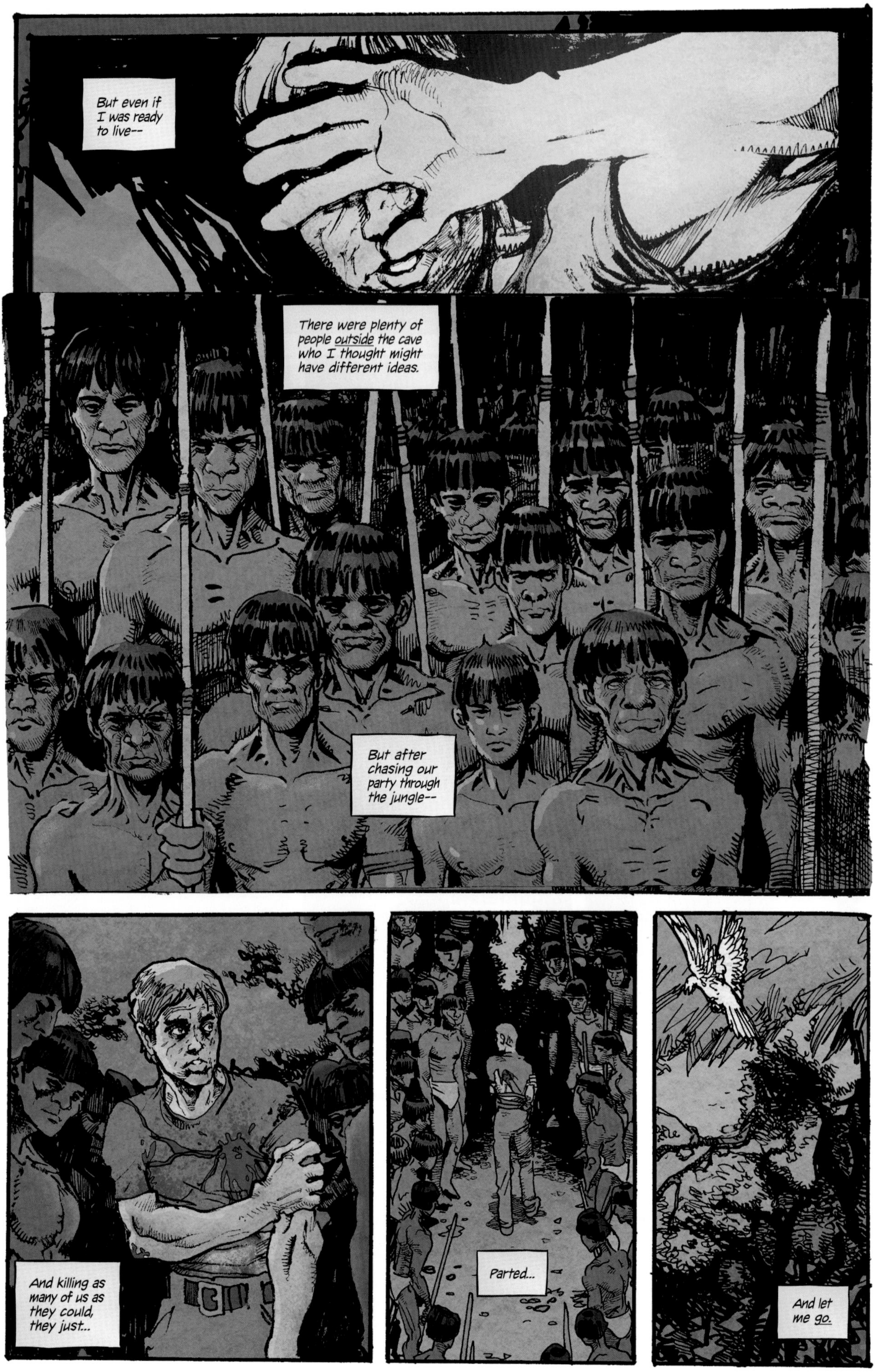

But even if I was ready to live--
There were plenty of people outside the cave who I thought might have different ideas.
But after chasing our party through the jungle--
And killing as many of us as they could, they just...
Parted...
And let me go.

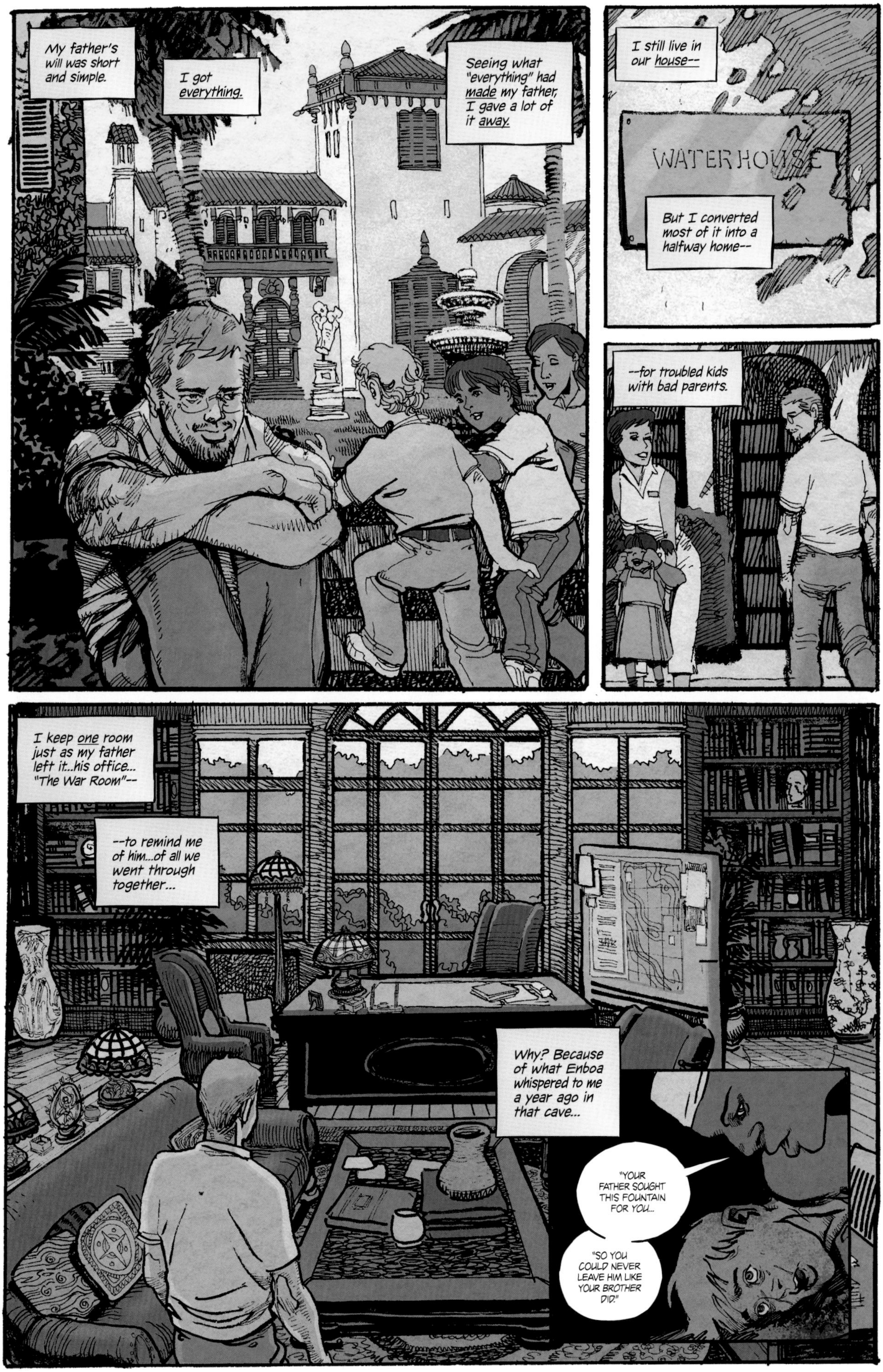
My father's will was short and simple.
I got everything.
Seeing what "everything" had made my father, I gave a lot of it away.
I still live in our house--
WATERHOUSE
But I converted most of it into a halfway home--
--for troubled kids with bad parents.
I keep one room just as my father left it...his office... "The War Room"--
--to remind me of him...of all we went through together...
Why? Because of what Enboa whispered to me a year ago in that cave...
"YOUR FATHER SOUGHT THIS FOUNTAIN FOR YOU...
"SO YOU COULD NEVER LEAVE HIM LIKE YOUR BROTHER DID."

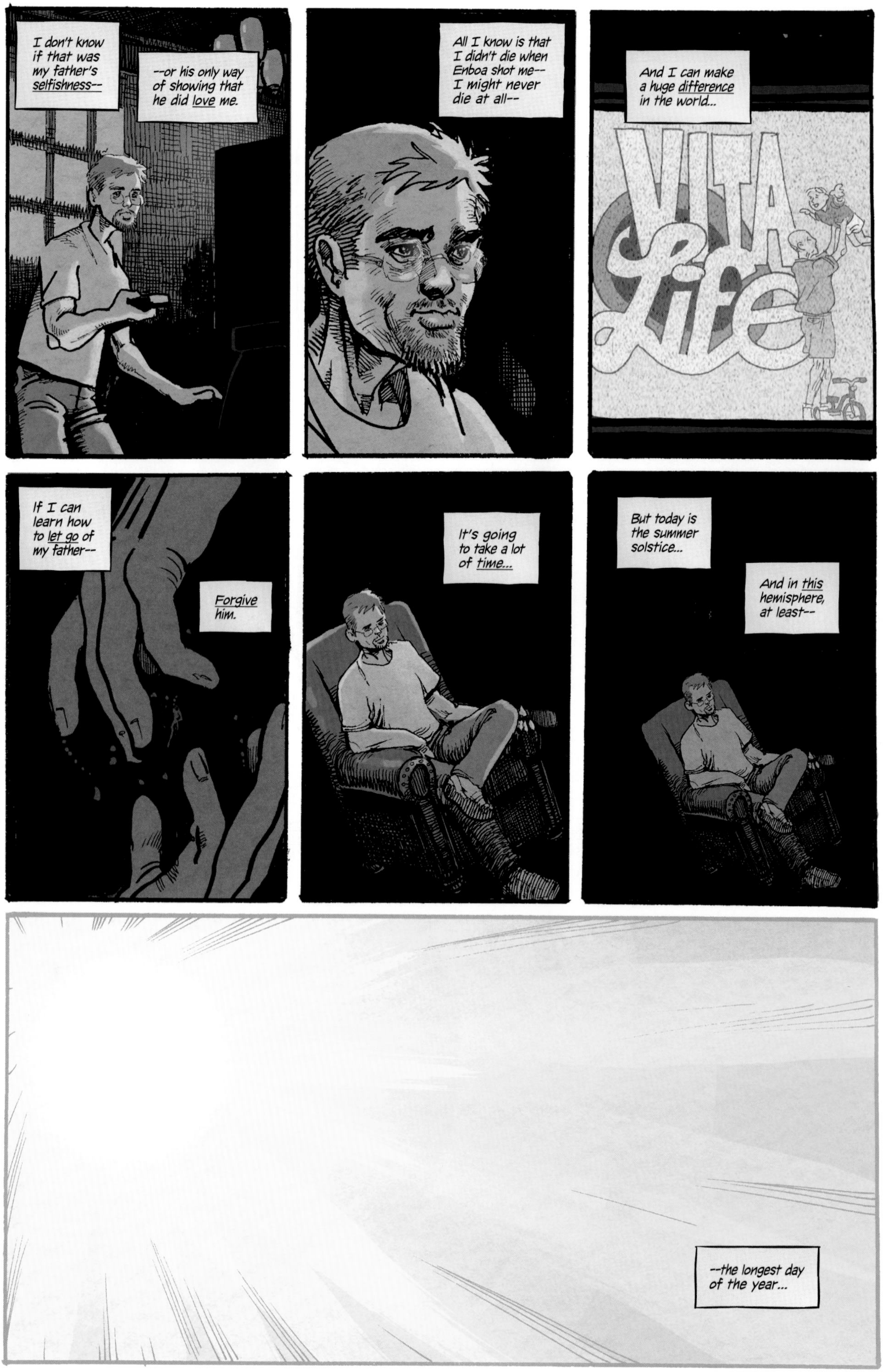
I don't know if that was my father's selfishness--
--or his only way of showing that he did love me.
All I know is that I didn't die when Enboa shot me-- I might never die at all--
And I can make a huge difference in the world...
VITA Life
If I can learn how to let go of my father--
Forgive him.
It's going to take a lot of time...
But today is the summer solstice...
And in this hemisphere, at least--
--the longest day of the year...

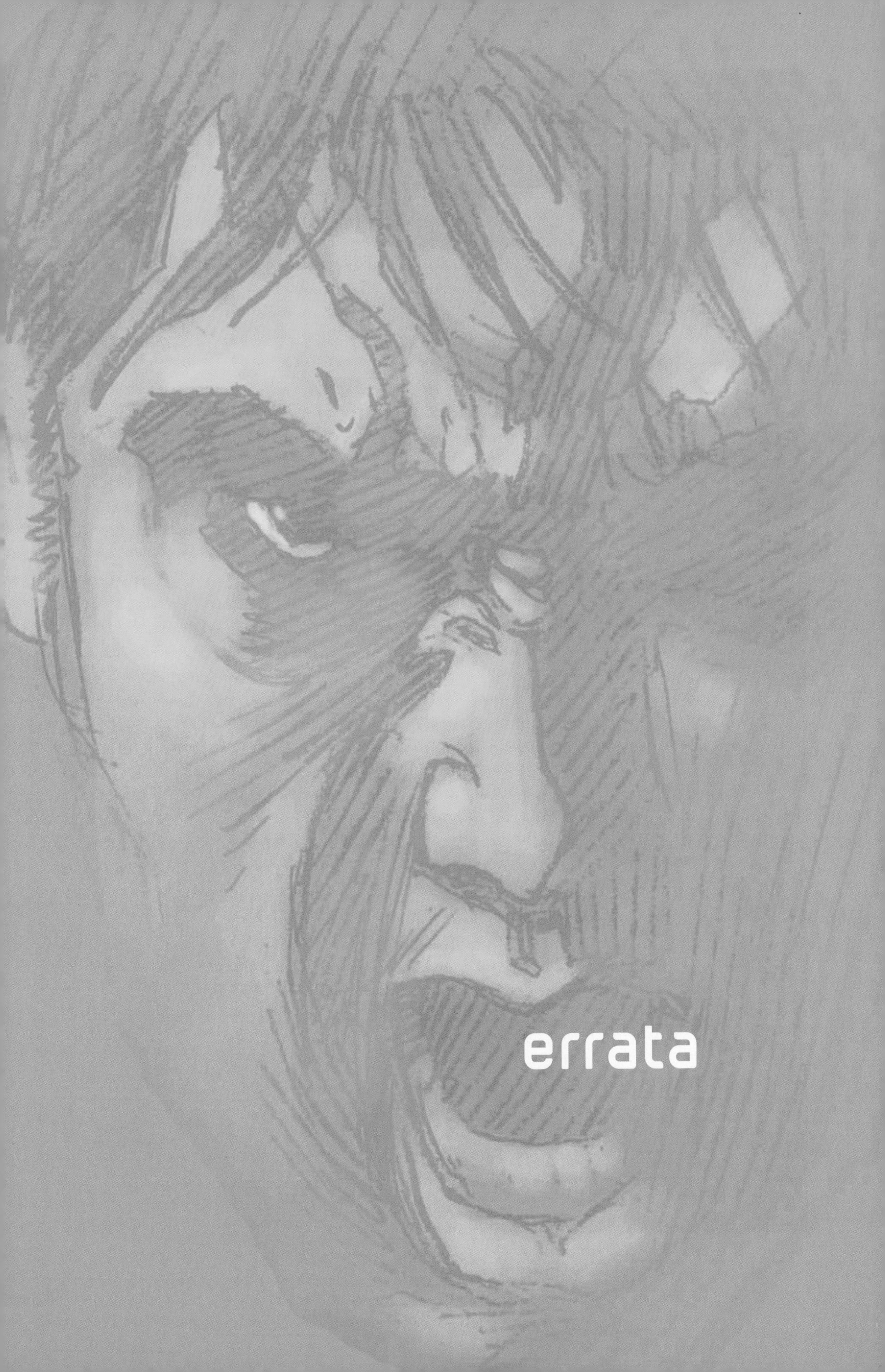

errata

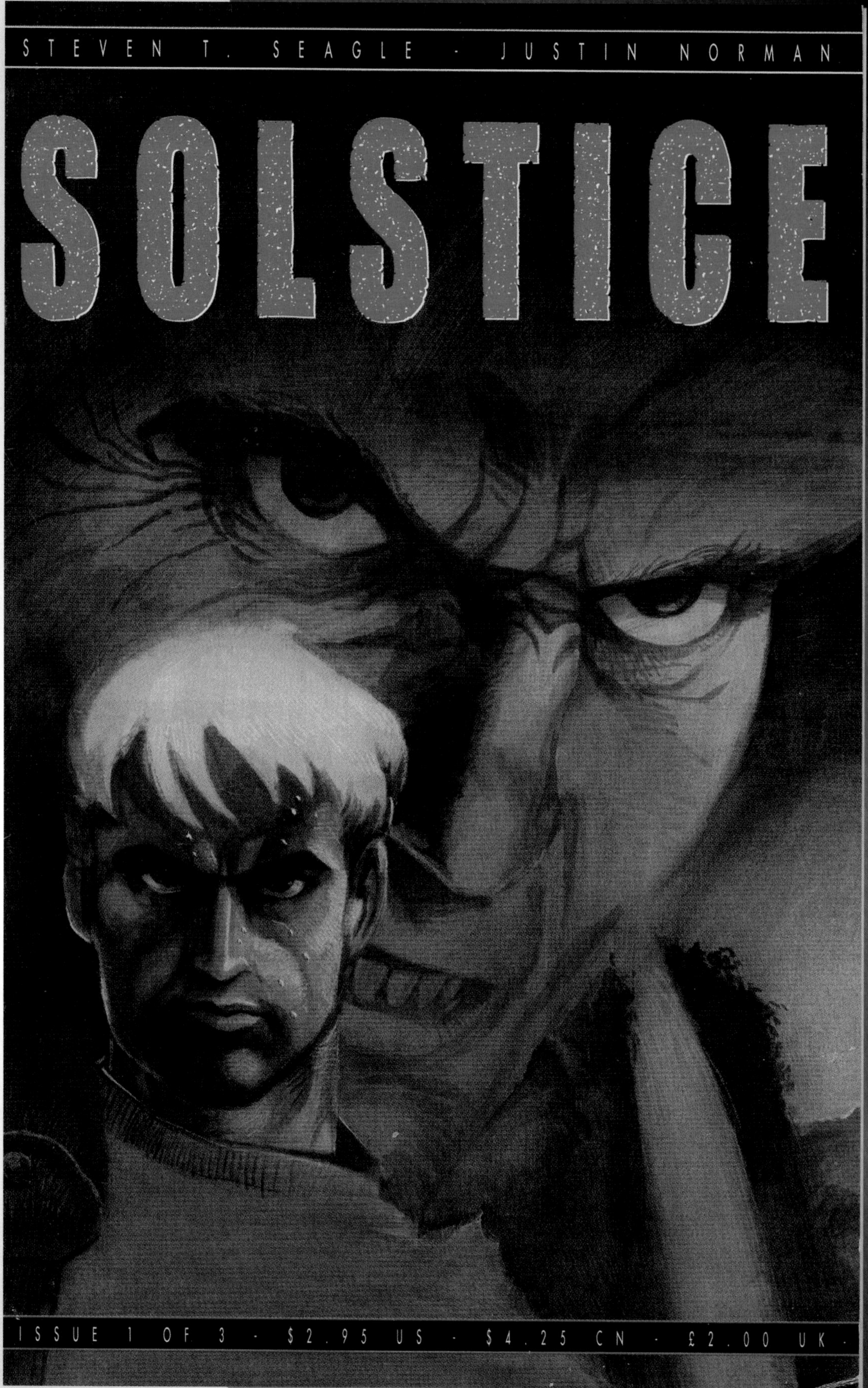
STEVEN T. SEAGLE - JUSTIN NORMAN
SOLSTICE
ISSUE 1 OF 3 - $2.95 US - $4.25 CN - £2.00 UK

above and opposite - Covers for SOLSTICE 1 and 2 published by Watermark. The issues were released in May and June, 1995.

It's a little ironic that the narrative stance of SOLSTICE is that of a young man looking back on a rocky experience that happened many years ago.

SOLSTICE first saw light of day as a three-issue miniseries published many years ago by a fearless upstart – Watermark Books.

Well...mostly published, that is.

After the first two issues shipped, its own rocky experience set in. Publisher E. Jordan Bojar called to commiserate that his publishing company had gone the way of water and evaporated. Production halted after issue 2 was drawn, and SOLSTICE was left unfinished.

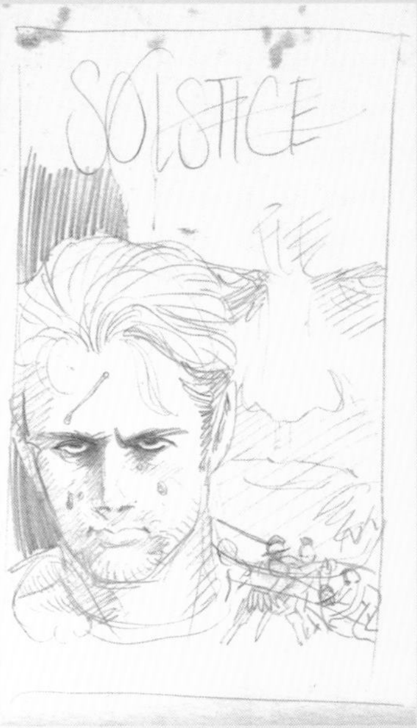
SOLSTICE

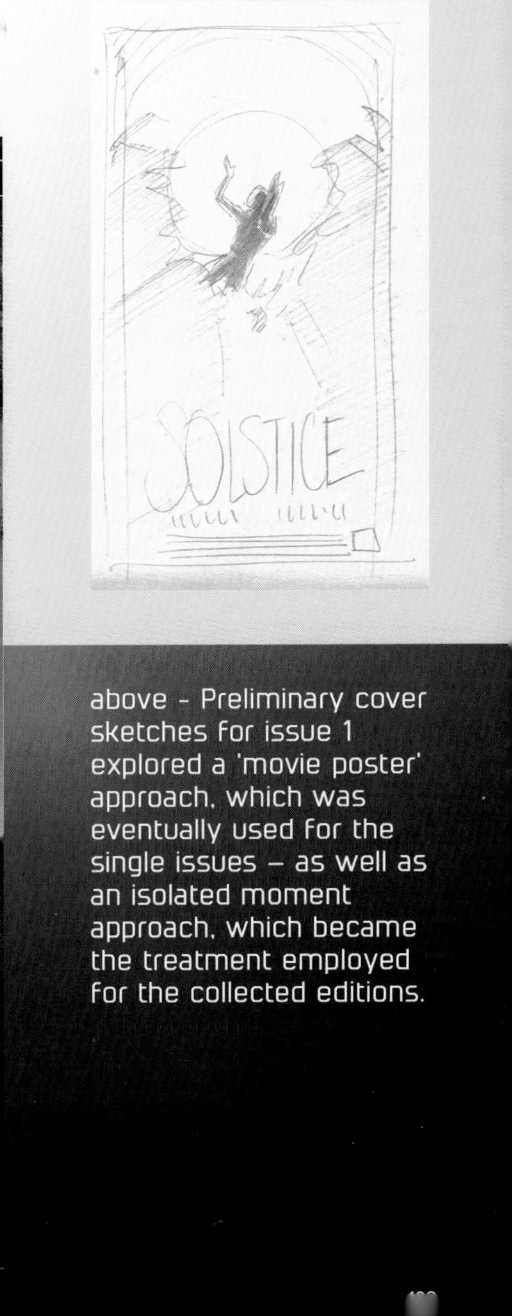
SOLSTICE

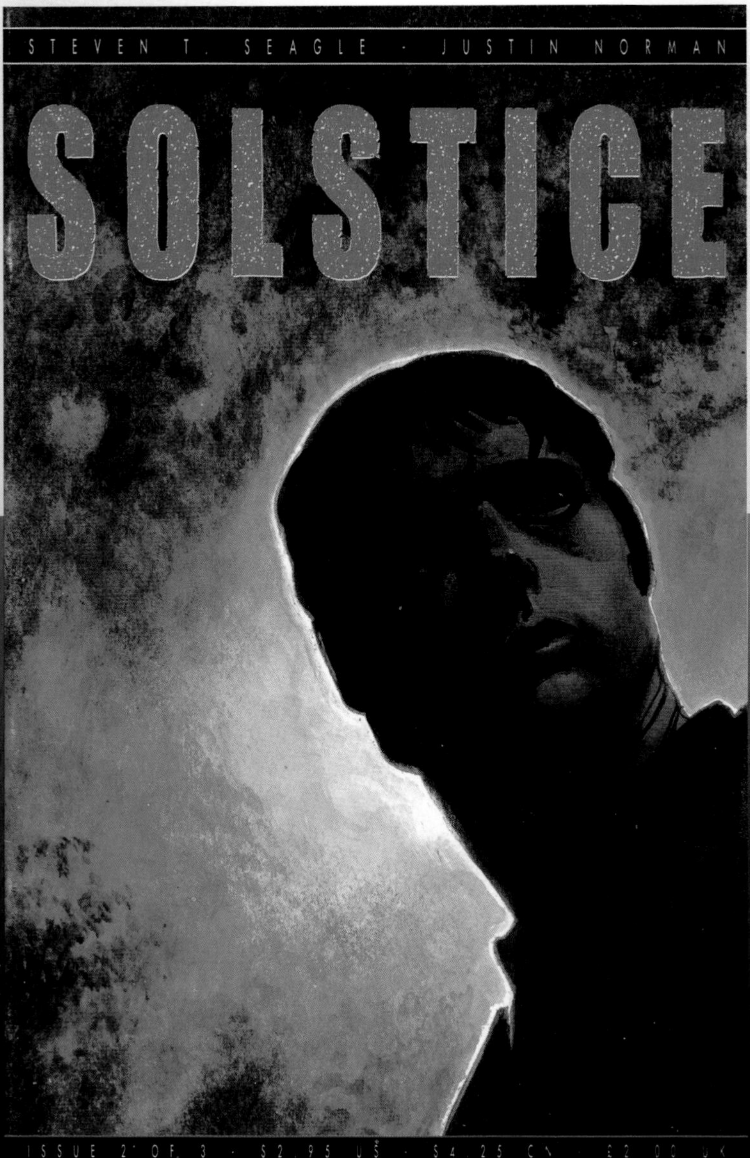
STEVEN T. SEAGLE · JUSTIN NORMAN
SOLSTICE
ISSUE 2 OF 3 · $2.95 US · $4.25 CN · £2.00 UK

above - Preliminary cover sketches for issue 1 explored a 'movie poster' approach, which was eventually used for the single issues – as well as an isolated moment approach, which became the treatment employed for the collected editions.

below – Moritat's film parody color study for the first issue cover pokes fun at just how bad the father/son relationship is, while the compositional layout draft that evolved out of it anticipates the final design for the issue's cover.

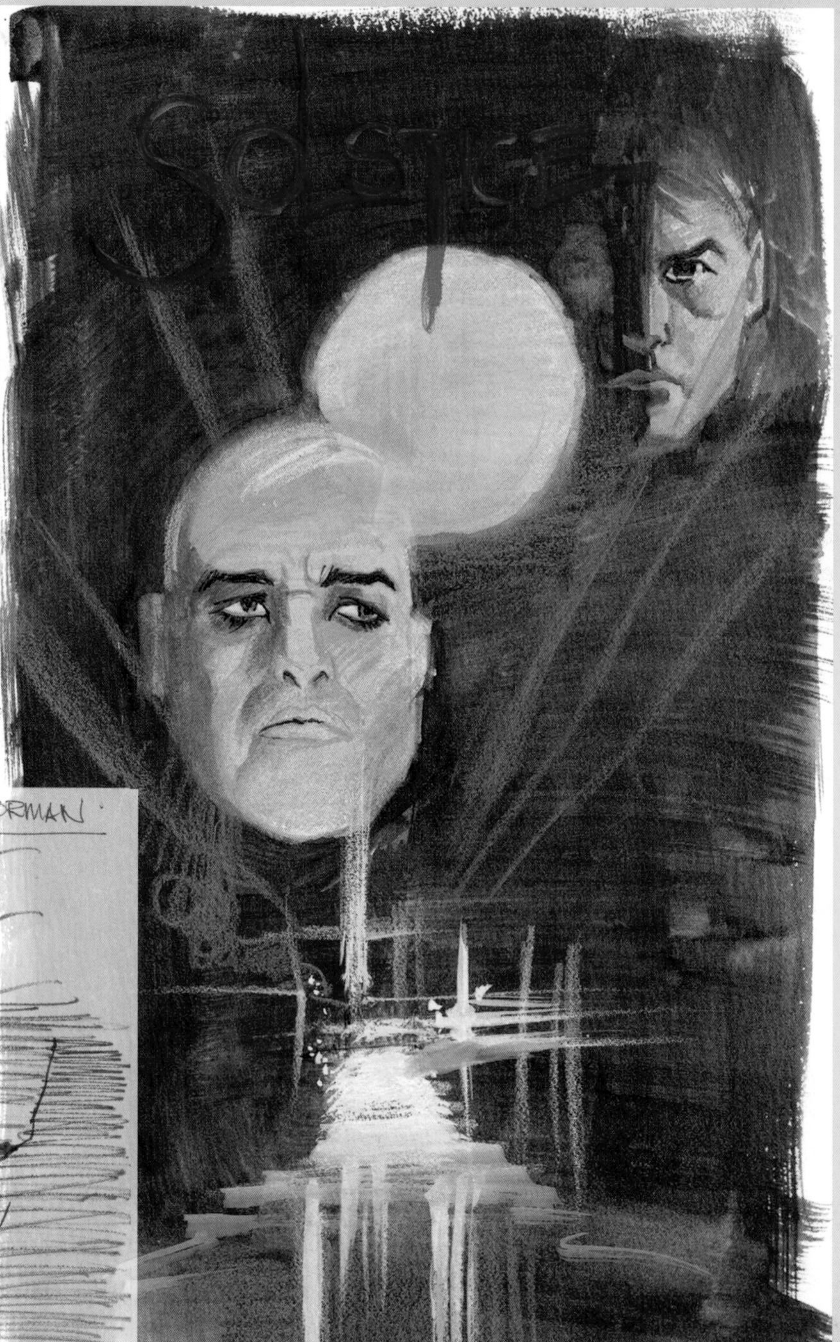
SOLSTICE

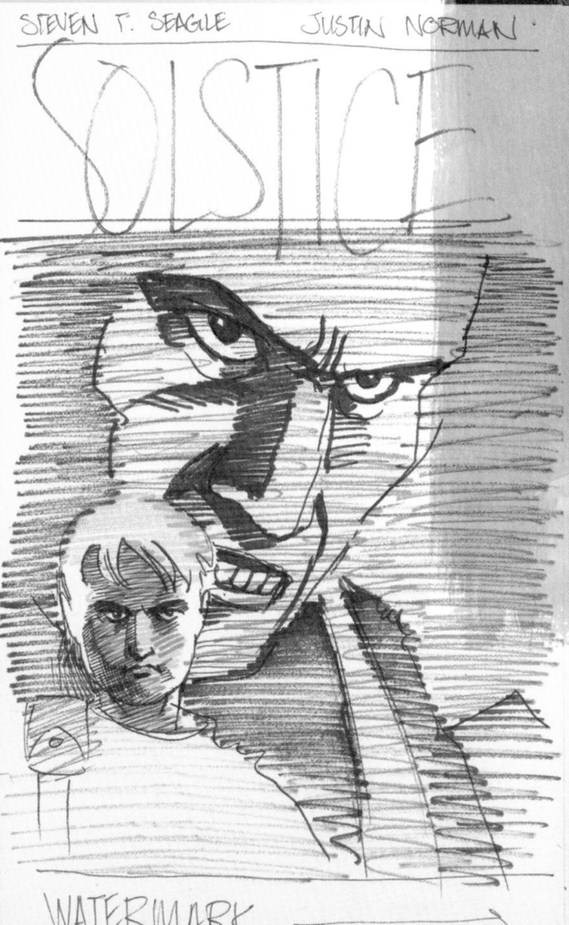
STEVEN T. SEAGLE
JUSTIN NORMAN
SOLSTICE
WATERMARK

Readers – having only two parts of a three-part story – were left hanging as to why Russell Waterhouse sought the Fountain of Youth and what eventually happened to his son, Hugh.

below - The interior front and back covers for issues
1 & 2 of the comic book featured original artwork by
Moritat. The page of statues was repurposed for
chapter interstitials in the first collected edition.

E. JORDAN BOJAR · PUBLISHER
TOIVO ROVAINEN · PRODUCTION ASSISTANT
RAE DINSMORE · ADMINISTRATIVE ASSISTANT
COLOR PRE PRESS BY DIGICOLOR
PRINTED AT QUEBECOR PRINTING INC.

SOLSTICE #1 (of 3). May 1995. Published monthly by WATERMARK, 916 N.E. 65th #400, Seattle, WA 98115.
SOLSTICE is ™ and ©1995 Steven T. Seagle. Illustrations ©1995 Justin Norman. All other material ©1995 E.
Jordan Bojar. All rights reserved. This is a work of fiction. Any similarity to actual individuals, institutions,
or situations purely coincidental. PRINTED IN CANADA.

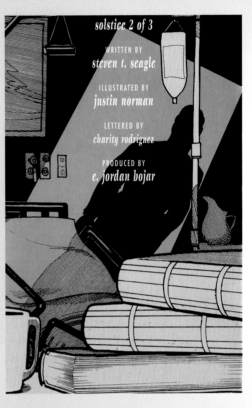

solstice 2 of 3

WRITTEN BY
steven t. seagle

ILLUSTRATED BY
justin norman

LETTERED BY
charity rodriguez

PRODUCED BY
e. jordan bojar

solstice 1 of 3

WRITTEN BY
steven t. seagle

ILLUSTRATED BY
justin norman

LETTERED BY
charity rodriguez

PRODUCED BY
e. jordan bojar

E. JORDAN BOJAR · PUBLISHER
TOIVO ROVAINEN · PRODUCTION ASSISTANT
RAE DINSMORE · ADMINISTRATIVE ASSISTANT
COLOR PRE PRESS BY DIGICOLOR
PRINTED AT QUEBECOR PRINTING INC.

SOLSTICE #2 (of 3). June 1995. Published monthly by WATERMARK, 916 N.E. 65th #400, Seattle, WA 98115.
SOLSTICE is ™ and ©1995 Steven T. Seagle. Illustrations ©1995 Justin Norman. All other material ©1995 E.
Jordan Bojar. All rights reserved. This is a work of fiction. Any similarity to actual individuals, institutions,
or situations purely coincidental. PRINTED IN CANADA.

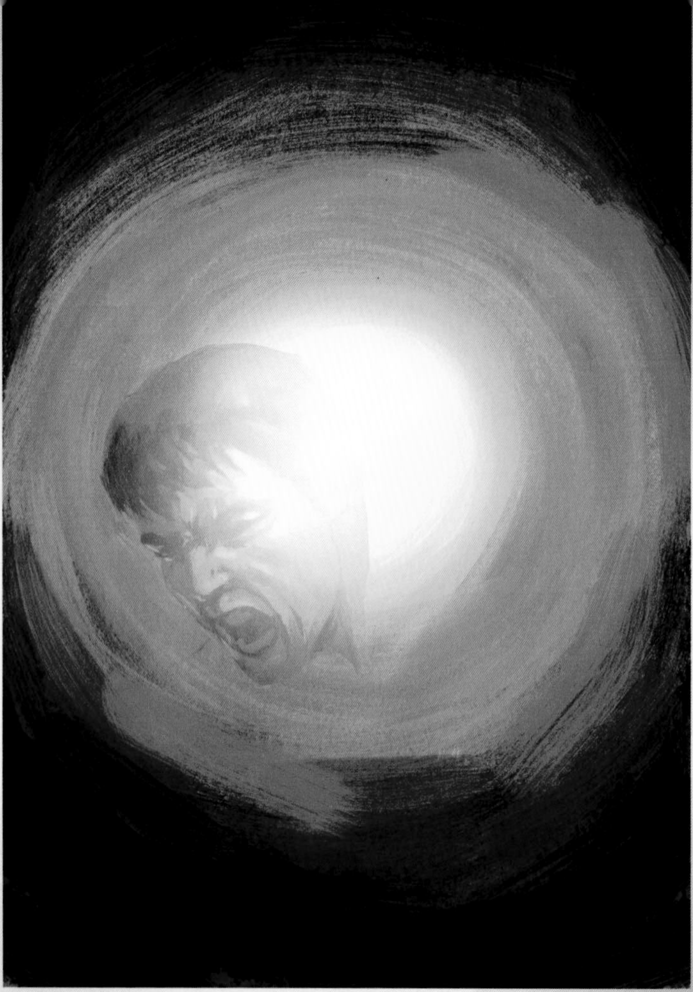

left and below - Color studies by Moritat for the first collected edition cover. The sun-scream motif won out over Hugh's calm reach for The Fountain.

far below - The full wraparound cover design for the Active Images trade paperback – logo by Richard Starkings.

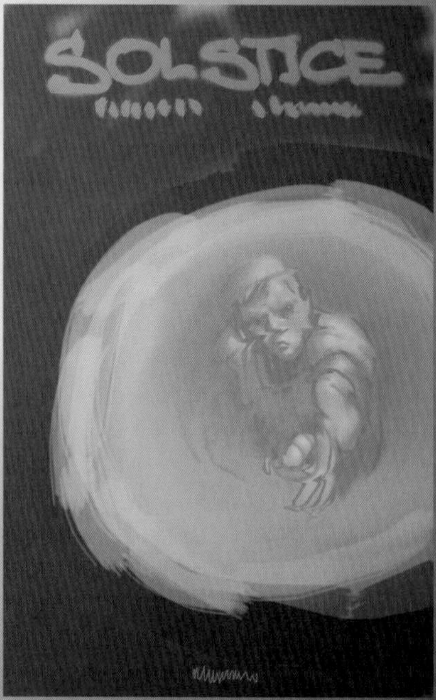

SOLSTICE

A decade later...

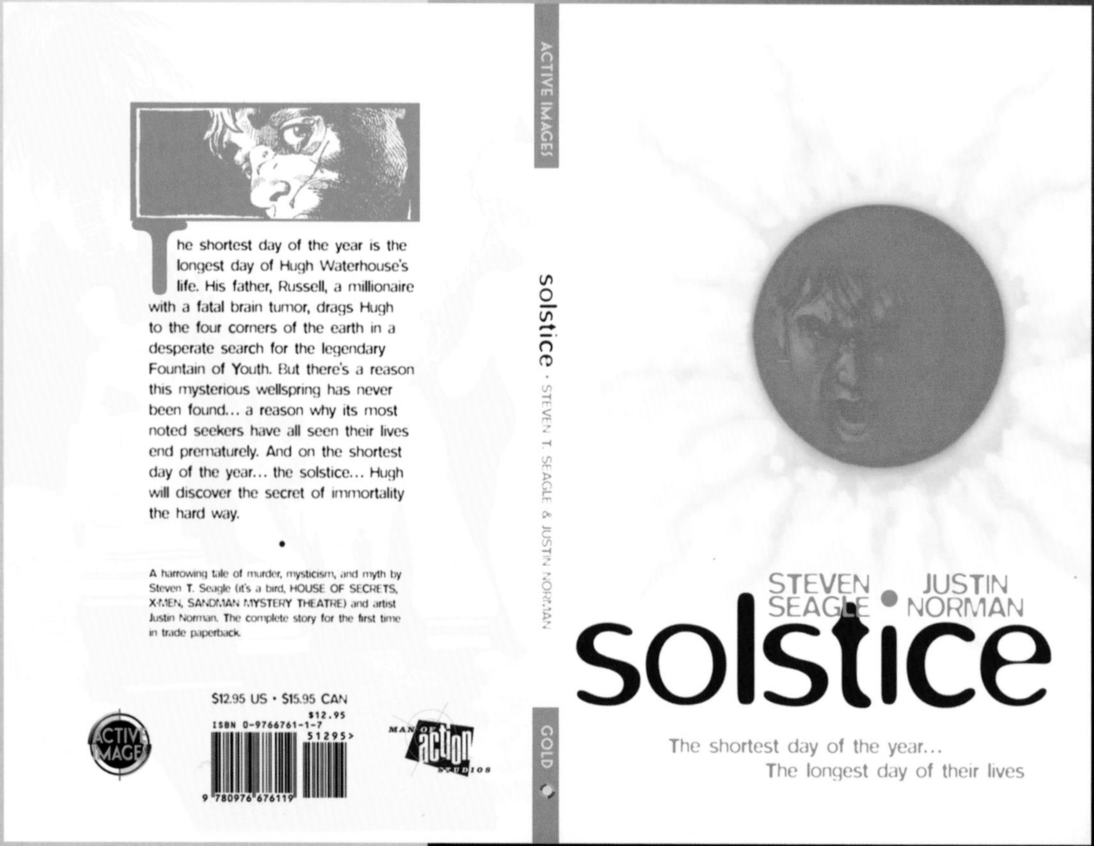

ACTIVE IMAGES
The shortest day of the year is the longest day of Hugh Waterhouse's life. His father, Russell, a millionaire with a fatal brain tumor, drags Hugh to the four corners of the earth in a desperate search for the legendary Fountain of Youth. But there's a reason this mysterious wellspring has never been found... a reason why its most noted seekers have all seen their lives end prematurely. And on the shortest day of the year... the solstice... Hugh will discover the secret of immortality the hard way.
A harrowing tale of murder, mysticism, and myth by Steven T. Seagle (it's a bird, HOUSE OF SECRETS, X-MEN, SANDMAN MYSTERY THEATRE) and artist Justin Norman. The complete story for the first time in trade paperback.
$12.95 US • $15.95 CAN
$12.95
ISBN 0-9766761-1-7
51295>
9 780976 676119
solstice • STEVEN T. SEAGLE & JUSTIN NORMAN
GOLD
STEVEN SEAGLE
JUSTIN NORMAN
solstice
The shortest day of the year...
The longest day of their lives

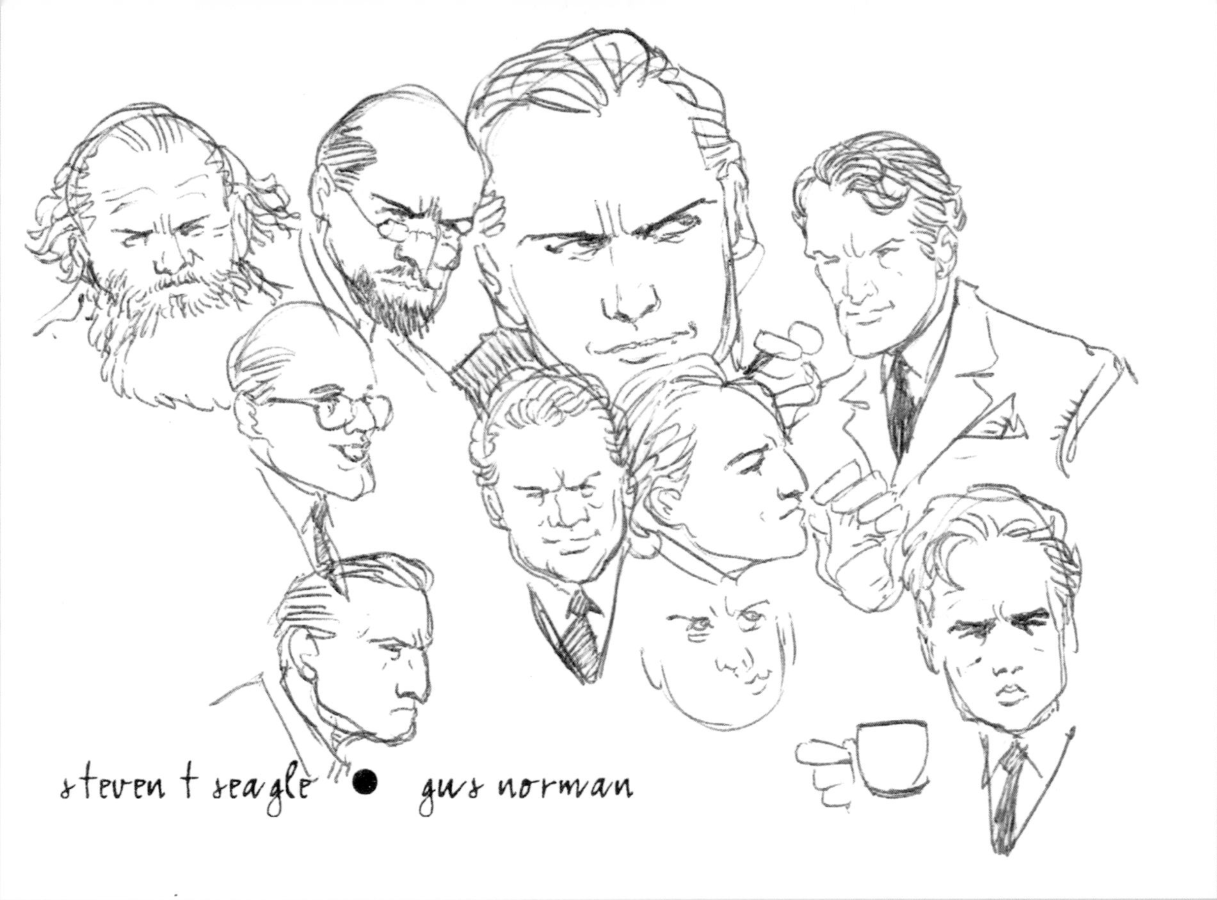
steven t seagle • gus norman

Writer Steven T. Seagle and artist Moritat ("Justin Norman" to some, "Gus" to Steve) found themselves exhibiting in adjacent booths at the San Diego Comicon in 2003. Reminiscing about their never-completed SOLSTICE series, both men agreed to revisit it, plow forward, tackle the third issue, and finish the series. But there were some "rocks" on the road...

While the original plot for issue three was written at the time of the first two, the full script had never been completed. Putting himself in the minds of characters he'd last considered ten years prior, Seagle wrote. With the script finished, Moritat, who had drawn in radically different styles in the intervening years, had to re-learn his old "hand" to draw pages that would mesh seamlessly with the previous issues his younger self had illustrated. The new pages were ready to be lettered.

But lettering was another complication...

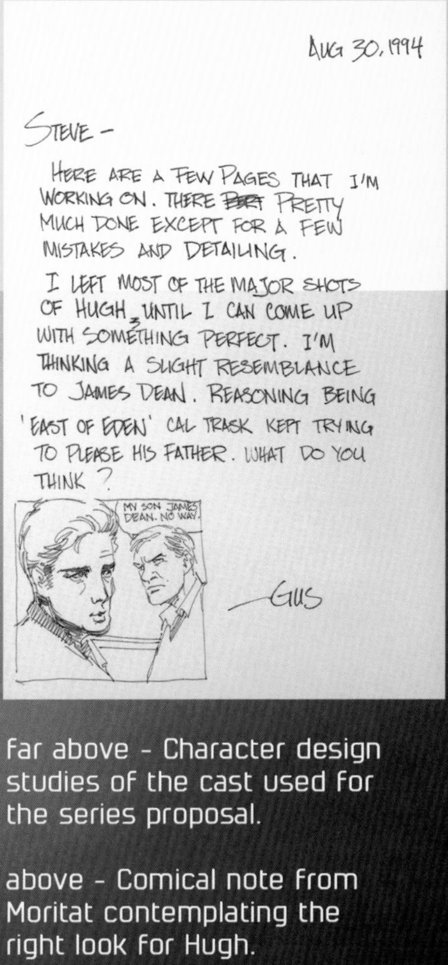
AUG 30, 1994

STEVE -

HERE ARE A FEW PAGES THAT I'M WORKING ON. THERE PRETTY MUCH DONE EXCEPT FOR A FEW MISTAKES AND DETAILING.

I LEFT MOST OF THE MAJOR SHOTS OF HUGH, UNTIL I CAN COME UP WITH SOMETHING PERFECT. I'M THINKING A SLIGHT RESEMBLANCE TO JAMES DEAN. REASONING BEING 'EAST OF EDEN' CAL TRASK KEPT TRYING TO PLEASE HIS FATHER. WHAT DO YOU THINK?

MY SON. JAMES DEAN. NO WAY.

— GUS

far above - Character design studies of the cast used for the series proposal.

above - Comical note from Moritat contemplating the right look for Hugh.

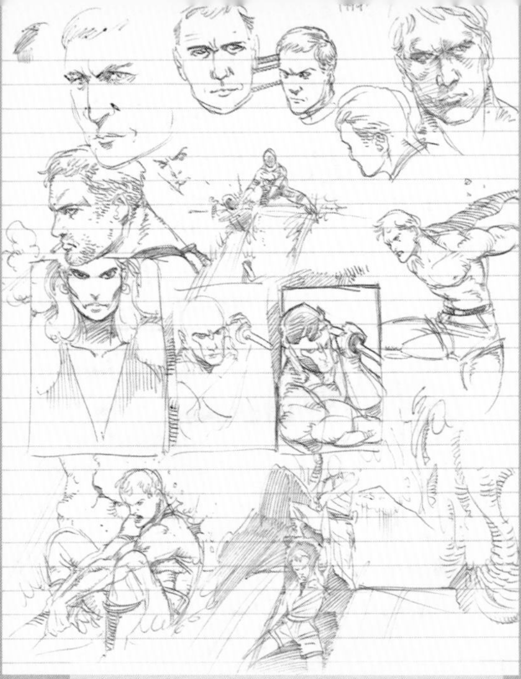

In the intervening years, former next-door neighbor and original series letterer Charity Rodriguez Stukenborg had become a mother (to adorable Dorothy and adventurous August) and followed husband Henry's job to Florida. If the look of the first two chapters couldn't be matched, the entire issue would have to be redone. Enter: Comicraft. Richard Starking's studio re-lettered the entire book from scratch, including the now-completed third chapter.

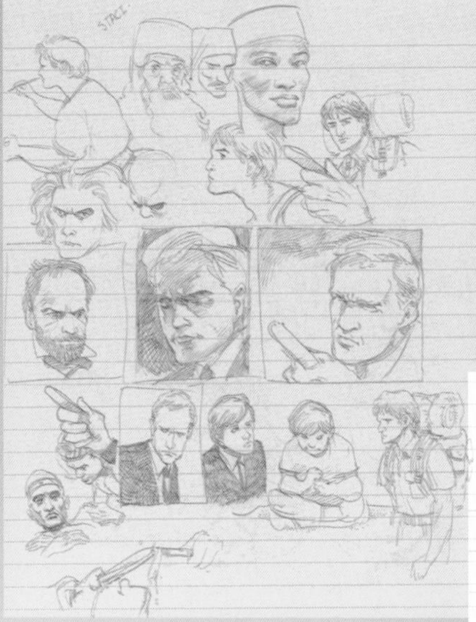

The publishing arm of the Starkings Empire – aided by John "JG" Roshell, Rob Steen, and Jimmy Betancourt – agreed to act as designer and publisher for the collected edition. That volume was released in 2005, and SOLSTICE was finally complete.

Kind of...

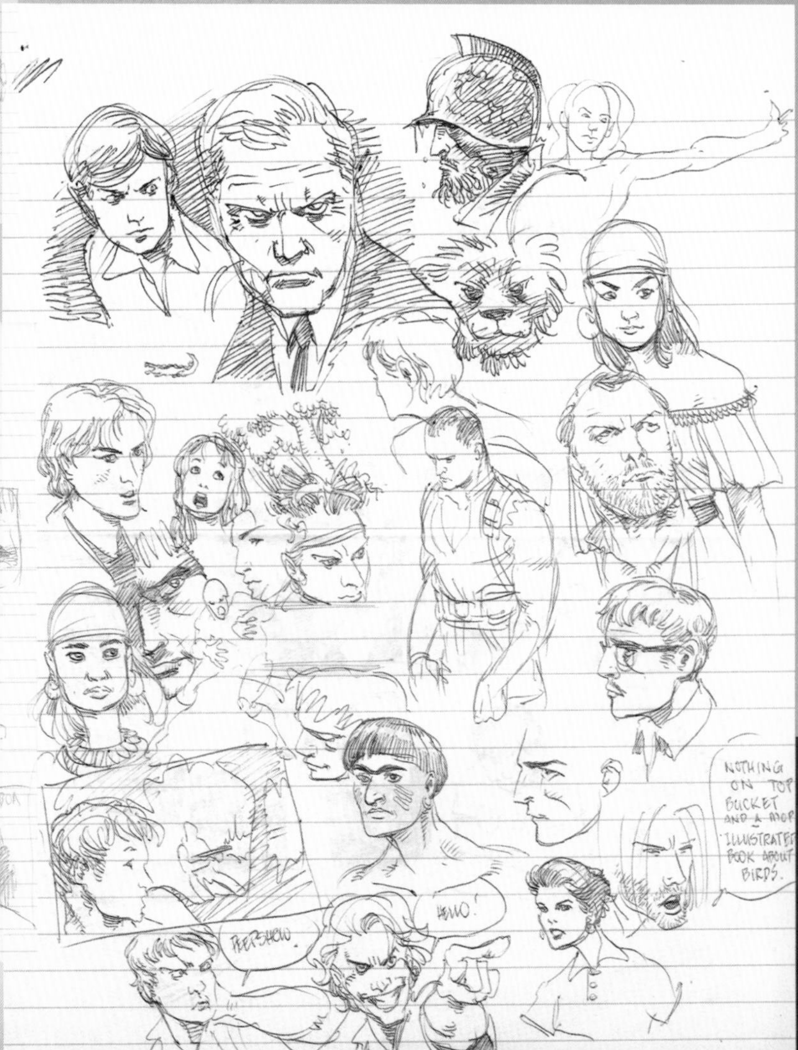
HELLO!
NOTHING ON TOP
BUCKET AND A MOP
BOOK ABOUT BIRDS.

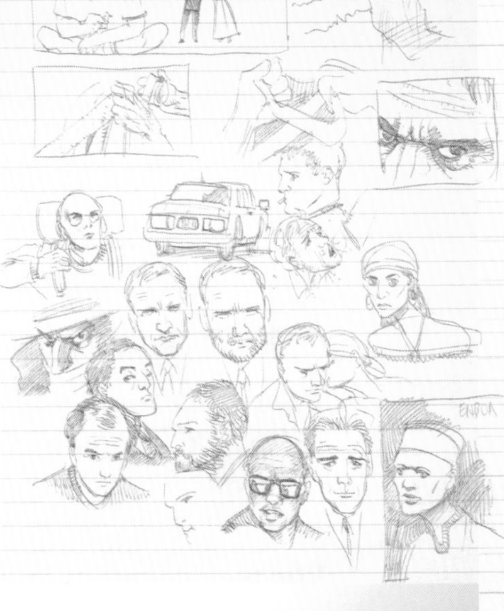

above - An alternate panel design of Hugh emerging from the cave discovered under a fallen patch of the image used in the book.

center - Early sketch of Peck.

opposite - A series of legal pad sketches Moritat drew as preparation studies of characters and panel designs for various issues.

A decade later...

Seagle had completed a new edition of his Eisner-nominated graphic novel KAFKA. The deluxe edition was larger, remastered, and in color for the first time. Given the positive reception to that volume, Seagle pitched Moritat the idea of embarking on a new journey — give the same upgraded treatment to the out-of-print SOLSTICE.

Unfortunately, more "rocks" hit their path. The files for the previous edition had decayed. The new volume would once again be starting from scratch. Each page was re-scanned from the original boards, then re-lettered by Thomas Mauer from Seagle's Image comic IMPERIAL. And for the first time, the book was colored in order to give the whiplash nature of the narrative more clarity — each time/location having its own color palette provided by IMPERIAL's Brad Simpson. New book design by Seagle employed solar and lunar photographs contributed by renowned voice actor Roger Craig Smith.

And SOLSTICE was complete. Maybe...

Check back with us again...

A decade later...

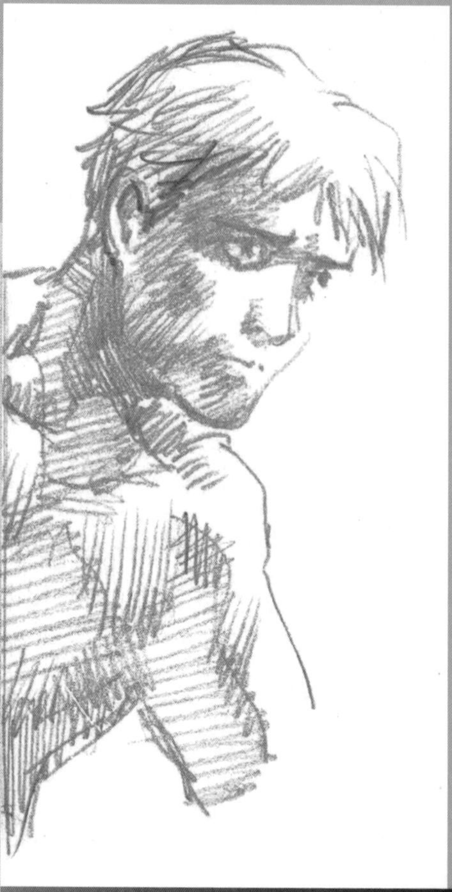

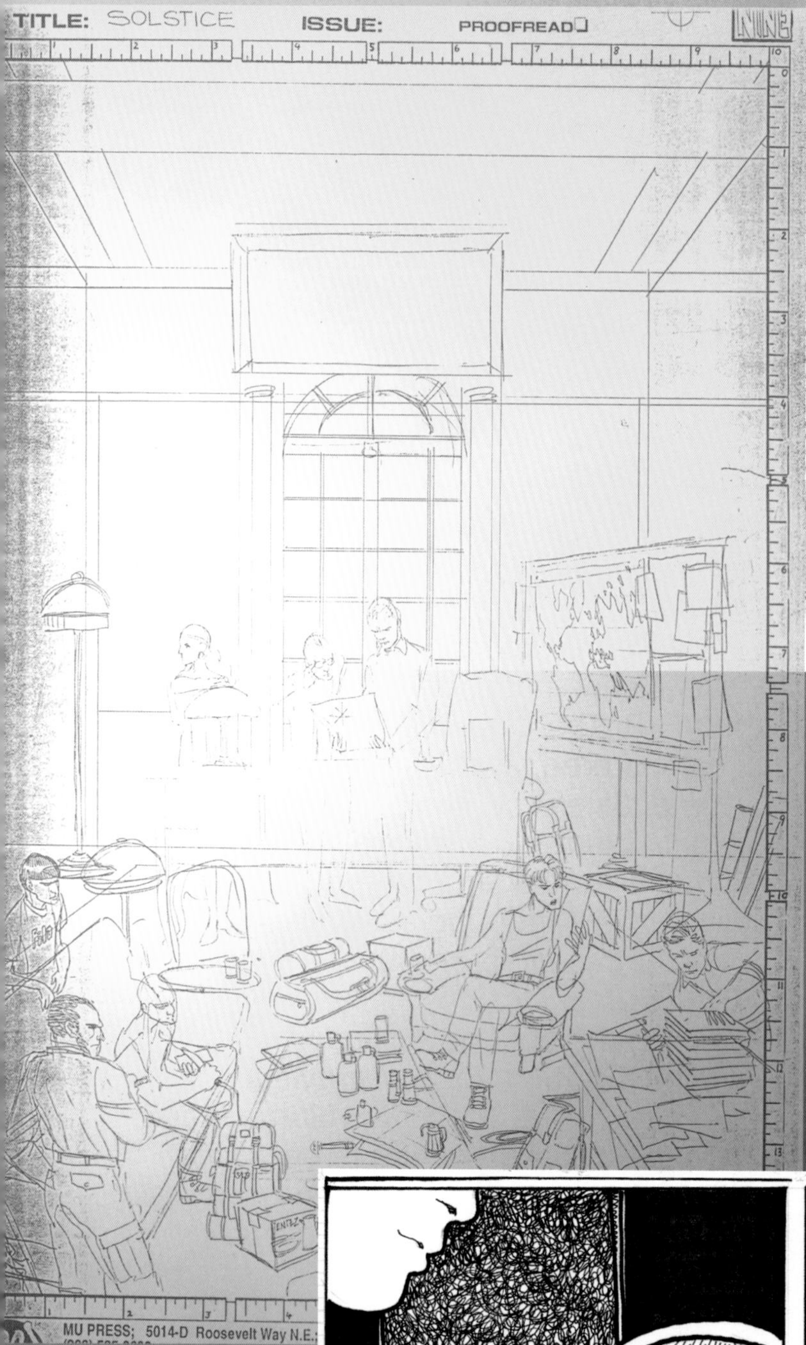

TITLE: SOLSTICE
ISSUE:
PROOFREAD
MU PRESS; 5014-D Roosevelt Way N.E.;

above - An early pencil examination of Hugh.

left - A photocopy of the pencil layout of Page 13.

below - Another early version tier of panels discovered beneath paste-up during the new scan of the original art.

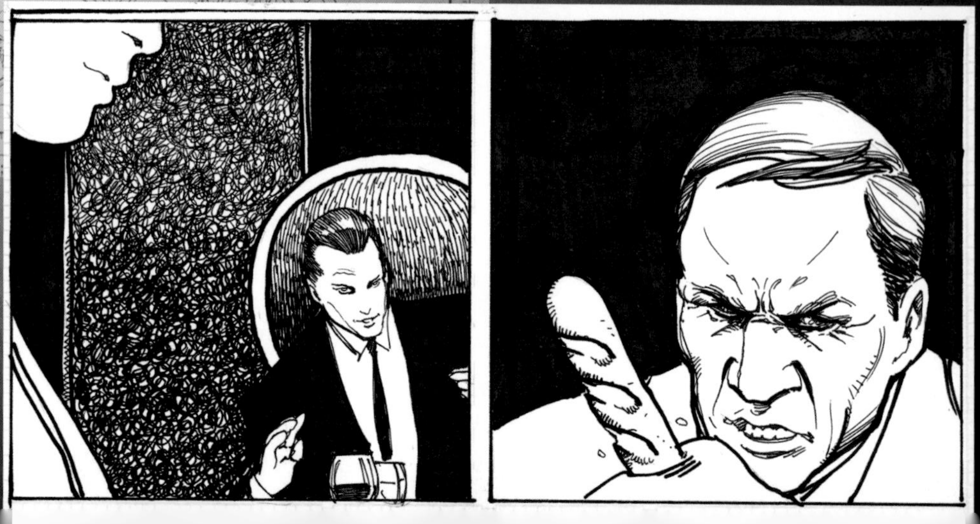

below - An unused cover illustration of "sun-scream" Hugh. The final art featured the character looking directly out from the sun instead of in profile.

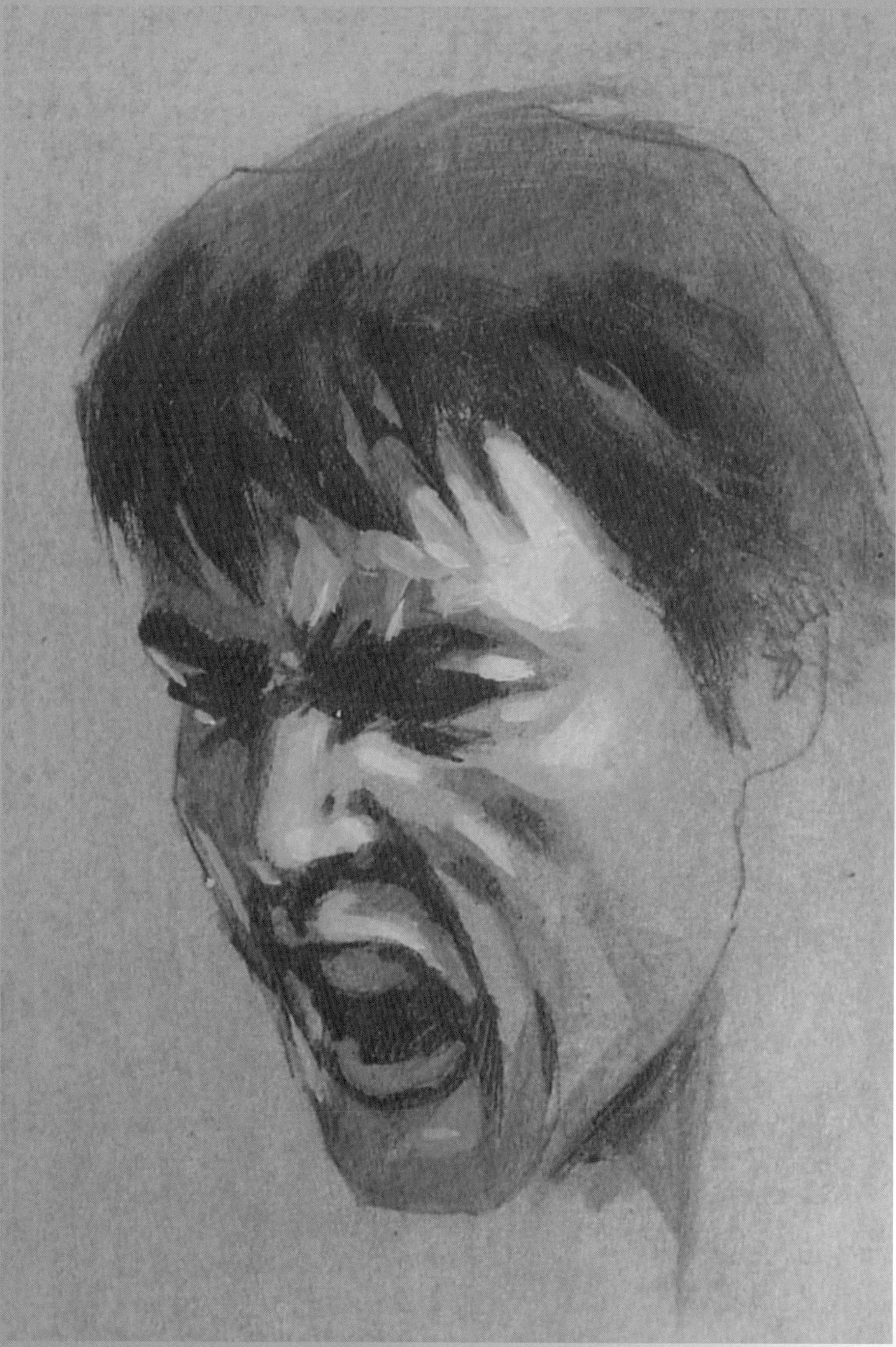

STEVEN T SEAGLE

Steven is a founding MAN OF ACTION – creators of BEN 10 and BIG HERO 6. His graphic novels include GENIUS, it's a bird...., KAFKA, HOUSE OF SECRETS, CAMP MIDNIGHT, and THE CRUSADES. His cat GAUDI proved not to be immortal this year.

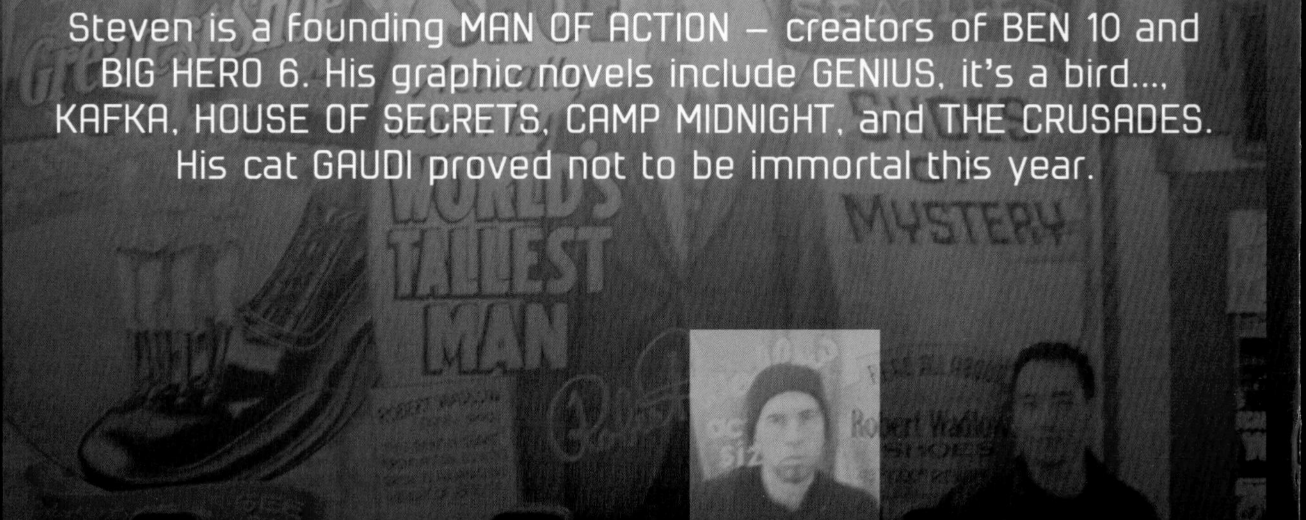
WORLD'S TALLEST MAN
MYSTERY

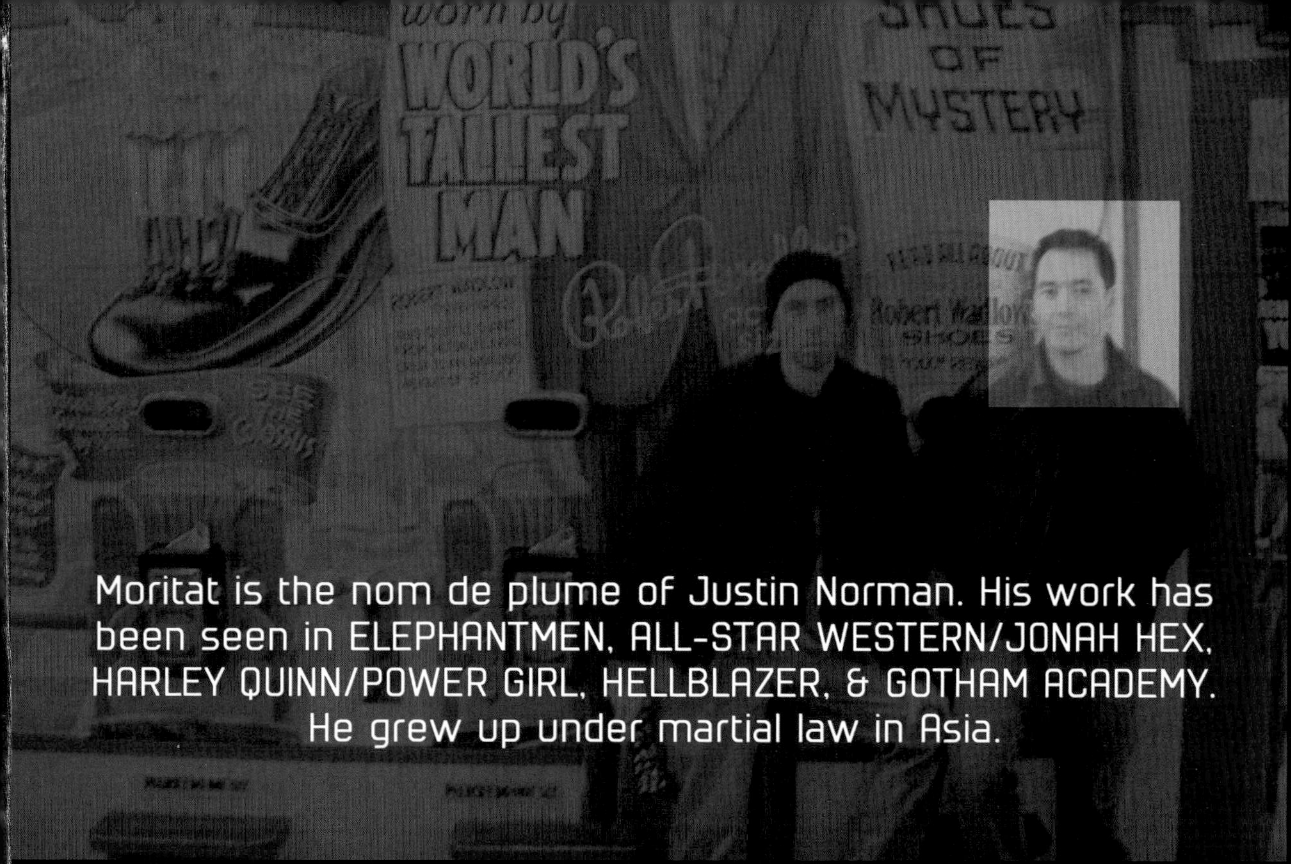
WORLD'S
TALLEST
MAN
OF
MYSTERY

Moritat is the nom de plume of Justin Norman. His work has been seen in ELEPHANTMEN, ALL-STAR WESTERN/JONAH HEX, HARLEY QUINN/POWER GIRL, HELLBLAZER, & GOTHAM ACADEMY. He grew up under martial law in Asia.

MORITAT

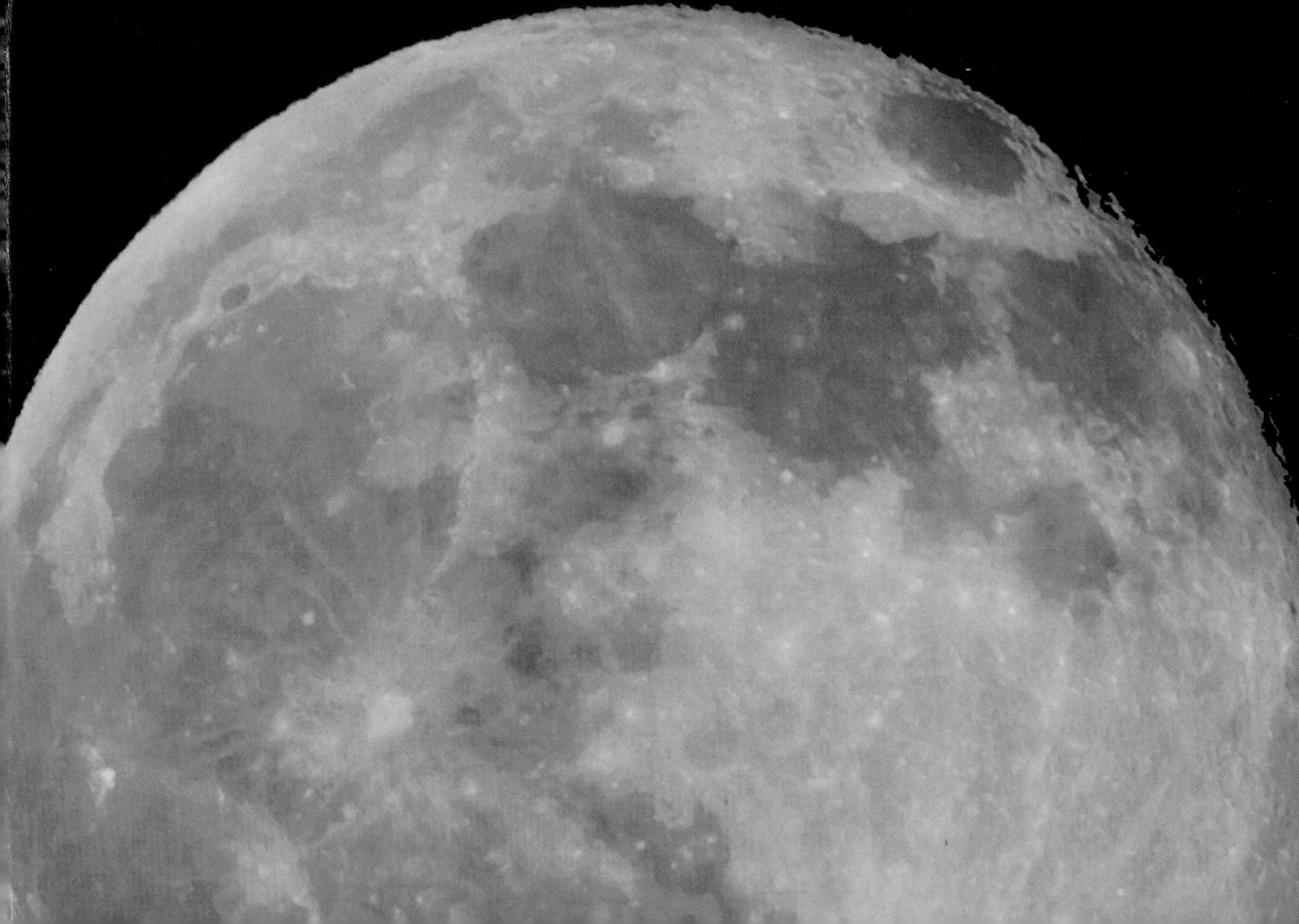

Image Comics, Inc.

Robert Kirkman – Chief Operating Officer
Erik Larsen – Chief Financial Officer
Todd McFarlane – President
Marc Silvestri – Chief Executive Officer
Jim Valentino – Vice-President
Eric Stephenson – Publisher
Corey Murphy – Director of Sales
Jeff Boison – Director of Publishing Planning & Book Trade Sales
Jeremy Sullivan – Director of Digital Sales
Kat Salazar – Director of PR & Marketing
Branwyn Bigglestone – Controller
Sarah Mello – Accounts Manager
Drew Gill – Art Director
Jonathan Chan – Production Manager
Meredith Wallace – Print Manager
Briah Skelly – Publicist
Sasha Head – Sales & Marketing Production Designer
Randy Okamura – Digital Production Designer
David Brothers – Branding Manager
Olivia Ngai – Content Manager
Addison Duke – Production Artist
Vincent Kukua – Production Artist
Tricia Ramos – Production Artist
Jeff Stang – Direct Market Sales Representative
Emilio Bautista – Digital Sales Associate
Leanna Caunter – Accounting Assistant
Chloe Ramos-Peterson - Library Market Sales Representative

www.imagecomics.com

www.manofaction.tv

SOLSTICE
ISBN: 978-1-63215-943-4
September 2016. Published by Image Comics, Inc.
Office of publication: 2001 Center Street, Sixth Floor, Berkeley, CA 94704.